The Poet's Chair
The First Nine Years of the Ireland Chair of Poetry

The Poet's Chair

The First Nine Years of the Ireland Chair of Poetry

John Montague
Nuala Ní Dhomhnaill
Paul Durcan

foreword by Seamus Heaney
preface by Donnell Deeny

THE LILLIPUT PRESS
DUBLIN

First published 2008 by
THE LILLIPUT PRESS
62–63 Sitric Road, Arbour Hill,
Dublin 7, Ireland
www.lilliputpress.ie

A CIP record for this title is available from
The British Library.

1 3 5 7 9 10 8 6 4 2

ISBN 978 1 84351 094 9 (cased)
ISBN 978 1 854351 095 6 (paperback)

Set in 10 on 15 pt Trump Mediaeval
Printed in Ireland by ColourBooks of Dublin

Contents

Contents

Paul Durcan

Foreword
Seamus Heaney

Remarks on the occasion of John Montague's appointment to the post of Ireland Professorship of Poetry, 14 May 1998

The Ireland Professorship of Poetry is an honour as well as an office. To hold this Professorship is to stand as a representative of the art within the Irish university system. The post is intended to manifest the value of poetry within our cultural and intellectual life, north and south – and nobody is better fitted to do this job than John Montague. In the course of a lifetime, his fidelity to his vocation and his fulfilment of its public demands have been ready, steady and characteristically vigorous.

I was proud to be associated with the establishment of the Chair and delighted with the outcome of this first appointment – an appointment, it must be said, regarded with the utmost seriousness by the universities concerned. They liaised and debated, evolved a job description, a well-ordered appointments procedure and have managed to agree upon certain services that will be required from the holder of the post.

The Arts Councils, north and south, were also crucial to the inception of the scheme and to the maintenance of momentum. They and their officers were aware of the complexity and challenge of what they were taking on, but did not flinch at the difficulties. They knew that when it comes to making decisions and judgements about poets and poetry in contemporary Ireland, you need the wisdom of Solomon and the decisiveness, if not the ruthlessness, of Procrustes – and it also helps to have the sanity of a Portia and a bit of the recklessness of King Lear. But one feature of the process deserves special mention: not only is the successful candidate informed ahead of time, but other poets on the short list are also made aware of the decision and are thus spared the indignity of discovering their un-success in public at the official announcement ceremony. That embarrassment, unfortunately, is too often the penalty of being short-listed for some other important literary awards in Ireland and in Britain. In this case, however, the poets concerned were informed privately of their candidacy and of their standing after the final, very difficult decision had been taken.

In the end, John Montague's name prevailed and it is a pleasure for me to make the formal announcement of his appointment. What we are honouring is not only John's achievement as a poet: equally important on this occasion is his critical acuity about poetry in Irish and English; his long and passionate involvement with the land of Ireland, north and south; his concern with the significance of its landmarks and the meaning of its place names, from the Glen of the Hazels in Tyrone to Mount Eagle in Kerry. Nor should we overlook his experience as a teacher in universities in France and Ireland and the United States, his international standing in the world of letters, his record as an active witness and committed participant at those moments of historical crisis that have marked each and every one of us. All of which makes John Montague an ideal first appointment to this uniquely important office.

I began to read John's poetry in what was for me the *annus mirabilis* of 1962–1963, the year when I came alive to the excitement of reading contemporary Irish and British poetry and yielded to the desire to write poems of my own – a desire that both ravishes and frustrates at the same time. I felt an almost literal quickening in my bones as I read for the first time poems that brought me to my senses in a new way, poems that would stay with me for a lifetime, such as Patrick Kavanagh's *The Great Hunger*, Ted Hughes's 'The Thought Fox' and 'View of a Pig', R.S. Thomas's 'Evans' and 'Iago Prytherch', and John Montague's 'The Water Carrier' and 'Like Dolmens round my Childhood, the Old People'. John Montague's essays and reviews were also appearing in those years, helping to establish a home-based critical idiom that was bracing and clarifying – as in his important early review essay (in *Poetry Ireland*) on the poetry of John Hewitt, and his reappropriation in the famous *Dolmen Miscellany of Irish Writing* of Goldsmith's 'The Deserted Village' as an Irish poem. Here was somebody sketching out a way of 'bringing it all back home', prefiguring the Hibernocentric reading of Anglo-Irish literature upon which academic critics would be engaged for decades to come.

This was also when I first met John in person, under the sponsoring eye of Mary and Pearse O'Malley in their house on Derryvolgie Avenue, and felt the reach of that long bony arm across my shoulder, and felt also the test and flush of his giddy, goading intelligence. Ten years older, farther travelled, more widely published, he arrived on the scene like a combination of talent scout and poetic D.I., a kind of government inspector from the government of tongue sent in by the *aos*

dana of the day, that body of unacknowledged legislators leg-
islating for all they were worth from Monaghan to MacDaids,
from rue Daguerre to Baggot Street Deserta. But there is no
need to wax nostalgic about those days: they generated inten-
sity and energy and edge, a combination of circumstances
that has continued through the decades and done us all good
as individual poets. In the course of the past few months,
therefore, it has been a moving and confirming experience for
me to re-read John's era-defining collections and to re-
encounter them in the magnificent *Collected Poems* – so
admirably produced by Gallery Press. Here is an œuvre that
inheres in and extends the tradition of Irish poetry – a tradi-
tion that began with the magical invocations of the *ur*-poet
Amergin and was reconstituted for our time by the transfor-
mative vision of W.B. Yeats.

For many of us, Montague's poems and individual lines
from his poems have attained 'that dark permanence of
ancient forms', forms which shadowed his own imagination
as he grew up in Garvaghey. It was there he became aware of
'lines of history, lines of power' in 'the rough field of the uni-
verse', aware of 'the sound a wound makes', of the stress of
violence. But there too he became capable of surmounting 'all
legendary obstacles', discovering 'the only possible way of
saying something as luminously as possible', expressing the
'small secrets' of childhood and the life-anchoring memories
of erotic experience. Montague's poetry has been fit to take
the strain of the big historical and political difficulties we
have faced in common and to register with honesty and deli-
cacy the most intimate felicities and desolations which we all
know (and can only know) alone. The poems are a 'source,
half-imagined and half-real', and what John once said in an
early poem about his musician uncle can now be said about
himself: he is one of those through whom 'succession passes'.

Preface
Donnell Deeny

The award of the Nobel Prize for Literature to Seamus Heaney in 1995 was greeted with enormous pleasure throughout Ireland and not least by both Arts Councils, each regarding him as their own, a distinguished northerner, resident in Dublin. All who know him combine enjoyment of and respect for his work with respect for and enjoyment of the man himself, generous as he is with his time and his talents.

There was a widespread feeling that this honour should be marked in some permanent way. That a small island such as ours with a population of five million people should have produced three previous Nobel Prize winners – W.B. Yeats, George Bernard Shaw and Samuel Beckett alongside James Joyce and Oscar Wilde and a chorus of eminent peers, was surely an extraordinary achievement necessary of celebration. But how to make it a permanent celebration?

Seamus would be the first to say that he did not stand alone, but was, in Yeats's phrase, 'true brother of a company' of Irish poets. As Arts Council Chairman, I had remarked more than once that if there were a World Cup in modern poetry, a first eleven from Ireland would be the undisputed favourite to carry off the laurels.

At an animated discussion of the matter at a luncheon party during the Wexford Opera Festival of 1995, Jean Kennedy Smith, the then American Ambassador to Ireland, said, 'What about a chair?' No sooner suggested than this did indeed seem the most elegant of tributes.

Perhaps surprisingly there had not been, until then, a chair of poetry in Ireland, despite our standing in that field. It was clear that we were not seeking a full-time academic chair. Such an institution would not only lack freshness for those who were already academics but would also debar many notable poets, who were not academics, from selection. We looked to the Oxford Chair of Poetry as a model, principally honorific, but with the duty to give one or more lectures a year and achieve some presence in the university and the community.

I felt our chair could be of even greater significance if it were held jointly between universities on either side of the border – a step manifestly appropriate in timing, recognizing the universality of learning in a burgeoning climate of peace and reconciliation on this island.

The choice of universities was obviously important. Discussions led to the proposal of Trinity College, Dublin, Queen's University, Belfast, and University College, Dublin. These proposals were unanimously endorsed by a joint meeting of the Arts Council of Northern Ireland and An Chomhairle Ealaíon, in Belfast in November 1995. All three universities enthusiastically accepted the invitation to participate, to our great delight.

Much remained to be done. To co-ordinate the workings of five institutions with their own internal rules and disciplines is no light matter. But with goodwill on all sides agreement was reached on every issue. These included the name – The Ireland Chair of Poetry – and that the tenure would be three years, with the incumbent, whilst Ireland Professor of Poetry, hosted in turn by each of the three universities.

In early 1998 we sought suggestions from the public for the first holder of the post by way of newspaper advertisements. Each of the five sponsoring institutions carefully considered the suggestions and prepared a short list of nominees. All five institutions were able to consult distinguished poets, critics and persons interested in the arts, in arriving at their views.

The final selection was made on behalf of The Ireland Chair of Poetry Trust by Professor Andrew Mayes, Vice-Provost of Trinity; Professor Robert Cormack, Pro Vice-Chancellor of Queen's; Professor Fergus D'Arcy, Dean of the Faculty of Arts at University College, Dublin; Professor Ciaran Benson of An Chomhairle Ealaíon; Professor Seamus Heaney; and my unprofessing self on behalf of the Arts Council of Northern Ireland.

We were delighted when John Montague accepted our invitation to become the first holder of the Chair. His œuvre marks him out as a poet of the first rank. He is a critic and prose writer of achievement. He is of the island as a whole and of its exiles. It is a pleasure to applaud the distinction and dedication with which he fulfilled the duties of the office.

He was succeeded, in 2001, by Nuala Ní Dhomhnaill. She brought with her great gifts as a poet, writing brilliantly in Irish, but widely translated into English by an array of distinguished peers. Like John she also enriched the literary enjoyment of many by her readiness to engage in widespread outreach with students and the public.

2004 saw the very welcome election of Paul Durcan. His voice in Irish poetry has been unique and carrying, his body of work remarkable. Paul has, with his scholarly lectures and successful engagement with all three universities, emphasized his ability as a critic of signal originality, having already shown himself a skilled broadcaster and prose writer.

The Chair is able to publish and to reach out to the public as a result of several donations, including a very generous gift from Mr William D. Walsh of California, through the Ireland Funds. I express my keen thanks to them and to Ms Belinda Conlan, the first administrator of the Chair, to Dr Maurice Hayes, and to Mr John B. McGuckian for their support.

This book brings together the public presentations of the three poets in the first nine years of the Chair. Some have been reworked to a degree for publication without compromising the palpable excitement present at their inauguration. One piece is new – John Montague's lecture on Samuel Beckett at Trinity in 2000 was later absorbed into his memoir, *Company*. 'The Challenge of Translation' takes its place. The Lagan Press previously published *The Bag Apron* in a limited edition pamphlet, and Matthew Hendry of the Arts Council of Northern Ireland ably helped in preparing two more quotidian but effective flyers as part of our public communications. Indeed, that council and its officers have consistently provided practical and invaluable assistance to the continuance of the Chair. For this book we much appreciate the skilful endeavours of the editor, Djinn von Noorden, the translator, Gabriel Rosenstock, the Irish scholar, Caoimhin Mac GiollaLeith and the publishers, Antony Farrell and Kathy Gilfillan, Chief Executive and Chair of Lilliput.

I am personally very grateful to the current administrator Alison Scott, for her gifted and fruitful management of the Trust and trustees for the last four years. I express my warm thanks to all the trustees over the last nine years who have generously given their time to positively assist the poets of Ireland.

May this volume not only add to the fame of Paul Durcan, Nuala Ní Dhomhnaill and John Montague but prove a first milestone on a long road of discovery and imagination.

The Poet's Chair

John Montague
Photograph courtesy of Peter Fallon, The Gallery Press

The Bag Apron
or The Poet and his Community

As I began this lecture I became all too aware that there were few recent precedents for my present post. There were the lectures that became his book, *Literature in Ireland*, by the young poet-rebel Thomas MacDonagh, at University College Dublin; his successor, Austin Clarke, describes MacDonagh absentmindedly placing a revolver on the desk. Then there were the lectures given by Frank O'Connor as a guest of Trinity College, lectures gathered in *A Backward Look*, which are among the very best causeries on early Irish literature. But O'Connor was more a translator than a poet, and we want a forward, not a backward look, especially at this time.

Later, I attended the extraordinary discourses of Patrick Kavanagh at UCD in the mid-fifties, performances organized by the then Taoiseach, John A. Costello, because of his barrister's guilt at having grilled Kavanagh to nervous exhaustion during the poet's foolhardy libel action against an impoverished Dublin periodical. Patrick consequently lost a lung through cancer, and he coughed and spluttered like an ancient motorcar, or a thrashing machine, relaxing now and then to quaver a ballad in his broken voice. His audience

3

were the wild young from the pubs ('Not to be exciting to the young is death,' was his Blakean epigram), and they cheered their man on as the Irish writers of the day were toppled like ninepins. I will try not to follow his example, but it was an exhilarating performance, delivered with the unmistakable roar of that particular poetic animal. In other words, he sounded completely like himself.

This process of discovering your own voice is both psychic and physical. 'She speaks in her own voice, even to strangers,' says Robert Graves of a friend, and that is the poet's task, to achieve authenticity, to speak in his own voice, 'the true voice of feeling,' in his own rhythms. It is a primitive process, with many parallels in nature, like the reptile sloughing off scales, or the butterfly emerging from its chrysalis. For young poets are like all adolescents: they imitate their heroes, nearly becoming them. With what psychic greed and astonishment I fell upon James Joyce, whose Catholic upbringing in Clongowes seemed like my own in Armagh College. But imagine my disappointment when I learnt that the stews of Dublin had been cleaned up by the Legion of Mary, and that my own sexual education would be delayed. Meanwhile, Tom Kinsella thought he was Thomas Mann's Tonio Kröger, as he prowled around the streets of Inichcore.

These early imitative efforts, actually more like possession than imitation, slowly give way to the real thing; as if in a room crowded with ghosts, the poet begins to speak in his or her own voice. Milosz writes: '… all my life I have been in the power of a daimon, and how the poems dictated by him came into being I do not quite understand.' The poet moves from being in thrall to the voices he or she admires, to possession by his or her own daimon. My friend Gary Snyder speaks of how one discovers one's rattle or rhythm in a dream, the kind of power vision the American Indians describe. For your way of talking is allied to your way of walking, and is as basic as your breathing. And so, when they have come into their own, poets start to look like their poems, or the reverse.

This could be the basis of an intellectual parlour game. When I first heard the languid, sardonic, rasping voice of Louis MacNeice, forty-four years ago, I though it sounded like the barking of a fox or a seal: 'I am not yet born, O hear me, / Let not the blood-sucking bat or the rat or the stoat or the club-footed ghoul come near me ...' The gangly and cantankerous figure of Kavanagh, with his hunched shoulders, seemed as uncompromising as the abrasive rhythms of *The Great Hunger*, just as the slow and melancholy movements of Austin Clarke were often echoed in his more private poems.

It could be amusing, but potentially dangerous, to move this intellectual parlour game to our own times. Ted Hughes looked and sounded like a Henry Moore rock sculpture from Yorkshire. Another American poet friend, the one-eyed Robert Creeley, is lean and over six foot two, and speaks hesitantly, as if he had marbles or precious stones in his mouth. I feel an affinity with him, because some of my more hesitating, wavering rhythms are linked to my stammer. Can one not say that the poems of Seamus Heaney often look as robust and sturdy as himself, as bulky as Robert Frost? Or that the verses of Michael Longley are as delicate yet ample as himself?

There are, of course, many obstacles to finding one's own voice, and they are partly due to education. The poets we responded to at school, where we had to endure poetry, had to have strong rhythms, like Alfred Noyes's 'The Highwayman': '... the road was a ribbon of moonlight / over the purple moor,' or, 'His eyes were hollows of madness / his hair like mouldy hay / But he loved the landlord's daughter, / the landlord's red-lipped daughter ...' Or John Davidson's 'The

Stag': 'When pods went pop on the broom, green broom, /
And apples began to be golden-skinned ...' Compressing my
education through Garvaghey and Glencull Primary Schools
to St Pat's Armagh, I think I had little or no sense of what
poetry could mean, except as a hurdle in the exam stakes, or,
occasionally, rhythms rousing as a song.

Indeed, you might say that we had a bias against poetry,
and here I must introduce an important character in my
development. Let us call him the Man from Keady, who
voiced our disgust at having to deal with such rubbish; the
Romantics especially were risible. His party piece was to
recite 'Ode to a Nightingale' in a strong Ulster accent: 'Thou
wast not born for death, immortal bird, no hungry genera-
tions tread ye down ...' he twanged.

As for Shelley's 'Skylark': 'Hail to thee, blithe spirit,' he
raised an imaginary shotgun, 'bird thou never wert ...'
Phrases like 'charioted by Bacchus and his pards,' (conjuring
up some celestial gambling saloon) or 'Here where men sit
and hear each other groan,' scrawled on a lavatory wall, dou-
bled us over with laughter.

Helen Vendler might not believe it, but I think that the
Man from Keady was trying to make an important point
through his parody: he was mocking a certain kind of English
speech, was saying crudely that all this had nothing to do
with him, that there was nothing in our English books which
directly concerned us. But something in me seemed to stir
when our Irish teacher, Sean O Boyle, intoned the local South
Armagh *Aislingi* in class. I can still try to sing them,
although they also seemed remote from our semi-urban,
wartime existence, or any possible future. A few poems in
the later part of our anthology, such as Stephen Spender's
'Landscape Near an Aerodrome' suggested a modern poetry,
unlike the Chesterbelloc Catholic formula promulgated by

our English master. (Many years later, sharing a platform with Sir Stephen, I thanked him so warmly that, in his turn at the podium, he praised the poems of 'John Montgomery'.)

You begin to find your own voice when you start to write not what you want to, but what you can, indeed must. In his Harvard lectures, Milosz speaks of 'the corner of Europe that shaped me and to which I have remained faithful by writing in the language of my childhood.' Or as Joyce said, in a famous exchange with a Waterford gentleman called Arthur Power who had come to Paris in order to learn how to write like Voltaire, 'You must write what is in your heart, not in your head.'

For a gifted and insufferable youngster who read everything, this truth took a long time to understand. There were several stages in the unfurling of the layers of the self. As a happy little Ulster boy in wartime, I read everything I could find: I moved from cigarette cards of our fighting ships and planes, to Jules Verne and H.G. Wells, with their pseudo-scientific view of the world. After that I advanced to the middlebrow epics of A.J. Cronin; I saw *Dr Wassell* in the Ritz Cinema in Belfast.

But Master MacGurren had leaned over my shoulder in Glencull School to tell me about things called 'Classics', implanting a deep curiosity. Soon the Tyrone Chief Librarian, a Mrs Tilly from Yorkshire, was wondering at the choice of books requested by my Aunt Winifred who ran our branch of the County Library. She could not believe that the local farmers were eager to plough through *War and Peace* and *Crime and Punishment* after a hard day in the fields.

It was still prose, of course, and the only part of Tolstoy's epic that I could relate to was Levin working in the harvest fields. The plot thickened when I moved to UCD and fell under the influence of my poetic contemporaries, and the spell of post-Emergency, melancholy Georgian Dublin, an atmosphere I try to convey in some of my earliest poems. But although Dublin was the first city I fell in love with, I was still eager for the larger world I had read and heard of, and to which I had briefly belonged, as a child in Brooklyn. I followed the tracks of the Sherman tanks which had crushed our hedges in Tyrone, when I made my first journey by bicycle through the battlefields of northern France, in 1948, awed by the lines of white crosses and crumbling helmets that strangely resembled vineyards of various vintages, from 1870 to 1945.

Now I had decided that I was Rimbaud, but a Rimbaud who could hardly speak French. After working in the wine harvest or *vendanges* on the Marne, my companion and I descended in search of the fleshpots of Paris, hoping, maybe, for a black mistress, like Baudelaire's Jean Duval. Instead we were waylaid by a bisexual Dutch friend and brought to a gay nightclub called Dr Moons, where I had to defend the Armagh virginity I had hoped to lose. Coming back to London through Charing Cross, I stocked up on the grim deities of the time, Kafka and Rilke, and the first translations of Hölderlin by Michael Hamburger. What Myles called 'the gentle art of Kafka-ing and Rilke-ing' was necessary for survival in literary Dublin. Or as my friend Brendan Behan said of our generation: 'Only a few hours out of the bog, and they're up to their arses in angst.'

It was the beginning of the Third Programme, and, during my holidays, my long-suffering aunts endured those discords that often sounded through the farmhouse, replacing their own favourite programmes, such as *Question Time* and the *Mansion House Ceilidh*. And in Fintona, my father, home from America, built shelves to accommodate books like André Gide's *Journals*, that he did not dare open, for fear that they would offend his Catholic *pudeur*. I suppose the climax for me and many of my generation, like the painter Barrie Cooke, and Ted Hughes, was the publication, in 1959, of ten Penguin editions of D.H. Lawrence. I began to see my own countryside through a sensual haze, to which, alas, the girls did not seem to respond. And when I showed *The Rainbow* to an older, farmer friend, Barney Horisk, he roundly declared, 'That man Lawrence knows buck-all about farming.'

Omnivorous, derivative, stumbling through French, German, Russian and Italian literature – to say nothing of the invading Americans – how did I extricate myself from this maelstrom of influences? It did not happen easily or quickly: precocity was nearly impossible during a period when so much was going on across the world. I admired the intense post-war literary life of France, startling in its energy, from Mauriac, Montherland and Gide, to Sartre and Camus. Again mainly prose, but I carried away a key phrase: *Il faut cultiver vos obsessions*. In other words, you must write out of your own wellsprings, write about what you have to; and slowly but surely your subject matter emerges.

There was the landscape of my upbringing, the hills of Tyrone, or 'the wild west' as a Belfast man in the Crown Bar recently observed to me. A landscape with figures, of course, the branches of my broken family tree, a tree splintered by politics and history. And the old people who hobbled down to our post office, through whom I came to know an older Ireland, before it would be swept away by factory farming.

Sometimes that intense feeling for the Ulster and Irish landscapes trembles towards an ideal patriotism, what one calls *tir grá* in Irish, or love of the land. In this connection, I recall a fierce discussion I had with Ted Hughes in Listowel, County Kerry, before he accepted the laureateship. I maintained that no one could be a simple patriot anymore, and quoted his own poem, 'Out': 'Let England close / Let the great sea anemone close.' He suggested that I was misreading the poem, which was really about the abomination of war, and began to speak of the British crown as a symbol of the unity of the tribe, like some ancient British chieftain: *Arturus, Dux Britanorum* ... As if Ted Hughes was the Merlin of the lost kingdom of Elmet.

Simpler than *tir grá* was *grá* itself, the effort to love. While not subscribing to the muse theory of Robert Graves, even under tonight's full moon, one can still recognize that there is an affinity between love and the lyric, though that love need not be limited to the chivalrous impulse of courtly love. It can be domestic love, between husband and wife, it can be directed towards the old mine workings of W.H. Auden, the hovering falcon of Hopkins, or the battle-weary comrades of David Jones – even the Fintona Horse Tram – anyone or anything cargoed with feeling. Milton surprisingly declared that poetry should be 'simple, sensuous, and passionate,' and it is this intensity that makes lines of Yeats ring in our ears, the most singable poet since the Elizabethans. Love of place, love of another – whether companion, child, or parent – love is the charge behind the lyric, technical mastery its muscle.

And there are deeper, underlying, almost inchoate concerns. Clio or History, for instance, is one of the Muses, but in this age of individual consciousness, public themes cannot be asserted, as in the *Aeneid*'s account of the founding of Rome, or the violent glory of war chronicled in the *Iliad*. My training as an historian in UCD helped, but I came to realize that for me as a poet history could only be 'his story', what I know about what had happened to my people, as I will explain later.

Then there are truly primitive and pre-historical powers working. Stones and water are among the enduring images in my work. Even when I translate, I instinctively turn to poems like the *Carnac* of Eugene Guillevic, who was born beside those ancient stones. Guillevic was a socialist, but then all great socialist poets seem to write paeans of mystic materialism, like Hugh MacDiarmid's 'On a Raised Beach', Pablo Neruda's 'On the Heights of Macchu Picchu', or the long promontory of his Piedras Negras. And when I am drunk out of my mind, I see behind my closed eyes water flowing over stones, perhaps my version of Eden, my primal landscape.

And there is the central irony of my career: the effort to be fluent about speechlessness. Being here in Belfast has for me the haunting quality of the road not taken. Omagh and Armagh were my two towns, but in my last year at school, as the wars ended, I began to come regularly to Belfast for speech therapy. My therapist was a lively young woman who taught me breathing exercises, placing a professional but distracting hand on my diaphragm. She had a passion for both opera and war poetry, introducing me to *Penguin New Writing*, and poets like Drummond Allison and Alun Lewis. I still went to see her all through the summer, cycling to now-closed railway stations, such as Beragh and Sixmilecross, spending a crammed day in Belfast, often taking in a film, as well as the dirty pictures of the Smithfield Market.

I was becoming dimly aware of something called Ulster Regionalism, but it seemed to deal mainly with matters east of the Bann, the Northern Pale, and was already fading. I called upon a gruff John Hewitt at the Ulster Museum, but he would soon go into exile, and it was in London or Dublin that I would meet MacNeice and Rodgers. So my poetic stirrings had to take place against the background of Dublin and UCD, where a new generation was beginning to emerge, not post-war, but a post-civil war that would take me years to understand. I did not know their provenance, but their passion for poetry was a prod in the right direction. Anthony Cronin from Enniscorthy spouting Auden, Ben Kiely singing Mac-Neice to MacNeice, John Jordan intoning Lorca, Pearse Hutchinson reciting everything! Despite the introverted gloom of post-Emergency Dublin, a new generation was cracking the egg, with the iconoclastic figure of Kavanagh as a goad. With such a cast of characters, my ambitions to be a bestselling novelist crumbled, although now I am glad to transfer them to my partner, Elizabeth.

My loneliness as a marooned Northerner and apprentice Southerner still kept me slightly apart. Gawky, red-haired, stammering in a Tyrone accent, I must have stood out amongst them: to the children of the new Free State, the North was a foreign country. And there was a further com-plication: my American birth. In due course, I would leave to explore that great country from end to end, meeting easier, less fractious contemporaries: Snodgrass and Bly in Iowa, Ginsberg and Snyder in San Francisco.

So you wander round the world to discover the self you were born with. But I had already made a start. I heard two of my poems being read out on Austin Clarke's poetry pro-gramme; another prize-winner was John Hewitt, which prompted my call on him in Belfast, when I was up to see my father in the Royal Victoria Hospital. And after my long American *hegira* I began again to publish poems, this time with an Ulster accent. Austin Clarke rang me up after he'd read 'The Sean Bhean Bhocht' in *The Irish Times*, a poem not about a national symbol, but a real poor old woman whom I had known: 'As a child I was frightened by her / Busy with her bowl of tea in a farmhouse chimney corner, / Wrapped in a cocoon of rags and shawls.' I had travelled far in order to write about homely things.

One grew up slowly then, through a clamour of influ-ences. My first wee book was called *Forms of Exile* (1958), something my generation specialized in, trying to escape the restrictions imposed by oppressive religio-political systems, both North and South, mirror-images of each other. But things were looking up. In 1960 a poem of mine won one of the first poetry prizes in this part of the world: the May Morton, and it was read by Sam MacCready in the Assembly Rooms of the Presbyterian Church in Belfast, though later it was docked a stanza in its transmission from the BBC North of Ireland. I was so pleased, I had it printed by my new pal, Liam Miller of the Dolmen Press, and sent one to Patrick Kavanagh. He stopped me in the street, to offer me a compliment: 'I see you got in the bag apron; I could never manage it meself.' Now that the bag apron had travelled all the way from Friel's Ballybeg to Broadway to Hollywood, it may seem a small matter, but it was a big step at the time.

Authenticity is the holy grail of the artist. To achieve 'Like Dolmens round my Childhood, the Old People', my experience of life in a country post office in County Tyrone and my dim sense of the deep archaeological past of the Clogher Valley came together under the influence of poems as diverse as the early Anglo-Saxon, Alan Tate's *Ode to the Confederate Dead*, and the bruised gloom of Wilfred Owen's 'Strange Meeting'. There is a line in my early work through *Poisoned Lands* (1961), *Death of a Chieftain* (1964) to *The Rough Field*, an exploration of the hidden Ulster west of the Bann, which, except for Ben Kiely, had not found expression since William Carleton's *Traits and Stories*.

In his study of the short story, *The Lonely Voice*, Frank O'Connor argues that the strength of the storyteller often comes from the pressure behind him of a community which has not achieved definition, a submerged population: Lawrence's coalminers, Joyce's mean Dubliners, Flannery O'Connor's Georgia grotesques. In the pre-literate Tyrone of

13

my past, there was a primitive respect for the poet, a kind of laughter and fear aroused by the idea of the local bard. I had a cousin, Tommy Montague, who was known as the Bard of Altamuskin, and whose verses appeared in the *Ulster Herald*. He had harps inset on the walls of his house, and a glass-walled study where he wrote old-fashioned novels. People thought he was a bit cracked, but, God bless him, he lent me Lamb's *Tales from Shakespeare* while he wallpapered our parlour. Then there was Michael Mullen, the Bard of Fore-mass, and the Farrells of Glencull, one of whose songs is included in *The Rough Field*: 'Glencull Waterside'. There were also the slightly more sophisticated voices of Matt Mulcahy and Barney MacCool of Coolaghy, in the *Tyrone Constitution*. And of course the Reverend Marshall's excursions into the Ulster dialect haunt me still: 'Concerning wimmen, sure it was a constant word of his / Keep far away from them that's thin / Their temper's easy riz / An' Margit she was very wee / And Bridget she was stout / But [and here comes the epic simile] her face was like a jail dure / Wi' the bowlts pulled out.'

Both sides of the house had retained some dim respect for the idea of verse, if not poetry, and occasionally somebody would raise the old canard that we in mid-Ulster still spoke the language of Shakespeare. Didn't Marshall organize a reading from *A Midsummer Night's Dream*, with Matt Mulcahy, my old Fintona neighbour, as Bottom? (The satirical side of the bard would now be best expressed by comics, like the deadpan ironies of Kevin MacAleer.) The truth was that Tyrone had not known a professional poet since the days of the O Neills, and through my long literary apprenticeship I was harnessing an artesian energy from many silent centuries. These hushed, orphaned voices whispered partly in another language, emphasizing the ironies of my own name:

Tadgh or Tague transformed into the more stylish Montague. The journey into this reservoir of silence was all the more ironical because I was born not in Ballygawley but Brooklyn, yet that distance may have made me listen more closely, like Sam Hanna Bell transported from Glasgow to the rural County Down of *December Bride*.

Among the welter of the world's voices, in the streets, on the airwaves, in the press, you find your own voice, yet this does not isolate you, but restores you to your people. Across the world, the unit of the parish is being broken down by global forces, and from Iniskeen to Garvaghey, from Bellaghey to Ballydehob, to the Great Plains of America, an older lifestyle, based on the seasons, is being destroyed. But it can still be held in the heart and the head. Although I know I will never be able to satisfy the Man from Keady, I have (echoing Nennius, the early British historian, as quoted by David Jones) 'made a heap of all I could find,' a cairn of the heart's affections.

Short Thoughts on the Long Poem: Words and Music

I say 'short thoughts' because the subject is a book-length one, like C.M. Bowra's study of the epic, or Auerbach's *Mimesis*. All I can bring to it is my own experience thinking of, and trying to write, long poems – three in all so far, with one to come, perhaps.

The Greco-Roman or classical epic dominates our view of the long poem, beginning with Homer's *Iliad*, described by Simone Weil as a 'poem of force'. Then there is the *Odyssey*, a more psychological and personal epic, the influence of which persists to our own day, in Joyce's great *Ulysses*. And in the background there is always the presence of the other world, disputing gods and goddesses playing havoc with human beings, backing their favourites, an atmosphere found also in the great tragedies. Virgil's *Aeneid* descends from the same tradition, Aeneas being a character in the *Iliad*. It also celebrates force, the matter of Rome, beginning '*Arma virum que cano*', 'Arms and the man I sing', although the most moving scenes are of Dido's love, and the doomed Turnus. Again gods and goddesses capriciously intervene, as in some rigged gambling saloon: as Hopkins says, they are not gentlefolk, but 'unnatural rakes'! Then we have the three books of *La Divina Comedia*, although Hell and Purgatory are far from our sense of the comic. To indicate the continuity of the tradition, Virgil is Dante's guide through Hell and Purgatory, where Ulysses reappears and is given a different destiny. Again we have the presence of the other world, but now hardened into the mighty Scholastic structure of medieval Catholicism, with its angels, saints and virgins.

The strength of such shared assumptions persisted until the middle of the twentieth century, or rather, could be said to haunt it, since the influence of Darwin, Frazier and Freud had made these beliefs so tenuous. Two poems by Americans who had emigrated to Europe evoke this broken tradition of the classical epic. Eliot's *The Waste Land* speaks of 'Falling towers / Jerusalem, Athens, Alexandria ...' but also reaches out towards meaning and salvation, which seem hard to find. The *Cantos* of Ezra Pound, a long 'poem including history' were begun in 1925, with a scene from the *Aeneid*, and evoking gods, goddesses, nymphs and sages from many societies, a poetic equivalent of Malraux's *Museum Without Walls*. But all his luminaries and talismanic figures, like Kung and Jefferson, and the Adams family, cannot be made to add up to a vision of order in our age: 'I cannot make it cohere,' is Pound's terrible cry in the late *Cantos*. The collapse of a whole system, Greco-Roman in structure, and Judeo-Christian in belief, haunts these poems. The so-called Modern Movement of the early twentieth century is as neo-classical as the Augustan age, with its rage for order (Wallace Stevens before Derek Mahon) and its revival of Imitation as a technique.

The desire for an English epic, encompassing and cele-
brating the matter of Britain, is something that recurs
throughout English poetry. *Beowulf* belongs in the context of
saga, or the home-made folk epic. The central English myth
is Arthurian, whether you follow Geoffrey of Monmouth, or
Malory who inspired Tennyson. I must make a confession
here: when I was reading E.M. Tillyard on Milton, I was fas-
cinated by those pages where he shows the great poet trying
to find his theme, being long-tempted by the Arthurian
before settling on his great Protestant subject. (Like Dante,
he fell back on the Bible, though, unlike that angry Floren-
tine, he did not commit his own contemporaries to hell or
purgatory.) I would like to think that as a little Ulster boy I
became infected with Puritanism, and like Seamus Deane I
can still read *Paradise Lost* in Protestant Ulster. Milton's is
the most deliberately epic effort in English, invoking the
example of the Ancients in his Preface: 'The measure is Eng-
lish heroic verse without rhyme, as that of Homer in Greek,
and of Virgil in Latin ...' Milton has '*la longue haleine*', the
long breath of the epic.

The Arthurian cycle still persists in the work of David
Jones's *Sleeping Lord*, and in English, Welsh, Cornish and
Breton mythology. But why is there no great long poem about
Arthur which is the English equivalent of the *Iliad*? One
would have to conclude that while there are many fine long
English poems, especially Romantic ones such as the *Prelude*
and *Don Juan*, there does not seem to be an English national
epic, encompassing that country's myths and history. I have
described how Milton hesitated over the Arthurian theme,
but instead chose the Fall of Man: *Paradise Lost* could be
regarded as the English Protestant epic. (And it is of course
composed in iambic verse, which, though a heavier style
than Shakespeare's, makes sonorous public reading, espe-

cially when Satan speaks, and the love scene in Paradise.)

There are other, less daunting long poems in English. Chaucer learnt from Ovid and Boccaccio how to weave tales together, and Langland has his wonderful medieval vision, a major influence on David Jones. But the *Faerie Queene*, meant to be the great English Renaissance poem, is even more daunting than Milton. Although I have lived beside the Lee, and seen Spenser's home in North Cork, I still prefer his shorter poems to his intended masterpiece. He wanted to write a Romantic epic, like Ariosto and Tasso, but he lacked the lightness of movement, and chose a lovely but slow-moving stanza, which was bound to obstruct his narrative, while the argument or structure he proposed was too weighty for any tale.

Every country, every nation, perhaps every province, aspires to an epic. Similar desires arise in music, with Sibelius echoing the *Kalevala*, Lonnrot's gathering of the tales of Finland. The northern folktales of the *Nibelungenleid* resonate throughout Wagner. But back to poetry. In Poland there is the *Pan Tadeusz* of Mickiewiecz, with its epic bear hunt translated by Donald Davie. From hunting to seafaring: the imperial voyages of Portugal are celebrated in the *Lusiad*, a direct echo of the *Aeneid*. But perhaps the most persuasive of all is the *Maharabata*, the great Vedic or Indian tale, which is also a religious statement, puppet-versions of which can be bought at street stalls. There, there are enough triple gods and goddesses, cowherds and *gopis*, to make even the deities of Olympus blush. Rituals that attracted a director like Peter Brook.

Many of these peripheral sagas or home-grown epics are concerned, like the *Iliad* or the *Aeneid*, with the clash of war. France has very few longer poems, but the best is the *Chanson de Roland*, dealing with the eternal strife between the

Moorish and Gallic worlds. As for the matter of Ireland, one of the great achievements of modern Irish literature is Kinsella's translation of the *Táin*, which illustrates the Irish theory of the epic, or long poem, using prose until the chariot wheels catch fire. If Spenser had learnt more Irish, he might have lit a fire under the Faerie Queene's tale.

The modern long poem is mainly American, the *Cantos* of Pound, the *Paterson* of his friend, William Carlos Williams, the *Maximus* poems of Charles Olsen. These are all poems about history, or at least a definition of a culture, and they all wage an only partly successful war against the iambic line, which, according to Williams, was not the natural tempo of American speech. There were false starts, such as Longfellow's *Hiawatha*, but the most original of contemporary long poets, perhaps the father of all modern epic poetry, was Walt Whitman, with his *Leaves of Grass*, a pantheistic and democratic vision of the universe. We know he loved the rhythmical structures of the Old Testament, and he adored opera, which may have inspired his exuberant arias, like 'Song of Myself'. 'He had his nerve', says Randall Jarrell, but he succeeded in doing what neither Pound nor MacDiarmid would manage, to weave a long poem out of the strands of himself. Although it contains beautiful individual volumes, like 'Drum Taps' from the Civil War, *Leaves of Grass* does add up, ironically as unified as the work of that decadent dandy in Paris, Baudelaire, with his *Fleurs du Mal* – flowers of evil instead of leaves of grass.

. America, being, seemingly, the most modern country, was fascinated by the adventure of modern poetry, and the most influential long poem of recent Anglo-American literature is, of course, T.S. Eliot's *The Waste Land*, which was originally called (before Pound's surgical editing) *He do the Policeman in Many Voices*. Eliot was part of a great generation: Pound, Stevens, Williams, Hart Crane. These last two especially thought that, when all the bets were off, Eliot had handed back modern poetry to the Academy. They thought of him as a traitor to the tenets of Modernism. Crane's hymn to *The Bridge*, under whose shadow I was born, is an attempt to find a myth to replace the Classical. In his letters you can follow his agonized debate with the implications of *The Waste Land*. And in *Paterson*, Williams tries to show that no land is waste; even in the most featureless American town, emotion blooms.

There is a line running through contemporary American poetry, from the optimistic vision of *Leaves of Grass*, through *Paterson*, to the desolation of Ginsberg's *Fall of America*. In my Californian days, my pals were people like Ginsberg and Snyder and Robert Duncan, all of whom seemed to be writing long poems. Olson's theory of Open Form – it seemed to me a contradiction in terms – was much debated, although I thought his better work was the earlier, more compact poems, like 'Kingfishers'. They were a fine company of poets, but I was not sure about their practice. Snyder was working on a long poem called *Mountains and Rivers Without End*, based upon the idea of unfurling a Chinese scroll. 'At least mine will be ended before yours', I said prophetically.

Then there is the Irish long poem. I spoke of the *Táin*, and there was a time when I hoped to weave together an even greater bundle of stories, the Fenian tales, especially the 'Conversation Between the Old Men', Oisin and Patrick, which Máirtín Ó Cadhain thought was the greatest work in Irish. And there are lesser stories, like the 'Frenzy of Sweeny', and the 'Vision of Mac Conglinne'. There is even an Irish version of the *Aeneid*.

In the eighteenth century, the two traditions and languages co-existed: the Anglo-Irish lament, *The Deserted Village*, the fierce pre-feminist humour of *The Midnight Court*, the heart-scalding drum beat of the 'Lament for Art O'Leary'. Allingham's *Laurence Bloomfield* has the amplitude of a Victorian novel. But when Patrick Kavanagh comes to write *The Great Hunger*, he channels both the erotic and economic frustrations of life on a small farm. I can testify from seeing the American anthologies in his flat that he was addicted to modern American poetry, and had read *The Waste Land*. Remember the scene in *The Green Fool*, when he asks for *The Waste Land* in the National Library?

'Without invention, nothing is well spaced.' Technical solutions are largely dictated by the material. Much as I loved Hart Crane, I could not be dithyrambic about Garvaghey, County Tyrone. Under my eyes it was becoming a no-place, like Paterson, or as Gertrude Stein said of Oakland, 'there's no there, there'. And there was not the belief that would underpin earlier long poems of the Christian period, but a conflict of attitudes, which I illustrate in 'The Bread God'.

PART II. WORDS AND MUSIC

Poetry flourishes where there is a natural connection between poetry and speech, the rhythms of the human voice, as in the Elizabethan period, when ordinary speech seemed to flow or fall naturally into iambics so that ostensibly abstract language could be understood even by the groundlings. The poetry that Shakespeare published in his own lifetime is much less accessible to the reader than the plays assembled by others in the first Folio. Perhaps because the poet was being more self-consciously literary when he composed his arcane verses, like *The Phoenix and the Turtle*, whereas the plays were invigorated by professional need, the pressure of many voices.

There is also another consideration, the relationship between poetry and music, which, practically speaking, assists the fluency of the verse. Behind much of Elizabethan poetry, one hears the phantom plucking of a lute or a psaltery, while many poems in Irish, especially in the seventeenth and eighteenth centuries, were also songs. Thomas MacDonagh, the most gifted of the poet martyrs of Easter 1916, has written on the connection between poetry and music in his *Literature in Ireland*; as well as Irish poetry, in both languages, he had studied the Elizabethan lyricist Campion. A change came when Cromwell and his pleasure-loathing ilk closed the theatres, and poetry returned to the intimacy of manuscript. Play-writing had been a public act, and publication in our modern sense of the book was still embryonic; besides, publication could be considered *infra dig* for a courtier. So Donne's poems were circulated, as were Marvell's. The critical unease of Ben Jonson, even with Shakespeare, is based on his being one of England's first professional poets, earning his living as such.

Poetry always has a political aspect. As the Scottish poet Hugh MacDiarmid has said, 'All poetry that is not conscious political propaganda, is unconscious political propaganda.' The political aspect was so prominent in the eighteenth century that many of the more successful poems of the period have the effect of pamphlets. The heroic couplet, introduced under the French influence of Charles II's court, gave a crispness to the message of poems such as Dryden's *Absalom and Achipotel* and Pope's *The Rape of the Lock*. But the restraining influence of the rhyming couplet, which has come to seem a necessity for poetry in the popular mind, is not entirely natural to English verse, and perhaps the greatest lyric poetry occurs where the naturalness of speech is only partly corseted by form, as in the best of Yeats.

The Romantic poets did not presume an audience, although Byron had one, being as potent an image in his day as Mick Jagger. Those we call the Lake Poets seemed to prefer isolation, especially Wordsworth, who often composed out of doors, as he strode along; a neighbour describes him as 'booming like a bee'. This brings us to the crucial question of the poet's voice, which is determined by his own bodily and psychic rhythms, the cadences of his heart and head. (There is a sense in which the poems should look like the person who composed them. The long lines of the American poet Robert Creeley, like a Giacometti figure, resemble his own lean form, while the short, gnomic verses of Guillevic echo the poet's short, taut steps.)

The first recording we have of a poet in English is Tennyson reading that very jingoistic poem, *The Charge of the Light Brigade*. His strong Lincolnshire accent and rhythms stayed with him all his life, as did Yeats's strong, slow-cadenced Sligo accent in the fragments that have survived from the programmes he recorded for the BBC. Since then, there have been many recordings of poets, especially those done by our own Claddagh Records in Dublin, on the principle that the poet should be heard reading his own work in his own voice, with its own rhythms.

In dramatising *The Rough Field*, I tried to do the same, blending or at least contrasting various voices. Like the harsh rasp of Pat Magee for whom Beckett wrote *Krapp's Last Tape*, the storytelling charm of Benedict Kiely with his honeyed singing voice, the young Seamus Heaney from Derry, and of course my own Tyrone-bred self. And weaving through all that matter of Ulster, the tunes played by the Chieftains. In other words, I was trying to compose and record an *Ulsteriad*, using a variety of forms and voices to suggest the complexity of the history of Ulster, thus placing the poem in the Western tradition of epic. For the problems raised by the Matter of Ulster are many: Celt and Saxon, English and Irish, Catholic and Protestant, the clash of the female and male principles inherent in these religions. The pressure of a community is often in inverse proportion to its size, and if anyone doubts the complexity of the struggle in Ulster, on Europe's western edge, they have only to drive through the small towns and villages of the North. The Catholic ghettos flaunt the colours of Palestine, while the Bible-thumping Loyalist enclaves are emblazoned with Israel's Star of David. Perhaps you could argue that this is history repeating itself as Comedy, after Tragedy, but the shafts that the Ulster problems send into the history of Western Europe are deep, and still unresolved, except in the harmonies of poetry and music.

The Challenge of Translation

I have been involved in, engaged with, translation for all of my creative life. The process has been a respite, a rest from my own work, but more often a challenge: how could this or that poem be made over into English? The great fertility of the Elizabethan period seems to me to come partly from that flow of other languages, Latin, French, Italian, into English. And when it comes to the Romantics, it is also the German language, Coleridge of course, and even Wordsworth composing the most exciting passage of *The Prelude* in Goslar. (Sometimes being surrounded by another language sharpens and strengthens one's sense of one's own. Think of Byron and Shelley in Italy, Joyce and Beckett in France.)

The obvious challenge for an Irish poet is the older language in which most of our earlier poetry was composed: our tradition is double-barrelled, or hybrid. I remember the Armagh afternoon when our Irish teacher, Sean O Boyle, began to sing in class, chanting harshly beautiful songs that were actually poems from South Armagh. That region is now known to the outside world as 'bandit country' but it was originally the site or seat of a Court of Poetry, to which Creggan churchyard still bears witness.

These were very formal poems, a bit like the contemporaneous verses of eighteenth-century England, Gray's *The Bard* or the more Scottish poems of James Thomson. But I was totally bowled over by the 'Lament for Art O'Leary', a wake song for a murdered man. Not until I read Lorca's dirge for his bullfighter friend would I meet its equal. Peter Levi declared 'Ag Caoineadh Airt Uí Laoghaire' one of the great poems of the world. I felt I had to hammer out my own version, though always halting even over the very first line. Should *'Mo grada go daingean tu!'* be 'My steadfast love'; 'My stalwart love'; 'My love, my stronghold' or; 'My dauntless love'? That phrase echoes throughout the poem, as in the passage describing how the speaker finds her dead husband, the cry of a woman whose heart has been seared:

> *My steadfast friend!*
> *I never believed you dead*
> *Until your horse came towards me,*
> *Trailing its bridle;*
> *Your heart's blood splashed*
> *From bit to polished saddle*
> *In which you rose and fell:*
> *I gave a leap to the threshold,*
> *A second to the gate,*
> *A third upon the horse.*

Early Irish poetry came later. When I undertook *The Faber Book of Irish Verse* I decided to overhaul the whole of Irish poetry although, lacking the exhaustive scholarship necessary for such a task, I obviously could not always succeed. Kinsella was working on the *Táin* at the same time, and I felt honoured to be involved in a somewhat similar enterprise, spiriting the power of our past literature over into the present. And of course Irish is the oldest vernacular in the West, and I loved the pen-point accuracy of the earliest lyrics, their precision and delicacy:

> *In Loch Leane*
> *a Queen went swimming;*
> *a redgold salmon*
> *flowed into her*
> *at full of evening.*

(from the Feliré Aengus)

Translating from the French was based upon a different impulse. Dazzled and dazed by the achievement of Joyce and the not yet acclaimed Beckett, I found my way to France after World War Two. I had had only a few classes in French during my last year at school, but I was fascinated by the drama of nineteenth-century French poetry, which seemed more glamorous to an eager adolescent than the poets of Victorian England. After *vendange*s along the Marne, harvesting the pale grapes for champagne, I descended on Paris on my bicycle, like Rimbaud swooping down from Charleville. I had his complete works in my rucksack, with a daft introduction by Paul Claudel claiming that Rimbaud was an embryonic mystic. I had begun to read Baudelaire's condemned poems as well, perhaps hoping that I, too, would find an exotic mistress, and I also sported the black flag of Nerval's melancholy. As I have said, both Baudelaire and Nerval seemed much more exciting than their English counterparts; the former drinking absinthe or black coffee and either working all night or making love to his sultry mistress, the latter sauntering through Paris with his lobster on a lead before hanging himself from a lamppost!

I did not really try to translate *les poêtes maudits*, these 'blighted bards', since many better hands had been there before me. But I became conscious that when the Modern Movement was beginning, France was a major influence, Flaubert on Joyce, LaForgue on Eliot, Gautier on Pound, and so on. Then quite suddenly there was a halt in the dialogue, and even a growing distrust. For instance, when I broached to Charles Monteith (the famous editor who fostered Golding and Heaney) a proposal for a *Faber Book of French Verse* to follow the success of my Irish one, his off-the-cuff dismissal was memorably succinct: 'I am afraid French poetry does not go down well in England. It would sell even less than Welsh.' And when, at his request, I sent a shoal of poems by my French poet pals to Alan Ross at the *London Magazine*, he commented dryly: 'The French really have peculiar poets.'

The initial problem is that the French expect the poet to be supremely intelligent. The marmoreal perfection of Mallarmé is an obvious example, but there is also Valéry's cry for clarity in his 'Complete Poem' (1903): 'The sky is bare. The smoke floats. The wall shines. Oh! How I should like to think clearly!' This attitude leads to the complexity of 'Le Cimetière Marin' or 'Seaside Cemetery' as Mahon calls it, with its motto from Pindar, and invocation of Zeno, the pre-Socratic philosopher. Rising at dawn to examine your own mind is a strenuous idea of the poetic vocation. And how far this is from Keats, who longs for a life of 'sensations' rather than of 'thoughts'. It seems that the Anglophone poet aspires to pure feeling, whereas the French poet desires pure thought, from Mallarmé and Valéry, to present mandarins like Jacques Roubaud and Michel Deguy.

I should reveal a prejudice. It seems to me that the great generation of French poets born on the hinge of the twentieth century, from writers like Jouve, Eluard, Aragon, Michaux, Ponge, to Follain, Char and Guillevic, are much more powerful than their contemporaries in English, aspiring to Plato's ideal of the Philosopher Kings. (It is in this company that Beckett found a natural place, translating Eluard and producing a belated prose poem of his own, *A Fizzle*, in which he declares morosely, 'I gave up before birth.') Surely they deserve a major bilingual anthology of their own? Stephen Romer, an English poet who teaches at Tours, has made a handsome start with his Faber anthology, and I have done my bit as well, contributing to the two translation series, Wake Forest in America and Bloodaxe in England, which have been trying to cross the divide.

For instance, there is the fascinating problem of the prose poem, a form beloved of the French since Baudelaire, but seldom found in English. It gave me great pleasure to translate some of Ponge's most endearing *pièces*, like 'The Horse', where that sly old Huguenot compares the Pope on his throne to an equine posterior, or in other words, a horse's ass. And his marvellous meditation on 'The Nuptial Habits of Dogs' makes me cry with laughter. Those translations, together with C.K. Williams's versions of *Le Partis Pris de Choses*, are reprinted in a Faber paperback, which seems, alas, to have received very little notice in England.

And then of course there is Guillevic's *Carnac*, that gnomic masterpiece by someone who was brought up amongst those mysterious standing stones, which I translated for the Bloodaxe series. I have also done his *Les Murs*, or *The Walls*, for a recent exhibition of Dubuffet. The erotic complexity of Jouve, the Norman terseness of Follain, the Burgundian gloom of Frénaud, I have tried from time to time to translate or transfer their qualities into English, and will continue to do so, as well as translating my near contemporaries, like Michel Deguy, Robert Marteau, and Claude Esteban. In one of Claude's last sequences, *Sur La Dernière Lande*, he seems to have combined sensation and thought. Although written in the lamenting voice of King Lear, it finishes with hope:

> *And maybe all was written in the book*
> *but the book was lost*
>
> *or someone threw it in the brambles*
> *without reading it*
>
> *no matter, that which was written*
> *abides, even*
>
> *hidden, another who has not lived*
> *through all that*
>
> *and without knowing the book's language, will understand*
> *each word*
>
> *and when he has read it, something*
> *of ours will yield*
>
> *a breath, a kind of smile between the stones.*

This optimistic note is not heard so much in the early Esteban. His first book, *La Saison Dévastée* or *The Stricken Season*, is very much the work of an alienated French intellectual:

> *Tree, bird, field:*
> *There is only this boat*
> *Mounting the black current*
>
> *Disjointed head, you*
> *Have come far …*

In his later years he suffered a terrible loss, the violent death of his wife, commemorated in *Elégie de la Mort Violente*

(1989). Yet despite this almost annihilating pain, he achieves a note of whimsical sadness, which prepares the way for his King Lear sequence:

> *When one has suffered too long, one should*
> *pause sometimes, and laugh a little, and share*
> *with friends some sweet cake since one is drinking*
> *sweet wine from the Canaries and let there be dances*
> *even a shade wanton, so once spoke a fool*
> *to distract his master who did not mend*
> *or who did not wish to mend from his malady,*
> *I know others like that.*

(From 'Someone Begins to Speak in a Room')

Michel Deguy is editor of the longest-lived poetry magazine in France, called simply *Poésie*, the only simple thing about Deguy's approach to poetry. His 'Chant Royal', for example, begins by invoking many precedents:

> *The poet in profile*
> *Set square to the body and the shadow on the sill*
> *The poet Gulliver retracing the pattern of winter brambles*
> *   with the pencil tip of Hopkins*
> *Or shrinking to align the grass and the Zodiac*
> *   with the compasses of Gongora*
> *A genie of Persian tales rejecting indifference ...*

A *philosophe* by training, Michel does not shirk the responsibility of our intellectual heritage, and describes poetry, or the act of writing, as follows:

> The belief is that this mental swarm, this ball of soot and fire, this obscurity that passes through the brain for an instant – *uno intuitu* – then the long labour of unravelling, of description, a devious and detailed analysis, ready to act again, with retro-

active force, will bring to a close the decoding, the *post parti-tum*, to only make an intelligible mouthful.

Yet despite this intellectual intensity, Deguy, like Esteban, was harrowed by the untimely death of his wife, which resulted in a departure from his previous work, a remarkable series of anguished prose poems, that form which seems to come naturally to the French poetic imagination.

Then there is Robert Marteau, from the Charente, who shares many of the mystical, even alchemical, ideas of Yeats, connecting them to the mysteries of earth, as in his native place, the forest of Chize. He is also profoundly influenced by ritual, an aficionado of the bullfight. Solitary, indeed almost hermetical, Robert is as intense in his way as Deguy, deeply conscious of how much we have lost in our exploitation of the world:

> *I say: nothing is tragic*
> *Since man's skull lost*
> *   the shape of the sky*
> *I say*
> *and (you will curse me)*
> *Eve's blessing on the treasure*
>
> *I say to the angel*
> *you are Thoth, you are great Hermes*
> *whom the serpents obey – and this quill.*

I continue to translate from the Irish, of course; there is a comradely exchange between Irish poets in the two languages. Nuala Ní Dhomhnaill, for instance, my successor in this Chair, has been translated by the top brass of Irish poetry in English. My own efforts include 'The Broken Doll' and her lovely love poem, 'Blodewedd' (the Welsh Lady of Flowers).

Trying to describe how Blodewedd exfoliates in her ardour, I borrowed a line from the American poet James Wright:

> *At the least touch of your fingertips*
> *I break into blossom,*
> *My whole chemical composition*
> *transformed.*
> *I sprawl like a grassy meadow*
> *fragrant in the sun;*
> *at the brush of your palm, all my herbs*
> *and spices spill open ...*

I read this aloud sometimes, startling my audience with a seeming sex change, since the final stanza opens with: 'Hours later I linger / in the ladies' toilet, / a sweet scent wafting / from all my pores ...' And this ambiguity in translation recalls me to my own 'The Trout', in which the speaker grasps the fish with his bare hands. Readers of the poem in English have wondered if it is a thinly veiled description of masturbation, but in the French of La Pleaide it is called 'La Truite', meaning that that particular argument does not arise.

I find Cathal O Searcaigh interesting because he writes in Ulster Irish, the Irish I tried to learn as a boy. In translating his 'Clabber: The Poet at Three Years', with its echo of Rimbaud's 'Le Poête a Sept Ans', I tried, of course, to render it in my own English Ulster-Speak: '... I heard a squelch in my wellies / and felt through every fibre of my duds / the cold tremors of awakening knowledge. / O elected clabber, you chilled me to the bone.'

I also contributed to Michael Davitt's *Selected Poems* and, sad to say, helped to translate his last sequence of poems, about his wanderings in Gascony. Perhaps it is fitting to end with these lines, the acute observations of an Irishman abroad in France:

Below us in the street
the argot of the teenagers,
bee-swarm of their scooters

up and down.
In the morning three old soldiers,
returning from the boulangerie

with their rifles of bread,
stand to attention beneath our window,
intently conferring ...

Nuala Ní Dhomhnaill
Photograph courtesy of Arts Lives

Níl Cead Isteach ag an bPobal

Tírdhreach Liteartha Neamhaitheanta na Gaolainne.

An Chéad Léacht de Dhámh Éigse na hÉireann.

Ba mhaith liom a shamhlú gurb é an leagan ceart Gaolainne ar an Ollúnacht seo ná Ollamh Fódla. Gabhann an t-ainm sin siar i bhfad i réimsí na staire agus na miotaseolaíochta. Deir *Lebor Gabhála Éireann* go raibh a leithéid d'Ollamh ann. Cailleadh sa bhliain 1390 RCh é agus is in Uisneach atá sé curtha. Chreid na luathársaitheoirí chomh daingean sin sa neach miotaseolaíochta seo gur dhein Macalister tochailt ar a uaigh, más fíor. Níor thángthas ar chorp ar bith san uaigh, ar ndóigh. Níor neach ceart é an tOllamh Fódla ach neach a fáisceadh as an miotaseolaíocht. Ach ní hin le rá nach ann dó go láidir mar mheafar. Meafar ab ea é. Meafar is ea é. Is cuid de réimse miotaseolaíochta agus samhlaíochta na hÉireann é, a d'fhág a mharc ar an litríocht riamh anall, go dtí an lá inniu féin. Is gné é seo atá cosúil go maith leis an gCúigiú Cúige a mhol Mary Robinson le linn a hUachtaránachta.

Is cóir mar sin agus is ceart má tá fáil ar a uaigh in aon áit gur in Uisneach a gheofaí í, croílár tíreolaíochta agus spioradáltachta na hÉireann, lár an Chúigiú Cúige. Imleacán na hÉireann is ea í, arb ionann í agus an chloch i lár shuíomh beannaithe Delphi na Gréige – *omphalos* nó imleacán an domhain. Agus go deimhin tá *omphalos* in Uisneach. Is cloch an-aisteach í a dtugann muintir na háite 'The Cat's Stone' uirthi sa Bhéarla agus ar a dtugtar Reann na Míreann sa Ghaolainn; glacaim leis gurb é an focal céanna é 'mír' agus 'curadhmhír', an chuid ab fhearr den bhfeoil go mbíodh na seanlaochra ag troid go bás ar a son. Seasann an mhír seo do chúig cúigí na hÉireann a tháinig le chéile ar an mball seo, de réir an tseanchais.

Bhí grianghraf den leacht neamhshuaithinseach seo, nach gallán, dolmain ná uaigh é, in eagrán den leabhar *An tAos Óg* a tháinig amach le déanaí agus ina bhfuil saothar le céad scríbhneoir Gaolainne. Is maith liom a shamhlú go bhfuil cuspóir leis seo go léir. Is maith liom a shamhlú go bhfuil ceangal éigin idir céad scríbhneoir Gaolainne a bheith ann agus leac uaighe Ollamh Fódla. Fé mar a d'éirigh sé aníos ionainne. Fé mar ba sinne go léir a chuid leanaí.

Bhain go leor scríbhneoirí leas as an gcloch seo. Is cuid de chosmeolaíocht phearsanta James Joyce í. Mar sin féin, agus is pointe é seo a bheidh á dhearbhú arís agus arís eile agam sa léacht seo, is beag le rá é i gcomhthéacs an tsuímh féin in Uisneach, i gContae na hIarmhí. Tá fána bheag ann, mar is léir ón ainm Uisneach, ón nGaolainn 'uisinn'. Tugann an Duinníneach 'a temple of the head' air chun nach gceapfaí gur teampall nó foirgneamh é. Tá comhartha beag dubh is bán in aice leis agus 'Uisneach' scríofa air ach ní thugtar a thuilleadh eolais don taistealaí neamhairdiúil ná d'éinne eile a bheadh ag gabháil na slí. Cén fáth gur dóigh liom gur mór an trua é seo? Cén fáth gur dóigh liom gur sampla maith is ea é de rúnoidhreacht na hÉireann nach léir in aon chor í don ghnáthshaoránach? B'fhéidir gurb amhlaidh is fearr é. B'fhéidir gurb é an rud deireanach ar fad atá uainn ná Ionad Oidhreachta ar an suíomh seo, rud a léireodh ní arbh fhearr leat a bheith clúdaithe le tost is mistéir, ní a chaithfeadh daoine aonair a aimsiú chun go mbeadh sé ina shuíomh oilithreachta inmheánaí dóibh, mar a déarfá.

Mar b'fhéidir an rud céanna a rá faoi Ráth Cruachan, tamaillín suas an bóthar i gContae Ros Comáin. An uair dheireanach a thugas cuairt ar an áit úd ní fhaca mé ach sreanganna agus feochadáin. Arís bhí comhartha beag taobh leis an ráth a dúirt go raibh cónaí anseo ar go leor de Ríthe Chonnacht. Ní luaitear Médhbh. Ní luaitear Ailill. Ní luaitear an Táin. Ní luaitear an comhrá cáiliúil idir an bheirt agus seo sampla de le go dtuigfí cad tá i gceist:

> 'Is fíorbhriathar é a 'níon ó' arsa Ailill, 'is maith an bhean bean dea-fhir.'
> 'Is maith cheana' arsa an iníon, 'ach cén fáth duit sin a rá?'
> 'Tá,' arsa Ailill, 'gur fearr tusa inniu ná an lá a thógas'sa thú.'
> 'Ba mhaith mise romhat' arsa Meadhbh.

Agus fé mar a deir siad, 'Chuadar ón bhfocal beag go dtí an bhfocal mór le chéile':

> 'Cibé a imreann méala nó meirtne nó mearbhall ortsa nil éiric ná eineachlann ann duitse ach a bhfuil domsa,' arsa Meadhbh, 'mar is fear ar tionchar mná atá ionat.'

A thuilleadh maslaí sa dá threo. Ansin:

> 'Mar sin féin,' arsa Meadhbh, 'is mó mo mhaithsa ná do mhaithsa.'
> 'Is ionadh liom sin,' arsa Ailill, 'mar níl neach is mó seod agus maoin agus ollmhaitheas ná mise agus tá a fhios agam nach bhfuil.'

Níl aon chúlántacht anseo. Níor shuáilce í an chúlántacht i measc na Sean-Ghael, bíodh an meon athraithe ó shin nó ná bíodh.

Bhuaigh Ailill i ndeireadh na dála, go sealadach, mar is aige atá an Finnebheannach agus níl a chómhaith ag Médhbh.

Bíodh sin mar atá, tugann sí faoi sheilbh a fháil ar an Donn Cuailgne, rud a chuireann tús leis an eachtra ar fad agus le téacs na Tána, an rud is cóngaraí d'eipic náisiúnta atá againn.

Nach cuma mura bhfuil macallaí na Tána le clos thart ar Ráth Cruachan mar atá sé inniu? Tar éis an tsaoil níl iontu ach scéalta. Scéalta fánacha a d'oirfeadh, mar a dúirt na manaigh féin a bhreac síos iad, *ad amusandum stultorum*, 'le haghaidh sult na n-amadán'. Ach sin é go díreach é. Níl againn ach scéalta. Insímid scéalta dá chéile le bheith beo agus chun leanúint orainn. Agus bhí suímh chomh hoiriúnach do na scéalta sin in Éirinn againn le fada an lá gur mór an trua nach féidir iad a aithint. Cuimhním agus ríméad ar leith orm ar rud éigin a thit amach nuair a bhí an dara hiníon againn, Ayse, thart ar a haon déag. An lá áirithe seo chuir sí ceist orm: 'T'ás agat, a Mham, na scéalta sin go léir sa Táin – Deirdre agus Naoise agus Cú Chulainn agus an stuif sin ar fad – ar tharla sé sin go léir?' 'Bhuel is scéalta breátha iad agus fiú munar tharla siad tá siad chomh maith sin mar scéalta gur chóir gur tharla. Ach pé acu ar tharla nó nár tharla, ar a laghad ar bith tá a fhios againn an áit inar tharla siad.' 'Is cén áit ab ea é sin?' 'In Eamhain Macha.' 'Tá a leithéid d'áit ann mar sin?'

Agus dúrtsa go raibh a leithéid d'áit ann go deimhin agus go raibh sé ann i gcónaí – tamall lasmuigh d'Ard Mhacha i dTuaisceart Éireann – agus má bhí fonn uirthi dul ann go raghaimís ann chun é a fheiscint. Rud a dheineamar. An chéad deireadh seachtaine tar éis don tsíocháin briseadh amach, thugamar seáp ó thuaidh agus roinnt cairde inár dteannta agus bhí saol an mhadra bháin againn. Ar an mbóthar abhaile bhí an trácht go hainnis timpeall na Teorann, ach fuaireamar amach nach raibh bac ná moill orainn toisc líon mór na ndaoine a bhí amuigh agus an fonn céanna orthu is a bhí orainn féin, sé sin cuid d'Éirinn nach bhfacamar cheana, nó nach bhfacamar i gceart, a aimsiú.

Sean-nath calctha a bhaineann leis an litríocht in Éirinn ná í bheith gafa le háiteanna. Cúis mhaith ba dhóigh leat go marcálfaí na háiteanna sin ar cuid dlúth den litríocht iad. Is dócha gur i mBinn Umha gar go leor dúinne anseo, a chónaigh éinín dil na Sean-Ghaolainne, Int én bec ro léic feit, lon dubh Loch Lao.

Agus ar ndóigh cathair liteartha nótáillte is ea Baile Átha Cliath. Ach i mBaile Átha Cliath féin, braithim easnamh. Gné iomlán liteartha in easnamh. Gné liteartha na Gaolainne. Sampla beag. Thuas ag Ardeaglais Naomh Pádraig tá plaic mhór tiomnaithe do na 'Writers of Dublin'. Tá scata ainmneacha luaite ann ach níl oiread is scríbhneoir Gaolainne amháin ina measc. Ba chuma liom ach an chuid seo de Bhaile Átha Cliath, go háirithe sna Libirtí taobh leis, ba nead scribhneoireachta agus scoláireachta Gaolainne í chomh fada siar le tús an ochtú haois déag. Lárnach ann bhí an file agus an scríobhaí Seán Ó Neachtain, fear a rugadh i gContae Ros Comáin ach a bhog go Baile Átha Cliath agus é ina fhear óg, áit a gcaitheadh sé an chuid eile dá shaol. Rugadh a mhac san, Tadhg Ó Neachtain, sa bhliain 1670. Chaith sé a shaol ar fad sna Libirtí agus áit chruinnithe a bhí sa tigh aige, ar dtús in Coll Alley, agus níos déanaí i Sráid an Iarla, ag scríbhneoirí agus scoláirí na Gaolainne, go dtí gur theip ar radharc an fhile sna 1740í. I ndán dá chuid 'Sloinfead scothadh na Gaoidhilge grinn' ainmníonn sé fiche is a sé scoláire Gaolainne a bhí ag saothrú leo i mBaile Átha Cliath agus máguaird. Bheadh aithne ag Déan mór na hArdeaglaise, Jonathan Swift, ar go leor acu agus chuadar i bhfeidhm air – a fhianaise sin an leagan atá aige de 'Pléaráca na Ruarcach':

> Orourk's *noble Fare,*
> *Will ne'er be forgot,*

By those who were there,
Or those who were not.
His Revels to keep,
We sup and we dine,
On seven Score Sheep,
Fat Bullocks and Swine.
Usquebagh *to our Feast*
In Pails was brought up,
An Hundred at least,
And a Madder our Cup.
O there is the Sport,
We rise with the Light,
In dosorderly Sort,
From snoring all Night.

Ach an luaitear an ghníomhaíocht liteartha, agus eile, ar an bplaic atá gar d'Ardeaglais Naomh Pádraig? Faic na ngrást.

Sampla eile. Ní fada ó shin ó thugas féin agus cara liom cuairt ar an teaghlach úd Baile na Corra, gar do Ghleann Molúra i gContae Chill Mhantáin. Is anseo a cumadh na danta cáiliúla a fhaighimid sa *Leabhar Branach*, leabhar na mBeirneach. Seán Mac Airt a chuir an *Leabhar Branach* in eagar sa bhliain 1944 agus sé atá ann duanairí de cheithre ghlúin ón teaghlach cinsealach, Gabhal Raghnaill i gContae Chill Mhantáin agus is iad na dátaí a thugann sé ná 1550 go 1630, go garbh. Seachtó trí dán atá sa duanaire seo. Is iad sin a haon go hocht déag, Duanaire Aodha mhic Sheaáin, a naoi déag go daichead a sé, Duanaire Fhiachaidh mhic Aodha, daichead a seacht go seasca a haon, Duanaire Fheidhlim mhic Fhiachaidh, seasca dó go seachtó trí, Duanaire Bhriain mhic Fheidhlim. Tríocha cúig file éagsúil atá sa *Leabhar Branach*. Tá cáil ar leith ar thriúr acu – Eochaidh Ó hEoghusa, Fearghal Óg Mac an Bhaird agus Tadhg Dall Ó hUiginn.

Ollamh le héigse ab ea Eochaidh Ó hEoghusa, an príomhbhard ag trí ghlúin de mhuintir Mhig Uidhir, taoisigh Fhear Manach. Duine acu, Aodh, a spreag mórdhán ar dhein James Clarence Mangan claochló air, 'O'Hussey's Ode to the Maguire'.

B'é Tadhg Dall Ó hUiginn, a bhfuil a shaothar curtha in eagar go slachtmhar ag Eleanor Knott, an duine ab aitheanta de theaghlach na mbard úd agus ba é tuairim a chomhfhilí gurbh é ab airde orthu agus is cruthú ar a cháil líon na gcóipeanna a deineadh dá chuid lámhscríbhinní.

B'fhéidir a áiteamh gurbh é Feargal Óg Mac an Bhaird, ball de theaghlach léannta Conallach, an chéad fhile 'nua-aimseartha' sa Ghaolainn sa mhéid gur scar sé ó nósanna a chomhphroifisiúnaithe agus in áit fulaingt sa dorchadas agus cloch anuas ar a bholg – cleachtas na mbard ag an am, deirtear – thug sé fén gcumadóireacht *al fresco*, uaireanta ar muin capaill de réir dealraimh. Nó sin a chuireann Fear Flatha Ó Gnímh ina leith:

> *Cuimseach sin, a Fhearghail Óig,*
> *fuarois tiodhloicthi ón Tríonóitt;*
> *gan feidhm ndaghoide ar do dhán*
> *ag deilbh ghlanoige ar ghearrán.*

Leanann sé air:

> *Gan boith ndiamhoir, gan deacoir,*
> *cead áinis as airdcheapaidh,*
> *scor raifhérach, radharc cnoc,*
> *amharc aiérach accat.*[1]

Ach fillimis ar an *Leabhar Branach*. Laighnigh ab ea scór de na filí a thugtar anseo. Den gcuid eile, Muimhnigh ab ea triúr acu, Ultach duine eile agus Laighnigh arís cúigear acu, ní folair. An dá phríomhshloinne ná Mac Eochadha agus Ó Dálaigh, baill de

theaghlaigh filíochta ó Loch Garman láimh leo, agus iad cean-
gailte le sinsearacht mar bhaird leis na Beirnigh, ach is léir go
dtugadh filí fáin cuairt an Bhaile na Corra ó thráth go chéile. Is
iomaí dán molta a scríobhadh i dtaobh Bhaile na Corra. Seo
ceann gairid le Donnchadh Ó Fíláin:

> *Beannacht ag Baile na Corra,*
> *mo chuairt ann is aithghearr liom;*
> *ní fhuil mo thol dún ag díorghadh*
> *[is] dol ón dún fhíonmhar fhionn.*

> *Baile na Corra ar gcuan sealga,*
> *seanróimh oinigh Innsi Néill,*
> *beag a t-iongnadh buadh 'gá bhuidhibh*
> *d'iolradh na sluagh suilbhir séimh.*

> *Mo bheannacht féin fágbhuim agaibh,*
> *a fhuil Raghnaill na reacht suairc;*
> *bhar meadh ga héineang a n-uighinn*
> *feadh Éireann dá gcuirinn cuairt?*[2]

Is geal liom an focal 'sean-Róimh' mar chur síos ar an mball
daoiniúil úd. Mheabhródh sé luathvéarsa duit a chuireann
síos go binbeach ar Ghleann Dá Loch mar 'Róimh' i gcom-
paráid le hEamhain Macha a bhí tráth fé ghlóir. B'in an uair a
raibh an mhainistir i nGleann Dá Loch i mbarr a réime agus
gan i mBaile Átha Cliath ach cúpla bothán cois Life.

Tagann an geimhreadh dian dubh agus tugaim cuairt ar
Bhaile na Corra, an teaghlach úd a mbíodh fáilte roimh fhilí
i gcónaí ann. Tá fonn orm féachaint ar thrí ráth nó lios a fhe-
icim ar an Mapa Shuirbhéireacht Ordanáis i mbaile fearainn
Charraig an Chróigh, an áit chéanna a luaitear sa *Leabhar
Branach* de réir dealraimh:

Iosdadh niamhghlan Cairrge an Chróigh
Nách iatar le haidhbhle sluaigh,
Traoi Laighion an síodhmhúr séimh,
Díobhdhúdh dom chéill m'aigheadh uaidh.[3]

Sé ata againn sa bhfocal 'cróigh' anseo ná an tuiseal ginideach den bhfocal *cróch* – planda. (Táim an-tugtha do na sonraí bith-luibheolaíochta seo). Ba gheal le filí riamh an áit seo, déarfainn. Chuirtí na muartha fáilte rompu. Tearmann ab ea é agus bia ar fáil ann, deoch, meas ar an bhfilíocht agus an saghas íocaíochta a bhí ag dul dóibh le sinsearacht, mar ba cheart – i bhfocail eile capaill, ar a laghad, seachas ba.

Luann Eochaidh Ó hEoghasa i ndán 47 trí lios nó ráth nó feirmeacha daingnithe mar chuid den áitreabh:

Ionmhuin teach ré ttugus cúl,
fionnbhrugh luchtmhar n alios mbán,
múr síodhfhoirfe sliombláith saor,
fionnráith chaomh líodhoilfe lán.[4]

Féachaim go grinn ar an léarscáil agus ansin féachaim tharam agus mé ag iarraidh an suíomh a shamhlú dom féin. De réir a chéile aithním an príomhráth dar liom, ráth na mban agus ráth na gcuairteoirí. Tá dhá cheann acu mar chuid de chríochghort agus ceann acu leathscriosta is iad faoi raon mo shúl. Más ann don gceann eile, caithfidh gur os mo chomhair amach atá sé lastall den gcnoc. Is lag íseal mílítheach é solas an gheimhridh, dath an chopair is na cré-umha ar an aiteann is ar an gcíb is ar an síoda móna a bhí corcra tráth is táim ag fiafraí díom féin an mbainfidh mé amach an ráth deireanach acu in aon chor. Ach ag bun an bhóithrín feicim comhartha a bhaineann stangadh asam – PUBLIC ACCESS DENIED. Ligim osna. Is dócha gur cheart go mbeinn sásta gurb ann dóibh i gcónaí mar ráthanna. D'fhéadfadh duine iad a leagadh le JCB i ngan fhios don saol Fódlach. Má moladh iad i ndán i ndiaidh dáin níl stádas leachtanna poiblí acu. Níl siad ar an liosta. Ritheann sé liom fiú dá mba leachtanna poiblí iad, ní bheidís saor ón loitiméireacht. Dá loitfí iad, chroithfeadh daoine a nguaillí agus bhainfí den liosta iad. Tá sé sin ag tarlúint go rábach ar fud na tíre.

Ba mhaith liom sampla a tharrac chugam anois ó Chúige Mumhan maidir leis an ngné neamhaitheanta sin de shaol na hÉireann ó thaobh litríocht na Gaolainne de.

Ar an gceathrú lá de mhí Bealtaine 1773, lámhachadh Art Ó Laoghaire i gCarraig an Ime, Contae Chorcaí. Ba chaptaen óg teasaí é sna Husáir Ungáracha, é tagtha abhaile ón Mór-Roinn agus é curtha ó choimirce an dlí mar gheall ar dhrochaighneas idir é agus Abraham Morris, Ard-Sirriam Chorcaí. Bhain an t-aighneas le capall a theastaigh ó Mhorris a cheannach ó Art ar chúig phunt, mar ba cheadaithe dó fé na Péindlíthe a bhí i bhfeidhm ag an am. B'in an luach ba mhó ar chapall, de réir an dlí, a cheadaítí do Chaitliceach. Ní raibh ann ach mioneachtra ag an am taobh leis an éagóir a bhí coitianta gach áit. Ní bheadh puinn eolais againn ina thaobh murach gur spreag sé ceann des na caointe is mó a scríobhadh riamh agus ceann de na dánta grá ab fhearr – 'Caoineadh Airt Uí Laoghaire', a chum a bhaintreach óg Eibhlín Dubh Ní Chonaill. Ina léacht tionscnaimh mar Ollamh le hÉigse in Oxford thug Peter Levi an dán ba mhó a scríobhadh sna hoileáin seo san ochtú haois déag air. Pé acu ar scríobhadh in aon chor é nó ar cumadh mar léiriú aithriseoireachta é nó pé acu go deimhin arbh í Eibhlín Dubh féin a chum, is ábhar mór díospóireachta ag scoláirí é sin fé láthair agus fágfaidh mé fúthu é. Ach is ann don dán agus seo chugaibh a thús le go mbraithfidh sibh an bheogacht agus an dobrón atá ann agus an chuisle dhúchasach:

Mo ghrá go daineagn tu!
Lá dá bhfaca thu
Ag ceann tí an mhargaidh,
Thug mo shuíl aire dhuit,
Thug mo chroí taitneamh duit,
D'éalaíos óm charaid leat
I bhfad ó bhaile leat.

Is domhsa nárbh aithreach:
Chuiris parlúis á ghealdh dhom
Rúmanna á mbreacadh dhom,
Bácús á dheargadh dhom,
Brící á gceapadh dhom,
Rósta ar bhearaibh dom,
Mairt á leagadh dhom;
Codladh i gclúmh lachan dom
Go dtíodh an t-eadartha
Nó thairis dá dtaitneadh liom.[5]

Is ann i gcónaí i Maigh Chromtha do 'cheann tí an mhar-
gaidh' agus aon uair go mbím ag dul thar bráid an aon iontas
é go mbíonn an dán mór seo á aithris agam dom féin os íseal.
Anuas air sin, suíomh seo an ghrá chomhlíonta a gcuireann
Eibhlín Dubh síos air, is ann dó i gcónaí i idtigh Airt Uí
Laoghaire i Ráth Laoich, gar do Mhaigh Chromtha. Nuair a
thosnaíos ar an léacht seo a bhreacadh síos bhí Tigh Ráth
Laoich ar díol agus bhí cás á dhéanamh ag scoláirí agus ag
scríbhneoirí go gceannódh an Stát é. Theastaigh ionad
cultúrtha uathu anseo a d'fhreastalódh ar leas an chultúir
dhátheangaigh agus ar leas na n-ealaíon scríofa agus léir-
iúcháin. D'fhéadfadh an tigh a bheith ina thearmann spio-
radálta, ina áit chruinnithe, ina thearmann do scríbhneoirí,
ina leabharlann, ina ionad acmhainní, ina amharclann agus

mar sin de. Is geata isteach i Múscraí Thiar é ina bhfuil an dá theanga fós á labhairt agus á gcanadh. Tháinig seanchaithe iontacha chun cinn i Múscraí Thiar – scéalaithe i nGaolainn agus i mBéarla – Amhlaoimh Ó Loinsigh a cailleadh i 1947 agus Tadhg Ó Buachalla, an táilliúir cáiliúil in 'The Tailor and Ansty'. Is ann a tháinig chun cinn amhránaithe móra dátheangacha ar nós Bess Cronin, gan trácht ar Chór Chúil Aodha a bhunaigh Seán Ó Riada, duine des na céad daoine a d'aithin saibhreas cultúrtha na háite. Áitíodh gurb é an chúis ar caomhnaíodh an tigh réamh-Sheoirseach agus an clós stábla mór daingnithe cloiche ná an meas a bhí ag na húinéirí i gcaitheamh na mblianta, i dteannta an phobail áitiúil, ar shuíomh 'Chaoineadh Airt Uí Laoghaire'. Deir Máirín Ní Dhonnchadha ó Ollscoil na Gaillimhe go bhfuil an tigh '... salvific in itself and can also stand for the good that poetry effects in people's lives when it is shared with them'.

Sé an caoineadh seo, a deir sí, 'ag Eibhlín Ní Chonaill an dán is aitheanta ó thraidisiún Gaelach an ochtú haois déag, nó go deimhin ó litríocht na Gaeilge trí chéile roimh an fichiú haois agus ar fud an domhain. Ach bhí stádas éiginnte aige san am ar cumadh é nuair ba mhó an meas a bhí ar fhoirmeacha ardstílithe filíochta ná ar an dán paiseanta a tháinig amach ón gcroí. Dá réir sin seasann 'Caoineadh Airt Uí Laoghaire' do ghnéithe dár n-oidhreacht atá fós le haimsiú agus le luacháil agus a athluacháil lenár linn féin.

Luadh tábhacht an cheantair chomh maith i gcomhthéacs dhá fhoirm lárnacha de litríocht Ghaolainne an ochtú haois déag – an barántas agus an aisling. Sa cheantar seo a rugadh beirt de mhórscríbhneoirí Gaolainne na haoise sin Aogán Ó Rathaile agus Eoghan Rua Ó Súilleabháin. Luadh leanúnachas an traidisiúin i Múscraí Thiar, mar shampla an mórfhile pobail Máire Bhuí Ní Laoghaire a rugadh anseo i 1771, bliain i ndiaidh bhás Airt Uí Laoghaire. Rugadh an

scríbhneoir agus an t-athbheochantóir an tAthair Peadar Ua
Laoghaire i bparóiste Chluain Droichead, nach bhfuil rófhada
ón áit, deich mbliana sular cailleadh Máire, agus rugadh Seán
Ó Ríordáin, an file Gaolainne ab fhearr sa chéad leath den
bhfichiú aois, rugadh eisean i mBaile Bhuirne tamall de
bhlianta tar éis bhás an Athar Peadar.

Ba mhún in aghaidh na gaoithe é. Tháinig litir ó rúnaí
príobháideach Shíle de Valera, a bhí ag an am sin ina hAire
Ealaíon, Oidhreachta, Gaeltachta agus Oileán, nach ndúirt
ach go raibh Tigh Ráth Laoich ar thaifid na struchtúr cosanta
ag Comhairle Chontae Chorcaí agus go raibh Tigh Thraolaigh
i gCaisleán an Bharraigh, Contae Mhaigh Eo, chun ligint don
Ard-Mhúsaem bailiúchán de lámhdhéantúsáin tíre a thais-
peáint i dtimpeallacht oiriúnach, agus go bunúsach go raibh
an oidhreacht ailtireachta á cosaint ag na hAchtanna
Pleanála. Brilléis! Cén bhaint atá ag Maigh Eo le litríocht na
Mumhan? Mar Mhuimhneach mé féin – (mheasas gur Éire-
annach a bhí ionam go dtí gur chuas chun cónaithe i mBaile
Átha Cliath agus mé i lár na dtríochaidí agus gur tuigeadh
dom gur sa Pháil a bhíos agus go dtí sin nár chónaíos in aon
áit in Éirinn lasmuigh de Chúige Mumhan) – faighim ana
bhlas ar línte deireanacha Chaoineadh Eibhlín Dubh.

> *Mo ghrá thu agus mo rún!*
> *Tá do stácaí ar a mbonn,*
> *Tá do bha buí á gcrú;*
> *Is ar mo chroí atá do chumha*
> *Ná leigheasfadh Cúige Mumhan*
> *Ná Gaibhne Oileáin na bhFionn.*[6]

An tábhacht a bhaineann leis an litríocht ina suíomh
nádúrtha, ba phointe é sin a chuaigh amú ar an Aire.

An sampla deireanach a theastaíonn uaim a thabhairt
anseo de litríocht na Gaolainne i suíomh nádúrtha, is sampla

é atá níos cóngaraí dúinn anseo i mBéal Feirste agus le bheith féaráilte ní sampla diúltach é. Baineann sé le hoidhreacht liteartha Oirghialla mar a thugann an tOllamh Breandán Ó Buachalla uirthi, sé sin Ulaidh Thoir Theas. De thairbhe an obair cheannródaíochta a dhein an Cairdinéal Tomás Ó Fiaich, nach maireann, agus é ina Ollamh le Nua-Ghaolainn i gColáiste Mhaigh Nuad, aithnítear an chuid seo de Chúige Uladh ar cheann de phríomhcheantair na gníomhaíochta liteartha Gaolainne iarchlasacaí sa tír seo. Agus tús curtha leis ag Séamas Dall Mac Cuarta (1647–1733) agus fad le hArt Mac Bionnaid agus Art Mac Cumhaigh, tháinig seoda chun cinn ón gcultúr sin i gcaitheamh tréimhse neamhbhriste de bhlianta fada. Áirítear anseo forbairt ar mheadaracht nua, trí rainn agus amhrán, 'sé sin le rá trí véarsa ghearra a bhí bunaithe ar mheadarachtaí fhilíocht na mBard agus véarsa deiridh bunaithe ar mheadaracht aiceanta na n-amhrán. I measc na saothar iontach caithfear 'Úirchill an Chreagáin' a lua mar cheann de mhóraislingí i stair an tseánra trí chéile. Tá binneas thar na beartaibh ann agus mairfidh sé fad a mhairfidh an Ghaolainn. (Tá leagan luathchlóite den téacs againn a d'fhoilsigh an scríobhaí Nioclás Ó Cearnaigh i dtuairiscí an Chumainn Oisínigh):

> Ag Úr-Chill an Chreagáin chodail mé aréir faoi bhrón,
> is le héirí na maidne tháinig ainnir fá mo dhéin le póig,
> bhí gríosghrua ghartha aici agus loinnir ina céibh mar ór,
> is gurbh é íocshláinte an domhain bheith ag amharc ar
> an ríoghan óg.[7]

Glaonn an tsí-bhean air chun domhan seo an dóláis a thréigint agus tar éis a bheith siar agus aniar lei diúltaíonn sé don gcuireadh agus fógraíonn gur mian leis bheith curtha san áit ina bhfuil sé anois i reilig an Chreagáin:

má éagaim fán tSeanainn, i gcrích Mhanainn, nó san
 Éiphte mhór,
gurb ag Gaeil chumhra an Chreagáin a leagfar mé i gcré
 faoi fhód.⁸

Is ábhar sóláis dúinn a fháil amach gur fíoradh guí paiseanta
an fhile. Sa reilig shlachtmhar taobh le hEaglais na hÉireann
sa Chreagán tá leac uaighe ann a thaispeánann dúinn cá
bhfuil Art Mac Cumhaigh curtha. Lastall den bhalla íseal tá
abhainn agus lúb leathan inti. An uair dheireanach a bhíos
ann bhí an ghaoth ag siosarnach i measc na gcrann, an t-uisce
ag spraoi i lúb na habhann agus bhí séimhe ar fud na háite a
chuir le mo thuiscint de bhua na hinspioráide a bhi laistiar
den dán 'Úirchill an Chreagáin'. Níos spéisiúla fós, is ann atá
Néilligh an Fheadha agus a thuilleadh den treibh chéanna.
Fuarthas é seo amach trí thimpiste nuair a bhí athnuachan á
dhéanamh ar an reilig, gur ghabh meaisín tochailte isteach i
bpoll mór sa talamh. Nach spéisiúil le samhlú é go mbeadh
Art Mac Cumhaigh i bhfolach sa tuama céanna agus cnámha
mhuintir Néill thart air nuair a scríobh sé na focail seo:

Is é mo ghéarghoin tinnis gur theastaigh uainn Gaeil
 Thír Eoghain,
agus oidhríbh an Fheadha, gan seaghais faoi léig 'ár
 gcomhair,
géagaibh glandaite Néill Fhrasaigh nachar dhiúlt do
 cheol,
chuirefadh éide fá Nollaig ar na hollaimh bheadh ag géil-
 leadh dóibh.⁹

Domsa agus do go leor daoine eile chomh maith, déarfainn,
b'ionann teacht ar thuama na Néilleach mar sin agus tuama
Thútancámúin á oscailt. Tuigim go binn conas a scríobhadh
dán ina bhfuil sárliriciúlacht agus ana-áilleacht chaointeach

Nuala Ní Dhomhnaill

in áit mar seo. Cuireann sé scéal i gcuimhne dom a d'inis Mícheál Ó hAirtnéide dom tráth. De réir dealraimh, nuair a bhíodh corp na bhFarónna á n-aistriú i mbád óna dtuamaí síos feadh na Níle, leanadh muintir na háite, na *fellahin*, iad ar feadh dhá bhruach na habhann agus iad ag caoineadh is ag béicíl is ag scréachaíl ar feadh i bhfad i ndiaidh na ríthe a bhí orthu tráth. Domsa mar sin is sampla den iontas agus den draíocht í reilig an Chreagáin a thugann an traidisiún liteartha áitiúil dúinn ach beagán cúraim a ghlacadh leis.

Tagann dánta as gach aon áit. As an aigéan gorm agus as an spéir i bhfad uainn. Dá mbeadh a fhios agam cad is ábhar dáin ann chuirfinn i mbuidéal agus dhíolfainn é. Ach tá a fhios agam rud amháin go cinnte – gineann dánta dánta eile. Gineann scéalta agus amhráin tuilleadh scéalta. Tagann athrú ar an bhfoirm, ar an teanga is ar an seánra ach dá mhéad dá n-athinsítear iad is ea is mó a chuireann siad le pléisiúr iomlán agus sonas an duine.

Dá réir sin, is den tábhacht é ná deinimis dearmad ar an ngníomhaíocht liteartha *in situ* agus tá súil agam go mbeidh ardmheas ar na céadta bliain de ghníomhaíocht liteartha na Gaolainne mar ghné shuaithinseach de chultúr an phobail agus nach bhfágfar fé shainghrúpaí scolártha amháin í. Tá sé tábhachtach mar sin go n-éileofaí saorchead isteach ag cách sa traidisiún sin, ar ais nó ar éigean.

NOTES
1 Osborn Bergin, *Irish Bardic Poetry* (The Dublin Instiute for Advanced Studies 1970) 118.
2. Seán Mac Airt, *Leabhar Branach: The Book of the O'Byrnes* (The Dublin Institute for Advanced Studies 1944) 144.
3. Mac Airt, *Leabhar Branach*, 167.
4. Mac Airt, *Leabhar Branach*, 166.

5. Seán Ó Tuama, *Caoineadh Airt Uí Laoghaire* (An Clóchomhar Tta. 1961) 33.
6. Seán Ó Tuama, *Caoineadh Airt Uí Laoghaire,* 45.
7. Breandán Ó Buachalla, *Nua-Dhuanaire II* (The Dublin Institute for Advanced Studies 1976) 41.
8. Breandán Ó Buachalla, *Nua-Dhuanaire II,* 42.
9. Breandán Ó Buachalla, *Nua-Dhuanaire II* 42.

Public Access Denied:
or *The Unrecognized Literary Landscape of Irish*

I would like to think that the proper Irish translation of the Ireland Chair of Poetry is 'Ollamh Fodhla'. This is a name that goes back a long way and stretches into the distant reaches of history and mythology. According to *Lebor Gabhála Éireann* (*The Book of Invasions*), there was an Ollamh Fodhla. He died way back in 1390 BC and is buried at Uisneach. Early antiquaries believed so implicitly in this obviously mythological entity that MacAllister excavated his reputed grave. Of course, no body was found in the grave. Ollamh Fodhla was never a real person, in that he was a mythological entity. But that doesn't make him any less real in metaphoric terms. He was a metaphor. He is a metaphor. He is a marker of a mythological and imaginative dimension of Irish life that has been expressed since time immemorial in literature, and as such is being readily expressed today. This is a dimension akin to that Fifth Province espoused by Mary Robinson during her presidency.

It is therefore apt that if his reputed grave is anywhere, it should be at Uisneach, the geographical and spiritual dead centre of Ireland, the centre of the Fifth Province, the *imleacán*, or bellybutton, of Ireland, equivalent to the stone at the centre of the sacred site of Delphi in Greece – the *omphalos*, or navel, of the world. And there is an *omphalos* in Uisneach. A distinctly weird-looking stone, locally called 'The Cat's Stone' in English, and known in Irish as *Reann na Míreann*; *mír* being probably the same word as in *curradh-mhír*, the champion's portion, which the ancient warriors were wont to fight about to the death. This portion refers to the five divisions of Ireland that supposedly come together at that spot.

A photograph of this unprepossessing monument, neither a *gallán* (standing stone), dolmen nor grave, appeared in a recent edition of *An tAos Og*, a book containing the work of one hundred Irish-language writers. I like to think it is there for a purpose, that the possibility exists of at least a hundred writers in modern Irish who are somehow connected with the gravestone of Ollamh Fodhla. As if it were resurrected in us. As if we were somehow all his children.

This Cat's Stone has been important for many writers. It is a part of the personal cosmology of James Joyce. Nevertheless, and this is the point I will be making again and again in this lecture, it would be very hard to make anything of it on the actual site of Uisneach itself, in County Westmeath. The site has a slight gradient, as implied by its name, Uisneach, from the Irish *uisinn* or temple. Ó Duinnín calls this 'a temple of the head', no doubt to distinguish it from a temple which might be a building or edifice. There is a small black-and-white sign nearby marking it as 'Uisneach', but no extra information is given to the unwary traveller, or to anybody else who might come that way. Why do I think this is a pity? Why do I think that it is typical of the deeply coded heritage of Ireland, which is well-nigh invisible to the ordinary citizen? Maybe it is better so. Maybe the last thing on earth we want is a Heritage Centre on the site, making blatantly obvious what is best left half in mystery and silence, to be searched out by individuals, making it, as it were, a site of inner pilgrimage.

The same could be said for Ráth Cruachan, just slightly up the road in County Roscommon. On my last visit to the site there was nothing to see except razor wire and thistles. Again, a small sign beside the rath notes only that this was the dwelling place of many of the kings of Connaught. No Medhbh. No Ailill. No mention of the *Táin*. No pillow talk. Here are a few snippets of the very same pillow talk (translation from the *Táin* by Thomas Kinsella) by way of showing what is at stake:

> 'It is true what they say, love,' Ailill said, 'it is well for the wife of a wealthy man.'
>
> 'True enough,' the woman said. 'What put that in your mind?'
>
> 'It struck me,' Ailill said, 'how much better off you are today than the day I married you.'
>
> 'I was well enough off without you,' Medhbh said.

And as they say in Irish, '*Chuadar ón bhfocal beag go dtí an bhfocal mór lena chéile*', which you could translate as saying, 'They started out with the small insults and went on to the big insults with each other':

> 'So if anyone causes you shame or upset or trouble, the right to compensation is mine,' Medhbh said, 'for you're a kept man.'

More insults each way. Then:

> 'It still remains,' Medhbh said, 'that my fortune is greater than yours.'
>
> 'You amaze me,' Ailill said. 'No one has more property or jewels or precious things than I have.'

No false modesty here. The like was never considered a virtue in Old Irish, however mores may have changed in the meantime.

They end up with Ailill winning, temporarily, because he has the *Finnebheannach*, or white-horned bull, and Medhbh doesn't have its equivalent. Undaunted, she sets out to get possession of the brown bull of Cooley, creating a pretext for the whole adventure of the *Táin*, the nearest we have to a national epic.

Why should it matter that the echoes of the *Táin* are not heard around modern Ráth Cruachan? After all they are nothing but stories, idle tales, suitable, as noted by the very monks who wrote them down, *ad amusandum stultorum*, 'for the amusement of idiots'. But that is my very point. Stories are all we have. Stories are what we tell each other to keep going, to keep alive. And in Ireland we have had such a suitable setting for these stories for so long that it is a pity not to recognize it. I remember with particular joy something that happened when my second daughter, Ayse, was about eleven. She came to me one day with a question: 'You know, Mam, those stories about the *Táin* – Deirdre and Naoise and Cuchulainn and all that stuff? Did it really happen?' 'Well, they are very good stories, and even if they didn't happen they are such good stories that they should have happened. But whether they happened or not, at least we know where they happened.' 'And where was that?' 'At Eamhain Macha.' 'Is that really a place then?'

And it was with great aplomb that I insisted that yes, indeed it was a place and that is was still there – Navan Fort, just outside Armagh in Northern Ireland, and that if she wanted we could go and see it. And we did. The first week-end that peace broke out we made a jaunt with some friends to Armagh and parts north and had the time of our lives. On the way home the traffic around the border was dreadful, but we discovered that there were no hold-ups, or slow-downs, or checkpoints involved. It was due to the sheer number of people who had had the same idea as ourselves, and were out to discover a hitherto not so well-known part of Ireland.

One of the timeworn clichés about literature in Ireland is that it is very much a literature of place. All the more reason, one would think, that we should mark the actual places that are so much a part of the literature. Cavehill, just beside us here, is more than likely the dwelling of the first beloved bird of Old Irish, *Int én bec ro léic feit*, the blackbird of Loch Laoi.

And Dublin of course is a noted literary city. But in Dublin itself, I notice an absence. A loss of a whole literary dimension. The literary dimension of the Irish language. A small example: up by St Patrick's Cathedral there is a large plaque dedicated to the 'Writers of Dublin'. It gives many names but not one single Irish language writer is mentioned. I wouldn't mind, but this particular area of Dublin, especially the nearby Liberties, was a veritable hotbed of Irish writing and scholarship going back as far as the start of the eighteenth century. It centered on the poet and scribe Seán Ó Neachtain who, though born in County Roscommon, moved to Dublin as a young man and spent the rest of his life there. His son, Tadhg Ó Neachtain, born in 1670, lived all his life in the Liberties and his houses, first at Coll Alley, and later in Earl Street, were meeting places for Irish writers and scholars until his sight failed in the 1740s. His poem, 'Sloinfead scothadh na Gaoidhilge grinn' ('I will name the best of clear Irish'), names twenty-six Gaelic scholars working in Dublin and thereabouts. Many of them would have been familiars of the great Dean of St Patrick's, Jonathan Swift, who profited from them, if his version of 'Pléaráca na Ruarcach' ('O Rourke's Ructions') is anything to go by:

Orourk's *noble Fare,*
Will ne'er be forgot,
By those who were there,
Or those who were not.
His Revels to keep,
We sup and we dine,
On seven Score Sheep,
Fat Bullocks and Swine.
Usquebagh *to our Feast,*
In Pails was brought up,
An Hundred at least,
And a Madder our Cup.
O there is the Sport
We rise with the Light
In dosorderly Sort
From snoring all Night.

But is there any mention of all this literary and other activity on the plaque near St Patrick's Cathedral? Devil the whit. To give another example, not so long ago a friend and I visited the site of the household of Balinacor, near Glenmalure in County Wicklow. This is where the famous poems that make up the *Leabhar Branach* (the Book of the O'Byrnes) were composed. The *Leabhar Branach*, edited by Seán Mac Airt in 1944, comprises the poem books of four generations of the ruling family of Gabhal Raghnaill in County Wicklow, and he dates them from the period between roughly 1550 and 1630. There are seventy-three poems in this *Duanaire*, or poem book. These are made up of one to eighteen, the *Duanaire* of Aodh Mac Seáin, nineteen to forty-six, the *Duanaire* of Fiach Mac Aoidh, forty-seven to sixty-one, the *Duanaire* of Fheidhlim Mac Aoidh, and sixty-two to seventy-three, the *Duanaire* of Brian Mac Fheidhlim. In all some thirty-five different poets are represented in the *Leabhar Branach*. Three of these are particularly well known – Eochaidh Ó hEoghusa, Fearghal Óg Mac an Bhaird, and Tadh Dall Ó hUiginn.

Eochaidh Ó hEoghusa was *ollamh* or chief poet to three successive heads of the Maguires, chieftains of Fermanagh, of which one, Aodh, inspired a great poem, which was transmogrified by James Clarence Mangan into 'O'Hussey's Ode to the Maguire'.

Tadh Dall Ó hUiginn, whose work has been so eminently edited by Eleanor Knott, was the best-known member of the Ó hUiginn bardic family and was considered by many other poets as absolutely outstanding in his time – the sheer amount of manuscript copies of his work attests to this fame.

Fearghal Óg Mac an Bhaird, a member of a famous learned Donegal family, could by some rights be called the first 'modern' poet in Irish, in that he supposedly broke ranks with his fellow professionals. Instead of suffering in the dark with a stone on his belly, as was supposedly the bardic practice at the time, he took to composing *al fresco*, sometimes reputedly on horseback. Or so he is charged by Fear Flatha Ó Gnímh:

> *Cuimseach sin, a Fhearghail Óig,*
> *fuarois tiodhloicthi ón Tríonóitt;*
> *gan feidhm ndaghoide ar do dhán*
> *ag deilbh ghlanoige ar ghearrán.*

This was translated by Osborn Bergin as:

> *This is comfortable, O Fearghal Óg,*
> *Thou has gotten gifts from the Trinity:*
> *Without any need of a good teacher for thy verse*
> *You frame fine scholarly art on horseback.*

He goes on:

Gan boith ndiamhoir, gan deacoir,
cead áinis as airdcheapaidh,
scor raifhérach, radharc cnoc,
amharc aiérach accat.[1]

Without a dark hut, without hardship,
With leave to take delight in lofty invention,
A grassy scaur, a view of mountains,
An airy prospect are thine.

But to return to the *Leabhar Branach*, twenty of the poets arrayed here have been identified as Leinster poets. Of the remainder, three are probably from Munster, one from Ulster, and five probably from Connaught. The two main surnames are Mac Eochadha (anglicized as McKeogh) and Ó Dálaigh, members of two poetic families from nearby Wexford, who were attached to the O'Byrnes as hereditary bards, but it is evident that many other wandering poets visited Ballinacor from time to time.

Many poems were written in praise of Ballinacor. Here is a short one by Donchadh Ó Filáin:

Beannacht ag Baile na Corra,
mo chuairt ann is aithghearr liom;
ní fhuil mo thol dún ag díorghadh
[is] dol ón dún fhíonmhar fhionn.

Baile na Corra ar gcuan sealga,
seanróimh oinigh Innsi Néill,
beag a t-iongnadh buadh 'gá bhuidhibh
d'iolradh na sluagh suilbhir séimh.

Mo bheannacht féin fágbhuim agaibh,
a fhuil Raghnaill na reacht suairc;

61

> *bhar meadh ga héineang a n-uighinn*
> *feadh Éireann dá gcuirinn cuairt?*[2]

> *My fond farewell to Ballinacora.*
> *My visit there seems much too short for me.*
> *My heart is not happy*
> *Leaving that bright hall full of wine.*

> *Ballinacor of the hunting lodges*
> *An ancient Rome on O'Neill's isle.*
> *It was small wonder to be without worry*
> *In the multiplicity of its merry, happy crowds.*

> *I leave you with all my blessing*
> *People of Clann Raghnaill of the pleasant rule.*
> *It is a great loss for me to leave you*
> *Though I visit all the length and breadth of Ireland.*

I especially like the word *seanróimh* – the 'Ancient Rome' that is used to describe the populous quarters. This reminds me of an early verse that rather vengefully calls Glendalough a *ruam* or 'Rome' compared with the erstwhile glories of Eamhain Macha. This from a time when the monastery of the Valley of the Two Lakes was a hive of human activity, while Dublin was still a barely identified ford of hurdles on the River Liffey.

In the slanting, early winter light I visit what can be safely identified as the once poet-welcoming household of Ballinacor. I especially want to check out what appear on the Ordinance Survey Map as three otherwise unmarked *liosanna* (raths or fortified farmhouses) in the townland of Carrigroe, which would seem to be the Cairrgre an Croigh mentioned in the *Leabhar Branach*:

Iosdadh niamhghlan Cairrge an Chróigh
Nách iatar le haidhbhle sluaigh,
Traoi Laighion an síodhmhúr séimh,
Díobhdhúdh dom chéill m'aigheadh uaidh.[3]

Carrigroe a house made of shining osiers.
A dwelling place of strength and ease
A fortress for people in this sublunary world.
A foremost example of fondness and peace.

Here *cróigh* is the genitive of *cróch*, a saffron plant. (This is the king of bio-botanical detail for which I am an absolute sucker.) It was obviously a place beloved of poets. A house where they were always welcome. A haven where they could be sure of food, drink, respect, and the kind of payment for their poems, which for centuries they had considered their due – in other words, at least horses, not cows.

Eochaidh Ó hEoghasa, in poem forty-seven, mentions the three *liosanna* that were part of the premises:

Ionmhuin teach ré ttugus cúl,
fionnbhrugh luchtmhar n alios mbán,
múr síodhfhoirfe sliombláith saor,
fionnráith chaomh líodhoilfe lán.[4]

Beloved house on which I must turn my back.
Abundant hostel of the white raths.
Rampart without drawbacks, free with flowers
White rath full of happiness.

I look carefully at the map, and then I look around again and try to position myself in the countryside. Gradually I begin to make out what may have been the main rath, the rath of the women and the rath of the visitors. Two of these, one half-destroyed and incorporated into a field boundary, are within sight. The other still exists, just up over the hill in front of me. In the wan, low, wintry light, with the nearby hill copper and bronze from dying bracken and sedge and the once purple moor grass, I wonder if I can make it up to see the last of the three raths. But at the foot of the *bothreen* a sign stops me dead in my tracks – PUBLIC ACCESS DENIED. I sigh. I suppose I should be pleased that the raths are still there at all. At any moment someone could take a JCB to them and no one would be any the wiser. For all their praise in poem after poem, they have no public monument status. They are not listed properties. It dawns on me that even if they were public monuments, it would not help them much against wanton destruction. If they were to be destroyed, people would just shrug and promptly 'de-list' them. That is what is happening wholesale throughout the country.

Now I want to give an example from Munster of the unrecognized Irish-language literature-based dimension of Irish life. On 4 May 1773 Art Ó Laoghaire, a young hot-blooded captain in the Hungarian Hussars, back from service on the continent and outlawed because of a bitter quarrel with Abraham Morris, the High Sheriff of Cork, was shot at Carraig an Ime, County Cork. The quarrel was over a horse, which Morris, according to the penal laws in force at the time, wanted to buy from Ó Laoghaire for five pounds. This was the maximum value of a horse that a Catholic could own, according to the law. The event was to everyone except the immediate victims, a more-or-less minor episode in a time of much more serious injustices. We would probably not know anything much about it, were it not for the fact that it became the occasion of one of the great laments and also love poems of all time – 'Ag Caoineadh Airt Uí Laoghaire', the 'Lament for Art O'Leary', composed by his young widow,

Eibhlín Dubh Ní Chonaill. Peter Levi, in his inaugural Oxford lecture as Professor of Poetry, calls it the greatest poem written on these islands in the eighteenth century. Whether it was actually written at all, or was composed basically as an oral performance; whether, indeed, it was actually composed by Eibhlín Dubh herself – these are all moot points, and a source of major contention to many great scholars at the moment, and I will not deem to point my toe where angels fear to tread. But it does exist, and let me quote a little from its beginning to give a feel of its vivacity, intense grief, and remarkable immediacy and verve:

> *Mo ghrá go daineagn tu!*
> *Lá dá bhfaca thu*
> *Ag ceann tí an mhargaidh,*
> *Thug mo shuíl aire dhuit,*
> *Thug mo chroí taitneamh duit,*
> *D'éalaíos óm charaid leat*
> *I bhfad ó bhaile leat.*
>
> *Is domhsa nárbh aithreach:*
> *Chuiris parlúis á ghealdh dhom*
> *Rúmanna á mbreacadh dhom,*
> *Bácús á dheargadh dhom,*
> *Brící á gceapadh dhom,*
> *Rósta ar bhearaibh dom,*
> *Mairt á leagadh dhom;*
> *Codladh i gclúmh lachan dom*
> *Go dtíodh an t-eadartha*
> *Nó thairis dá dtaitneadh liom.*[5]

Here the translation is from *A Celtic Miscellany* by Kenneth Jackson:

> *My steadfastly beloved, on the day that I saw you beside the*
> *market-hall, my eye gave heed to you, my heart gave love to*
> *you; I stole away from my family with you, far from home*
> *with you.*
>
> > *Nor did I repent it. You gave me a parlour brightened for*
> *me, rooms decorated for me, the oven heated for me, loaves*
> *made for me, roast meat on spits for me, beeves butchered for*
> *me, sleep on duck's feathers for me until high morning, or later*
> *if I chose.*

The *ceann tí an mhargaidh* or market-house gable men-
tioned here is still a noted landmark in the middle of Mac-
room and every time I pass it, I start murmuring parts of this
great poem to myself. More to the point, the site of such nup-
tial bliss described by Eibhlín Dubh, is still extant in Art Ó
Laoghaire's house in Rathleigh, near Macroom. Around the
time I was originally writing this lecture, Rathleigh House
was up for sale, and a group of scholars and writers were mak-
ing a case for it to be bought by the state. The case was that
a cultural centre based here would have a justified claim in
serving the interests of a dual-language culture and also of
the performing and written arts. The house could well be a
spiritual home, a meeting place, a writers' retreat, a library, a
resource centre, a theatre, and much else besides. It is the
gate to West Muskerry, where two languages and two litera-
tures are still spoken and sung. West Muskerry has produced
amazing *seanchaithe* – storytellers – in Irish and English:
Amhlaiomh Ó Loingsigh, who died in 1947, and Tim Buck-
ley, the famous tailor of 'The Tailor and Ansty', as well as
great dual-language folk singers such as Bess Cronin, and the
Cúil Aodha Choir, founded by Seán Ó Riada, who was one of
the first people to recognize the particular cultural richness
of the area. It was argued that the reason the pre-Georgian
house and extensive fortified stone-built stable yard had been
conserved was largely because of the respect of the successive

owners and also of the local community for the setting of Caoineadh Airt Uí Laoghaire. Máirín Ní Dhonnchadha of UCG wrote: [The house was] '... salvific in itself and can also stand for the good that poetry effects in people's lives when it is shared with them.'

Eibhlín Ní Chonaill's *caoineadh* is the best-known poem from the eighteenth-century Gaelic tradition, perhaps from all of pre-twentieth-century Gaelic literature in Ireland and beyond. Yet it had a more ambiguous status in its contemporary culture, some of whose brokers placed less value on passionate, spontaneous expression than on highly stylized forms of poetry. Consequently, 'Ag Caoineadh Airt Uí Laoghaire' is well placed to symbolize what is yet to be discovered from our heritage, how we evaluate and re-evaluate it in our own time.

Appeals were made for the importance of West Muskerry with regard to two vital forms of Gaelic literature in the eighteenth century – the *barántas* and the *aisling* – and that the area was home to two of the greatest Irish writers of that century, Aogán Ó Rathaile and Eoghan Rua Ó Súilleabháin. The continuity of tradition in West Muskerry was singled out – for example, the outstanding folk poet Máire Bhuí Ní Laoghaire was born here in 1771, the year after Art Ó Laoghaire's death. The writer and language activist an tAthair Peadar Ua Laoghaire was born nearby in Clondrohid parish, some ten years before her death, and Seán Ó Ríordáin, Ireland's best Gaelic poet in the first half of the twentieth century, was born in Baile Bhuirne a few years after an tAthair Peadar's death.

The appeals fell on deaf ears. A letter from the private secretary of Síle de Valera, then Minister for the Arts, Heritage, Gaeltacht and the Islands stated only that Rath Laoich House was on Cork County Council's record of protected structures, that Turlough House in Castlebar, County Mayo, was being developed to allow the National Museum to put on display a collection of folkloric artefacts in a suitable setting, and that basically the architectural heritage was being protected through the planning acts. I think that was fudging the point, to put it mildly. Where is Mayo when you are talking about the literature of Munster? As a Munster woman myself – I thought I was Irish until I went to live in Dublin in my mid-thirties and realized it was beyond the Pale – I identify deeply with the last lines of Eibhlín Dubh's lament:

> *Mo ghrá thu agus mo rún!*
> *Tá do stácaí ar a mbonn,*
> *Tá do bha buí á gcrú;*
> *Is ar mo chroí atá do chumha*
> *Ná leigheasfadh Cúige Mumhan*
> *Ná Gaibhne Oileáin na bhFionn.*[6]

> *And on my heart there is a grief for you*
> *That the whole wide province of Munster could not cure*
> *Nor all the craftsmen of all of Ireland.*

The importance of literature in its natural setting, obviously the whole point of the exercise, was entirely lost on the Minister.

The last example of Irish-language literature in its natural setting I would like to give is one closer to us here in Belfast. And to be fair, it is not a negative example. It concerns the literary legacy of Orghialla, or south-east Ulster, as it has been called by Professor Breandán Ó Buachalla. Largely because of the pioneering work done by the late Cardinal Tomás Ó Fiaich when he was Professor of Modern Irish at Maynooth College, this area of Ulster has now been recognized for what it is, as one of the main areas of poet-classical Gaelic literary activity in the country. Starting with Séamus

Dall Mac Cuarta and lasting up to Art Mac Bionnaid and Art Mac Cumhaigh, the unbroken years have yielded the culture many felicities. These include the development of a metrical form – *trí rainn agus amhrán* – three short stanzas based on the metres of the older bardic poetry plus a concluding verse based on the accentual song metre. Among other outstanding achievements must be 'Úirchill an Chreagáin', easily considered one of the most outstanding *aislingí* or vision-poems in the history of the whole genre. A work of astounding lyrical sweetness, it will live on as long as Gaelic lives:

> *Ag Úir-Chill an Chreagáin chodail mé aréir faoi bhrón,*
> *is le héirí na maidne tháinig ainnir fá mo dhéin le póig,*
> *bhí gríosghrua ghartha aici agus loinnir ina céibh mar ór,*
> *is gurbh é íocshláinte an domhain bheith ag amharc ar*
> *an ríoghan óg.*

An early printed version of the Irish text published by the scribe Nicholas Kearney in the *Transactions of the Ossianic Society* has an accompanying English translation:

> *Near the clay of the church of Creggan I slept last night*
> *in Sorrow,*
> *And with the dawn of morning a maiden approached*
> *me with a kiss,*
> *Her cheeks blushed like the rose and her hair glistened*
> *like gold.*
> *Twas the pleasure of the world to be gazing at the*
> *young princess.*

The fairy calls the poet to come away from the worries of this world, and after much to-ing and fro-ing he finally denies the invitation and declares that he wants to be buried where he is now, in the graveyard of Creggan:

> *má éagaim fán tSeanainn, i gcrích Mhanainn, nó san
> Éiphte mhór,*
> *gurb ag Gaeil chumhra an Chreagáin a leagfar mé i gcré
> faoi fhód.*[7]

> Though I die by the Shannon, in the Isle of Man or in
> great Egypt
> It is in sweet-scented clay of Creggan that I shall lie
> under the sod.

It is a comfort to know that Mac Cumhaigh's fervent and
heartfelt wish came true. In the beautifully kept graveyard
beside the Church of Ireland in Creggan is a gravestone,
which shows where Art Mac Cumhaigh is buried. Just
beyond the low wall there is a river and a wide bend in the
river. When I was last there, the rustle of wind in the trees,
the play of water on the bend in the river and the general
peacefulness of the place added up to an understanding of
how the gift of inspiration for a poem like 'Úirchill an
Chreagáin' could come. Interestingly, in the grounds of the
churchyard is the actual tomb of the Ó Néills of the Fews,
where many other Ó Néills are also buried. It was discovered
accidentally when the graveyard was being renovated, and an
excavating machine ploughed into a hole in the ground. It is
intriguing to think that Art Mac Cumhaigh might have been
sheltering in the very tomb, with the bones of the Ó Néills
all about him when he wrote:

> *Is é mo ghéarghoin tinnis gur theastaigh uainn Gaeil
> Thír Eoghain,*
> *agus oidhríbh an Fheadha, gan seaghais faoi léig 'ár
> gcomhair,*
> *géagaibh glandaite Néill Fhrasaigh nachar dhiúlt do
> cheol,*

*chuirefadh éide fá Nollaig ar na hollaimh bheadh ag géil-
leadh dóibh.*

Tis my sore wounded plague that we have lost the Gaels
of Tyrone
And that the heirs of the Fews sleep without pleasure
under the stone hard by
The comely shoots that sprang from Niall Frasach who
would not leave music without its reward,
Who would give raiment at Christmas to the Ollamhs
who owned their sway.

For many of us, the finding of the tomb of the Ó Néills like this is something akin to the opening of the tomb of Tutankhamen. It seems to make perfect sense why a poem of such incomparable lyrical sweetness and deep elegiac beauty could have been written in a place like this. It reminds me of a story once told to me by the late Michael Hartnett – that when the bodies of the Pharaohs were being moved from their tombs by boat down the Nile, the *fellahin*, the local people, followed for ages on both sides of the river, crying and wailing and ululating in mourning for the bodies of their erstwhile kings.

The graveyard at Creggan is an example of the wonder and magic that a little care and consideration of the importance of local literary tradition can grant us. Poems can come from everywhere and nowhere, out of the deep blue sea and out of the elusive sky. If I knew what made a poem, I would bottle it and sell it. But one thing I know for sure – poems create other poems. Stories and songs beget other stories. They change form, language, genre, but the more they are retold, the more they add to the sum total of human pleasure and happiness.

We must not to forget the importance of literary activity *in situ*, and I hope that the centuries of literary activity in Irish will be cherished as an important dimension of our popular culture and not left purely to the devices of the scholarly elite. Public access to that tradition, one way or another, will not be denied.

NOTES
1. Osborn Bergin, *Irish Bardic Poetry* (The Dublin Instiute for Advanced Studies 1970) 118.
2. Seán Mac Airt, *Leabhar Branach: The Book of the O'Byrnes* (The Dublin Institute for Advanced Studies 1944) 144.
3. Mac Airt, *Leabhar Branach*, 167.
4. Mac Airt, *Leabhar Branach*, 166.
5. Seán Ó Tuama, *Caoineadh Airt Uí Laoghaire* (An Clóchomhar Tta. 1961) 33.
6. Seán Ó Tuama, *Caoineadh Airt Uí Laoghaire*, 45.
7. *Breandán Ó Buachalla, Nua-Dhuanaire II, 42.*
8. Breandán Ó Buachalla, *Nua-Dhuanaire II*, 42.
9. Breandán Ó Buachalla, *Nua-Dhuanaire II* 42.

Kismet
or The Workings of Destiny

When I left Holland on our 'final return' to Turkey in the autumn of 1974, I had no idea what was ahead of me. All I knew was that I was five months pregnant and, by a miracle of bad timing, out to see the world. We travelled first by train to Zurich to visit my husband's favourite sister, Aysel, who was bringing up two small children while her German husband Nick, an ornithologist, was finishing his PhD on the bird-breeding patterns of Mt Oerlikon, or whatever it was. On the night train from Utrecht I caught an early glimpse of the real world beyond my sheltered life as a *Luftmensch*, or sky-cadet, from which I had been used to looking at things. When the night porter suggested that for twenty Dutch florins he would ensure we were not disturbed, I was not so dumb as not to understand what that meant – turn him down and he would see to it that every other passenger was dumped into our compartment at all hours of the night. He would also see to it that the customs and immigration officers in Switzerland gave us a thorough going-over in the depths of the night. I was genuinely horrified. This was an abject bribe, and I could hardly believe my ears to hear it coming from a smiling young Dutchman. Where was all that Lutheran probity? Where was the genial image of the friendly Dutch? They were nothing to the Dutch idol of worship, which was money. Needless to say, we gave him the bribe, and slept soundly until we reached our destination.

For the second time in my life I was taking part in an unseasonable contraflow migration, just like in the fifties when my family returned to Ireland as everyone else was going in the opposite direction. In Zurich my sister-in-law gave us sound advice while we made final preparations to return to a country that most people at the time were fleeing, mostly for economic reasons. Most importantly, she gave us food for the journey – *yolluk*, consisting of a large batch of *bosnak* or *kol boreghi* or potato pastries in the Bosnian style, which was a speciality of her mother's side of the family. This and two cooked chickens made up the bulk of a hefty amount of food that was to bring us safely to Turkey.

We were to travel on the Orient Express. At the time it had come down enormously from the high-class railway immortalized by Agatha Christie in *Murder on the Orient Express*, and was a mixum-gatherum of two different trains, one starting out from Paris and the other from Munich. They met in Belgrade and from there trundled on as best they could as far as Sirkeci Station in Istanbul – the modern, luxurious equivalent of the old train was not even a gleam in the eye of some clever travel operator. We took a train from Zurich, which travelled over the famous Simplon Pass and Tunnel. I only realized we were climbing the mountain in spiral fashion from the inside when I noticed, in one of the odd breaks into the outside, that I had seen the same landscape at least three times already – truly an extraordinary act of modern engineering.

We reached Milan and changed trains, and there I had another glimpse of what lay before me. Near where the trains for the east came in stood a man with a small kiosk selling the life-size, elaborately dressed dolls in large boxes ostentatiously displayed on many young marriage beds, which were particularly loved by Yugoslav workers travelling home. 'Watch him, and keep a good eye on the luggage,' Dogan said, as he went to get cigarettes and a train timetable for the rest of our journey. He was right. Your man did seem a shifty type. Dark, with a large moustache, he was nevertheless dressed in an impeccably cut mohair camel coat. Something did not ring right. What was such a well-dressed man doing selling gee-gaws on a station platform? Was he a pickpocket? Did he make off with unaccompanied luggage? Or maybe he was no more than a small entrepreneur, impressed by the pervasive Italian idea of the *bella figura*. I never found out.

The pleasant journey along the great plain of Lombardy was made somehow mysterious by the great, heavily pollarded trees that loomed out of the mist. Short stops in Venice and Trieste were not long enough to take in anything more than the Square of St Mark and the Bridge of Sighs. Then we travelled through a rolling, well-farmed landscape studded with new chalet-type houses all the way to Belgrade. The level of housing was impressive and so was the intensive farming. Not an inch was wasted. Knowing that these houses had been built mostly by remittances sent back by members of farm families working in the parts of Europe we had come from, mostly Holland, France and Germany, did nothing to lessen their pleasantness. Actually, coming from a family which a generation before had sent huge remittances (half my mother's pay as a GP in England) back home to educate her siblings and keep up the farm, made me particularly susceptible to enjoying the pleasant industriousness through which we passed. Once, very early in the morning, I saw a pheasant roosting on the lowest branch of a tree at the edge of a tidy beech forest. Years later during the Bosnian war, as Serb and Croat forces thrashed each other back and forth through the *Krajina,* news footage of the same areas showed unforgettable scenes of those beautiful chalets in still-smoking ruins and the good farmland between them desolate and either overgrown or shattered by craters.

During the journey we met a Turkish girl called Ayse who was bringing – I am loath to say smuggling – two heavy suitcases of designer clothes from Milan back to sell in a boutique in Istanbul. When we got to Belgrade she and my husband went to get a couchette, for the rest of the journey. They both knew the score, that if you didn't manage to get a bed you had to sit it out all the way to Istanbul. I was left with the enormous pile of luggage. The train shunted back and forward. There was an incessant cacophony of shouts in languages I couldn't understand. It seemed to go on for ever. I stood out on the little balcony at the door of the end carriage hoping against hope that either of the two would turn up. No such luck. More shunting back and forward. The part of the train we were on seemed to have ended up on another platform altogether. I definitely began to panic. I also began to feel distinctly queasy.

As I was blocking the passage to the door with my enormous stomach, some men whom I took to be Turkish workers began to speak to me. At this stage I had got as far as chapter sixty-two (the related past-perfect conditional) of *Türkische Sprachlehre für Ausländer* from the School of Oriental Studies in Vienna – the only book that I have ever read that in its method does justice to the logicality of the Turkish language. It had been a hard slog, necessitating I learn as least as much German as Turkish, but it meant that I now had some knowledge of a subject that I have always loved and have prided myself as being quite good at – grammar. So I knew, in theory at least, all about gerunds and gerundiums and present and past particles and the myriad suffixes and affixes, prefixes and postfixes from which a Turkish sentence is constructed. In my sheer terror I heard myself blurting out a sentence of perfect agglutinative construction – '*Kocam gelecegim diye, gitti gelmedi,*' ('my husband having said he would be back soon, went away and hasn't come back'), all of which is only five highly inflected and conjugated words in Turkish and which persuaded the listeners that I was an excellent speaker of that language. This sentence drew forth a torrent of speech, of which I understood only one word in ten. Little did anybody around me know at how much of a loss I was. It would take at least five years of living in Turkey before I could make a complicated sentence like that with anything resembling a similar insouciance. As they say in Irish – *múineann gá seift.* Necessity is the mother of invention.

Eventually my husband and Ayse turned up and we manoeuvred ourselves into the part of the train that had the couchettes. My queasiness having turned into an honest-to-God bout of vomiting, we settled in for the last part of the journey. Thank God for the *yolluk*, which saved our lives, as there was no restaurant car between Belgrade and Istanbul. We shared it with a young American student, who was travelling to Pakistan to study the sitar under Ravi Shankar. Or at least that is what he thought he was doing. A product of your average middle-class Western democracy, like me, he was actually clueless. If it hadn't been for Aysel's carefully packed hamper he would have died of inanition even before reaching Istanbul. Before leaving us he solemnly presented us with an American silver dollar in a little gift box as a thank-you for having kept him from starving. His father had assured him that nothing else would be as welcome a gift in the countries he was travelling through. Even then, despite my innocence, I had a suspicion that a few paper dollars, actual everyday currency, would be a much more effective, more appreciated, and lighter stash of gifts. I don't remember whether we exchanged address or not. Anyway, we never heard from him again. I wonder if he ever did make it to Pakistan. Iran was particularly tricky at the time, it being shortly after the popular revolution had ousted the Shah, and just before the mullahs hijacked the uprising of the mostly left-wing *muhajaddin*. I somehow doubted that Ravi Shankar would have accepted him as a pupil on the sitar, unless he had shown very particular musical talent. Maybe he was just a slightly belated hippy going on to Nepal and either making it home eventually or not. I never found out.

We on the other hand had enough on our plate. The train eventually limped into Sirkeci Station in Istanbul ten hours late. We had been held up by the Bulgars insisting on exorbitant transit visas, smiling and calling us '*komsu, komsu*' ('neighbour'), while perpetuating highway robbery. Then there was the long wait at the Turkish border station of Kapikiri. As we had slept mostly through Bulgaria it was morning when we travelled through the countryside of East Thrace or Trakya, the European province of Turkey. After the rolling farmlands and tidy chalets of Yugoslavia it seemed irredeemably run down – nothing but small, one-storey houses in villages that often seemed little more than an assortment of badly built shanties. The harvest of hay and maize was already gathered, and the fields looked poor and bare under the looming fog. Preparation of the fields for the planting of winter wheat had already begun, and the only movement in the whole countryside was that of the odd tractor making straight brown lines in the yellow stubble. Dogan and I stood side by side, not saying a word – he because he was deeply ashamed of the first appearance of his country, and I because I didn't want to make him feel ashamed. It was all very much a sorry sight.

An even sorrier sight awaited us in Sirkeci. The poor Turkish workers, coming by longer train journey rather than by coach because it was cheaper and easier to bring more stuff, were beset by, shouted and screamed at by the customs officials. Miserable cardboard boxes tied up with string were torn open and their contents strewn all over the place. Again, all this shouting in a language I could not understand. I wondered what the fuss was about. Later I discovered that being a customs official was a big deal, and entitled you to bribes both small and large for letting people bring into the country material, some of which was their constitutional right, most of which was not. The really big bribes – mostly for contraband – went to those stationed in Kapikiri, and the officials in Istanbul were pretty pissed off at only having the poorest and most innocuous workers on whom to vent their anger. Turkey at this time had a high-tariff protectionist economy, for all the world like the Ireland of the fifties. One of my earliest childhood memories dates back to that decade and it is of being so tiny I had to take two steps for my father's every one step. All I could see was the holed pattern on my father's brown leather brogues as he held my hand and walked back and forth in a small lean-to near the customs post off the boat from Liverpool. Don't ask me what they were looking for being smuggled in from the austerity of post-war England. Nylon stockings and the likes, I suppose.

There is a great story of my grandfather taking my granny to Paris after the war. It was the first time he had been back there since his stint at the Sorbonne, where as a student from the College des Irlandais he had got an arts degree way back in the year dot, sometime at the turn of the century. My granny had a great friend, a Mrs McCurtain, to whom she had

promised to bring back a hat from Paris. 'Do you have any-
thing else to declare, Ma'am?' said the Customs Officer,
unable to bring himself to look in the direction of her ample
bosom. 'Not in the least, young man,' said my granny
blithely, only afterwards realizing that all the time an enor-
mous pheasant feather had been sticking up out of that part
of her anatomy, in the depths of which she had secreted the
notorious hat.

But fraught and all as such minutes were, they were noth-
ing to what I witnessed in Sirkeci. It was like a scene out of
Hell. The poor unfortunate workers, mostly from Germany,
were the targets of great jealousy and resentment by the
petits fonctionnaires back home. If that was what Turks do
to their own countrymen I dreaded to imagine what the
scenes at the end of the long train journeys to, say,
Auschwitz, must have been like. We, on the other hand, were
whisked through on the strength of Dogan's student passport
and my Irish one and my by now obvious condition. Our lug-
gage wasn't as much as looked at. It was smiles for us all
around. I felt terribly guilty. Relieved in part that we were
not being subjected to such dreadful behaviour, but at the
same time guilty for what seemed to be a totally unfair priv-
ilege. It all reminded me of being back in National School in
Nenagh, Tipperary, where kids around me were being beaten
with well-worn sticks for not knowing Irish. I, on the con-
trary was above reproach because I had better Irish than the
teachers and spoke in *tuiseals*, automatically inflecting
words, because that is what you do when you know an
inflected language. Once again, I had got away with murder.
Or that was how it seemed.

But that moment didn't last for long because shortly we
were descended upon by the extended family – Dogan's
mother, his two sisters and his youngest sister's husband

Emin, who was the only car owner and designated to bring us all the way across the Bosphorus to where Dogan's mother lived in a small ground-floor flat of a two-storeyed house in Kucukyali. They had come to collect us at five in the morning, when the train was supposed to have got in. After waiting a few hours, they had gone back home, had a few hours' sleep, and were back waiting for us again. They seemed to think nothing of the ten-hour *retar*, as goes the Turkish word, borrowed from the French. I was gradually learning that time in Turkey was different from time in Northern Europe. More like Irish time in fact, these still being the days when to give a person a time to meet in Ireland meant at the very earliest twenty minutes later. I had always found this a problem because for my surgeon father, good timekeeping was of the essence: in an operating theatre, where people's lives are at stake, one is scrubbed up and ready for work at half past eight on the dot. It is just not up for discussion. Later I found out that Turks, when they want to be, are very good timekeepers. It is not for nothing that they are called the Prussians of the Levant. But that is something I discovered much later, in my professional life. Right now I was just *yenge*, the auntie that married in. And having no obvious or ostensible family structure or kin to back me up, I was an *el kizi*, literally 'hand maiden', which, in a society of complicated kin structures, was the lowest possible form of life within the family.

First there was the Bosphorus bridge to be marvelled over. It had been opened just before in 1973 to celebrate the fiftieth year of the republic, and was an object of great national pride. Although we mostly used the ferryboats back and forth to the Old City from the Asian coast where most of the family lived, it was still a remarkable experience. Built perfectly on time by a British engineering firm, it was the first time the Bosphorus had been crossed by bridge since Roman times or even further back since Darius the Persian had built a pontoon to ferry his huge invading army across into Greece. My first footfall in Asia. I paid special attention to what seemed to me an important building, a rectangle of white marble, boarded up and abandoned just beside the deep cut the new road had made as the bridge abutted on the Asian shore. I later found out it was a military kiosk and given the ubiquitous ancientness of Istanbul's antiquities, quite unspectacular. But to me that day it was important. I still mark it off mentally every time I cross the bridge.

Later, visiting Dogan's brother in the old business centre of Bakircilar Caddesi in Tahtakale, across from the wall of Istanbul University and just up from the Suliemaniye *cami* or mosque, it became the most natural thing in the world to travel from continent to continent. You bought your little disk for the turntable for a risible amount, checked to see you were on the right boat, crushed up to the open deck in the front if it was a fine day, or to one of the enclosed decks if it was cold, and waited until the boat was full, and off you went across to another continent. To take the ordinary, workaday ferries across the Bosphorus is still one of my heart's delights. Leaving the Old City in the evening with the sun setting behind the Aqueduct of Valens, the fire tower of Istanbul University on the horizon, the kiosks of Topkapi Palace at the edge of the sea, and the main mosques of the Muslim world straddling the city's seven hills, is to my mind the most beautiful man-made skyline in the world. San Francisco has a fine skyline and the evening view of Venice across the Arno is also breathtaking, but I have never in my life seen a skyline like that of Istanbul's Old City at sunset, seen from a ferry chugging along and minding its own business as it deposits the city's tired workers over to the Asian suburbs.

The journey itself is never boring. First, there are the

inevitable *chaycis* offering hot ruby-red tea in little thin-waisted glasses. You can usually buy kitchen coffee or some kind of herb tea as well. You don't pay for it immediately, but just when the boat is approaching the shore and you think it will be too late (or you will get away with a free one, depending on your mentality), up springs the *chayci* and asks for payment, more or less at your own discretion, or so it seems. On the other hand I have never come across a case of him being short-changed. The price is so tiny, and the self-respect of your average Turk so strong, that often I have seen people in a crowd charging backwards against the wave of people and running after the *chayci*, insisting they pay for whatever it was they had drunk. Then there are the travelling salesmen who will offer you the chance to buy every kind of useful gadget from carpet cleaner to egg beater – all this accompanied by a demonstration of the article in question and a rapid-fire sales patter that is often worth listening to just for itself. No article is too small, no gadget too recondite, that it cannot be extolled to the skies as the best thing since the sliced pan. That it is in a highly demotic, and at the same time formulaic Turkish adds to the charm of the sales pitch. It is now as much a part of a vanishing sonic dimension of Istanbul as the cries of the *eskici*, the rag-and-bone man much like that of the Lancashire of my childhood, or straight out of *Steptoe and Son*, right down to the scrawny horse and cart. Then there is the whistle of each quarter's *bekci* or night-watchman, or the winter cry of the *bozaci* who in the depths of night sells a concoction of fermented millet much loved by all, which unfortunately I cordially detest.

But our first egress to the Asian continent was by car. We settled into Dogan's mother's one-bedroom flat in the mostly retirees' suburb of Kucukyali. The exact address was Magari Cikmazi, which I came to learn means 'the-one-way-street-leading-to-the-cave'. The cave in question was a Byzantine building with a courtyard, the stonework intercepted by lines of brick, typical of that type of architecture. Nobody had a clue what it might have been originally – a church, a sort of *caravan saray*, a monastery, or even a *han* of some kind, and I never managed to find out anything more about it except to notice that in spring the tumulus around it was covered with wild white anemones, *anemone nemerosa*, a sure sign that in the not-too-distant past the area had been woodland. Now it was a place where sheep were herded before their slaughter *en masse* at Kurban Bayrami, or the Feast of the Victim, held six weeks after the end of Ramadan, and one of the major dates in the Muslim calendar. It is held in memory of Abraham's attempt to honour God by sacrificing his only son, and the Muslim version of the story is remarkably like the Jewish and subsequently Christian version, the victim in question being poor old Isaac. This is a story for which I have always felt an innate distaste but have a positive detestation of since becoming a mother. That it is one of the major mythical images shared by the world's three monotheistic religions is a very disturbing idea: the unquestioned sacrificing of the son to the father, and that on what seems the pathological idea of being asked to do so directly by God. Mind you, Isaac does escape in each version of the story, but just by the skin of his teeth. To my mind it is a legend that does no justice to any of the three religions that believe in it.

On the other hand the actual killing of the sheep on the feast day, usually by each head of household or by a special ritual butcher who will come and do the dirty deed for a small financial recompense or even the gift of the sheepskin, never bothered me at all. I am a confirmed meat-eater and the respect with which each sheep's neck is cut over a small hole in the ground, and the way the earth is allowed to soak in the blood, is deeply sacramental in its ritual. It is done mercifully and swiftly to the accompaniment of a prayer and has always made me and other observers of the act aware of the basic fact that our lives are lived at the expense of the lives of other animals. It has always left me speechless for a long time afterwards and very aware of some of the conundrums and deepest realities of human existence. Later on I was to have a son who at the age of ten quite cold-bloodedly filmed the whole ritual on a video, including all the gory bits, while a daughter ran in horror into the bedroom, hid under the bed, and could not be coaxed out for over two hours. Another younger daughter, just barely able to speak, remarked quite nonchalantly '*Mey et oldu*', 'The sheepy-weepy has become meat' – proof of the fact that such things affect everybody quite differently.

Magari Cikmazi was also the place where the sheep were penned for the lambs to be milked in the spring. You could buy the sheep milk to boil and use in making the most wonderfully creamy yoghurt imaginable. I was a strictly European eater of fruit yoghurts only until I became acquainted with sheep-milk yoghurt. It became an addiction. The only thing that was even better was a yoghurt from the town of Yalova made from water-buffalo milk. It had a large head of cream on it and was so thick you could cut it with a knife, and this was without the addition of clotting agents such as carrageen, which are now commonplace, unfortunately even in Turkey. It became my *ash ermek*, or the food craving that pregnant women are allowed and even expected to develop in Turkey, where it is absolutely taboo to eat anything in the presence of a pregnant woman without offering her some. This is done in case she might develop a longing that she would be too polite to express. An unrequited longing for food in a pregnant mother is considered to be very harmful to the baby. It might mean the baby would be born with its tongue hanging out. Failing such an obvious symptom of foetal trauma, the baby might be born extremely greedy. Or impossible to satisfy. Or it might develop into a selfish and unsociable being, whose *gozu doymaz*, or 'eye', could never be replete – in effect, some- one who is always and ever 'on the make', and never at peace with themselves or their surroundings.

There are a lot of people of this sort in Turkey, as there are now in Ireland and in every other country I have ever vis- ited. Nevertheless, a certain peace of mind, or acceptance of one's fate, a type of active fatalism – to be able to learn what one can change and what one cannot change and to know the difference between them – seems to be deeply ingrained at the heart of civil Turkish society. So by allowing a pregnant woman to hanker even unconsciously after an item of food is a sure-fire way of creating a monster of the unborn child. Whether or not any of this has a whit of standing in scientific literature is totally beside the point. What it makes for is a great politeness and care generally shown to pregnant women in Turkey, which was exactly what was shown to me, and for which I remain eternally grateful.

But not every cultural difference was as easily recon- noitred. On the morning of the second day my mother-in-law put a large tray of string beans into my lap and said: '*Kiz, temizle bunlari.*' I understood I had to prepare them for cook- ing in some fashion or other but my only previous experience of any kind of bean having been those of Heinz in a tin I was at a complete loss. Dogan somehow explained to her that beans don't grow where I come from (a lie of course) and it got me off the hook. The late afternoon of the following day she had a *kris*, or some sort of nervous crisis. She shook and per- spired and huffed and puffed until we brought her by taxi to the doctor. He was pretty cursory in his diagnosis and it was obvious that she had presented at his surgery in the past with almost the same symptoms. It was all very mysterious. Now, it was not for nothing that for years I had been bringing the laden tea tray into the drawing room to my mother while she had been doing a roaring trade in psychosomatic diseases. I was convinced this was a disease of the same nature, and took it as a personal attack against me as a daughter-in-law, an incompetent and heathen one at that. But I kept my thoughts to myself and held her hand through her ordeal. Just because a disease is hysterical or psychosomatic doesn't necessarily make it hurt any less. Dogan also had his suspicions and he also kept them to himself. He was convinced that this was an attack directed not so much at me as at him for being an ungrateful son and having taken his time getting an education in Europe while leaving his poor mother to struggle at home. And then to cap it all, here he is at home without a fortune to spend on her and a heathen wife in tow to boot.

Only years later did we compare notes and realize that we had both understood what was up, only had each blamed ourselves for it. After a few weeks of this, Dogan's younger brother Ufuk had her admitted to hospital, where she had an operation for what she called kidney stones. These were large enough stones that she passed regularly in her stool, washed and collected and brought to the doctor. The surgeon was mystified, because the operation showed she had no such complaint. Nor had she gallstones or any other stones that the body could possibly manufacture. Only later did we find out that before breakfast every morning she religiously drank a whole glass of olive oil, mixed with the juice of one lemon. The olive oil solidified in her bowel and created the mysterious stones. This was at least her third operation and she went on to endure two more, the last one being in Ireland and netting her a 'European scar' which she was not loath to display to all and sundry as if it were a triumphal trophy. Five major operations and all for nothing. Because my mother-in-law's ailment was not of a physiological nature – she was suffering from Münchausen's disease.

Münchausen's disease is named after the legendary German fabulist. The patient learns to mimic the symptoms of a particular illness so brilliantly that physicians and surgeons submit the patient to an operation, where no sign of any disease is ever discovered. It is a very difficult disease to diagnose and to cure, being at its core a masochistic need for the patient to undergo the trauma of surgery and also to benefit from the attention that being a suffering victim calls forth. An even more serious condition is Münchhausen's by proxy, where the mother inflicts injuries on her child for the sake of the vicarious pity and attention she receives by being the mother of a suffering child – but this was something I learned about much later and had nothing to do with the problem at hand. I didn't know the exact diagnosis at this point but I had my suspicions. I distinctly remember feeling a bit miffed that she had only given us two days of relative peace before playing up. We had arrived on the Tuesday and she had had her first crisis on the Thursday.

Remziye Hanim, for that was her name, was in hospital for over three weeks and this period was like a honeymoon for us. We visited her every second day over on the European side of the city where her hospital, the Numune Hastane was. The journey back and forth was great fun, and we also frequently visited Dogan's brother amongst the myriad historical monuments in the Old City. In Holland I had got hold of *Walking the Streets of Istanbul*, by John Freely and Hilary Somner-Boyd, and came to know a lot of the Old City through it. We bought a Redhouse Turkish dictionary at the famous Redhouse bookstore over in its old premises in Tahtakale. We bought Geoffrey Lewis's *Turkish Grammar*, still my *vade mecum* when I run into some Turkish construction I cannot quite fathom. On rainy days we took the tram from Sirkeci but mostly, when the rain stopped, we walked and walked. The streets after rain were lakes of water. I noticed the beautifully crafted stone gutters around the old Imperial mosques and decided that Istanbul was definitely a city that had seen better days. In Ireland and Holland I had seen plenty of gutters but these were usually things that were being gradually improved over the years. Istanbul seemed to be the city that had invented gutters and then forgotten entirely about their existence. It was definitely like nowhere I had ever been before.

When Remziye Hanim got out of hospital, she was semi-invalid for a while. Then one day, when we had taken one of Dogan's nieces up the hills to look for *cighdem*, or winter crocuses – basically any excuse for a long walk on a fine day – we came back early to find her down on her hands and knees, scrubbing the floors. She had not been impressed by my standards of cleanliness. She was indeed highly vituperative because in my attempts to cook in her absence I had damaged her exaltedly valued European Teflon non-stick frying pan. I admit I was only learning to cook *a la Turca*, but her reaction seemed totally over the top. To me it was only a pan, but to her it was a both a status symbol and necessary for her minutely calculated diet, which was entirely low fat. There were bound to be difficulties between us.

I think, though, that one of the things that made her really angry with me was the fact that when we eventually went to Ankara, for Dogan to get work in MTA (Maden Tetik Arastirma), the Geological Survey of Turkey, we went to visit his father, her estranged husband, and I got on particularly well with him. This was entirely a surprise to everyone, especially to me, who had been fed up to the gills with stories of his perfidy and iniquity. Even the fact that Remziye Hanim called him *Kochero*, the name of an especially notorious bandit in what was then called Kurdistan and is now for political reasons called the south-east of Turkey, had pre-judged me against him to the extent that when we went to visit him it was in some fear and trembling on my part. We arrived at the train station in Ankara towards night, and immediately the smog had us holding our breath. It was mostly caused by the low-grade coal or lignite used in house heating during the very cold winters of Ankara's continental climate. On the advice of one of Dogan's geological acquaintances in Istanbul we went at once to the Uzun Oteli at Diskapi. The receptionist asked for our marriage certificate. And me in my condition! I was horrified, only to learn afterwards that there might have been a good reason for it, as the surrounding area had come down a lot in the world since Dogan's childhood and was full of tacky little hotels and night-clubs or *paviyon* of most dubious aspect. We went on foot to find where Dogan's father lived, in what Dogan remembered as a wooden house in a large garden full of all sorts of fruit trees, a duck pond at the front and a fountain playing in the courtyard. There was no sign of it. On every side of the large main thoroughfare that is Altindag Caddesi there were itty-bitty shanties, shuttered and derelict. We pushed through a wooden door beside a *hurdaci*, or scrap-metal collector, and there was a small glass lean-to with a large tree growing up through the middle of it. 'That is a mulberry tree, and I recognize it from my childhood,' said Dogan. We knocked at the door of the iron-roofed house beyond the glassed-in area. Dogan's stepmother opened it, and recognized him after a fourteen-year absence. We took off our shoes at the door and were ushered into a compact and clean little living room, in spite of the obvious poverty.

Dogan's father, the infamous *Kochero*, came forward, we kissed his hand, and we were home.

The usual tea and pleasantries ensued. When we finally got up and insisted we spend the night in our hotel, there was pandemonium. Stay in a hotel? This would never do. It was unthinkable that a young man and his wife would not stay in his father's home. We prevailed and spent the night in the hotel, only for the pair of us to come down the next day with a whopping case of the 'flu. When Dogan's half-brother Cihangir came by the next day to see why we hadn't turned up again, it was obvious that we would need looking after for at least a few days. So custom prevailed and, willy-nilly, we were moved bodily to Suleyman Leflef's house in the most insalubrious shantytown of Ankara, where we were plied with lemon drinks and aspirin and linden-blossom tea made from one of the last surviving trees in the once-glorious garden. We gradually got better. It seemed like a genuine case of *kismet* – destiny, or the hand of God, whichever way you prefer to look at it.

And so it happened that during the next five years, the person who had the greatest influence on me and who was my chief motivator in learning Turkish was my father-in-law, Suleyman Leflef. He was a great character, a genuine original. He had been the only male, and therefore literate person, left at home when the new surname law was promulgated in the 1920s and when he went to register a name for the family under the law he just took the ending –*oghullari* 'sons of', off the long-standing family nickname, and so their surname became *Leflef*. When his older brothers came back from military service, they were very annoyed with him: 'Why didn't you take the chance to give us a heroic name like everyone else is doing?' A name like *Safkan* 'pure blood', or *Ozturk* 'original Turk', or *Demirel* 'iron hand', or the likes. He demurred, saying that the name they had had for hundreds of years was good enough for him and should be good enough for them as well.

A former military officer, my father-in-law had never really enjoyed his years in the army. For one thing, though a crack shot, he never believed in killing people. I remember years later when we finally caught a rat that had been terrifying the household, especially me with a newborn baby, he wouldn't even kill the rat. I, on the other hand, with more important things than rats' lives on my mind, drowned it unceremoniously in the nappy bucket. It was by default that he had ended up studying in Harbiye, the military academy. He had wanted to study at the Academy of Fine Arts, but did not have the necessary mathematics to be accepted. I once saw his graduation diploma, where he got top marks only in marksmanship and horsemanship. He had only advanced to the grade of *yuzbashi*, or centurion when he was cashiered for having two wives.

Being Muslim, Turks are allowed up to four wives by their religion. Since the reforms in Turkey brought about by Kemal Ataturk in the 1920s, however, the secular, westernized state had outlawed polygamy. My father-in-law was given the choice of giving up the second illegal – but religiously accepted wife, or being court-martialled. As a good Muslim he felt conscience-bound to keep the second wife, who had done him no wrong. And so, as he always maintained, he had resigned his commission because of his religious scruples. That was his version of the whole affair, but Remziye Hanim had a very different take on the story.

His philandering was the cause of her very genuine grievance. She was his only legal wife. She had, with her sister Mediha, been looking after the children of her Aunt Latife in Ankara when they had been followed by a young officer on

Anafartalar Caddesi in Ulus, which was at that time the main street of the still tiny capital city. She was only fifteen years old at the time, and from pictures taken of her in Bosnian costume during her one year of schooling, was a remarkable beauty of the Balkan type. Suleyman Dede said he followed the girls because of their beautiful legs in short skirts, still a great novelty in the deeply Muslim but rapidly modernizing country. According to her sister, Remziye always said she wanted to marry an officer. Suleyman followed them home, noticed where they lived, one thing lead to another and in a short time he presented himself in his full formal military uniform to ask for her hand, which he was duly granted. In their wedding photos they look a very handsome couple. Remziye's dress is of white satin with a train almost a mile long. She isn't wearing a veil, but a satin headdress, which exquisitely frames her dark blonde hair and her impeccable features.

But life with an officer did not have the glamour she had imagined. As his first commission Suleyman was sent to a village near Mardin, on the border with Syria. A fascinating area, it is still home to the Assyrian Christians or *Suriyani*, who use Aramaic, the language that Christ spoke, for their liturgical ceremonies. Such things held no interest for Remziye, who hated the climate, the lack of such basics as olives and who all her life went on about how the water was from underwater cisterns and had to be sieved with muslin to take out the little red worms wriggling in it. Having her mother-in-law come to live with them was no help either. Fatma, or Hamine as she was called by her complicated and extended family, was a formidable character and as tough as old boots. When, after some imagined slight or other, Remziye moved her own woollen mattress into another room, to sleep apart from her husband, his mother seemingly acquiesced to his taking a Kurdish servant girl as a sleeping partner. And a bald one at that, insisted Remziye, who always referred to her as *kel kizi*, or the bald girl.

There were other surprises and alarms to be endured. Once a visiting senior officer asked Suleyman to take a certain soldier out of the ranks and to beat him. Suleyman refused, as there was no reason to punish the soldier and he would be damned if he did so purely at a senior officer's say-so. The senior officer knew that Suleyman was correct according to military rules, but was still incensed. That night he sent a party of soldiers to arrest him and he gave the *vur emri*, or order that he should be shot at sight. Suleyman escaped with the help of the villagers and having appealed his case to a higher authority was pardoned and reinstated. But life with such a difficult, wilful and selfish man was very hard on Remziye. She missed the warmth, civility and modernity of her large Bosnian family. She detested her mother-in-law. She dearly regretted her marriage. And the birth of Dogan, her first child, while she was still at sixteen only a child herself, was not enough to ensure her happiness. The birth was very difficult. The child was two months premature, and she was in labour for three whole days with the dubious help of a village midwife and her cruel but extremely practical mother-in-law. In an area noted for its huge instance of infant mortality, especially from diarrhoea and dehydration in the baking Mesopotamian summers, it was through an enormous effort on her part that she managed to bring Dogan to the age of two. In a picture of the family and guests taken at his circumcision at the time it is hardly possible to recognize the sullen, withdrawn, painfully thin and worn young woman as the radiant young bride of three years before. Her dreadful unhappiness is utterly palpable.

Worse was to follow. On a subsequent tour of duty on the

Black Sea, Suleyman took in another young woman called Lamiye. She was from a family of refugees from Thessalonica, and according to Remziye, a gypsy. When she arrived in the house, ostensibly as a servant, she had been so neglected that she had to be thoroughly washed and deloused. She regularly wet her bed. Then to top it all Suleyman went through a religious ceremony with her, a *hodja nikah*, that, to his mind at least, and actually according to Muslim law, if not the law of the land, made her his wife. She was to be his last wife, and if anything a *grande folie*. He was absolutely out of his mind about her. He played the *saz* and sang *uzun havas* (Turkish *sean nós*) and *Ezo Gelin* to her. He was prevailed upon, if only for the sake of his profession, to put her away time and time again, but each time he took her back. Remziye to her death declared that he had been given a love charm, that the girl's sister was a witch and knew how to bind a man irreducibly. Remziye, finally, throwing all hope of financial security and caution to the wind, complained to the military authorities. In the confrontation that followed Suleyman chose the young woman over a secure financial future and career in the military. He had been after all at Harbiye, the military academy, a classmate of Kenan Evren who lead the putsch in 1980, and who made sure in the following years that the military would live high and well. To everyone who knew him the decision seemed like madness. To Remziye it was the result of evil machinations and a tryst with the devil.

So when she discovered that he had been kind to me, and that we actually got on quite well, she was understandably very seriously put out. Certain things happened between us and when, as a new mother with a six-week-old child, the tension between us had become so bad that my milk almost dried up, Aysel, who was visiting Turkey, realized that things could not go on like this and brought me to Ankara to stay in the shantytown with her father. There, for all the restrictions of shantytown life, the tensions were resolvable and my milk came back in by the bucketful. It was here, with the help of my father-in-law, that I can say I finally began to crack the linguistically hard nut that is the Turkish language.

Suleyman Dede was an Ottoman to the end. So much so that he refused to call Ataturk by that name. He was perfectly prepared to allow him the honorific appellation of *Gazi Pasha,* because he was just that – a great war hero (*gazi*) who survives, as opposed to a *sheyit* who dies a martyr's death. Ataturk was also a great *pasha,* or general. But to his dying day he refused to call him Ataturk, 'father of the Turks'. This he considered presumptuous in the extreme: 'How could anyone call himself "Father of the Turks" indeed! He is not my father.'

Not that he had any good words to say for his own father either, who had been an *ulema* or religious teacher in the local religious school, the *medrese.* He had also been a howling dervish, who with his fellow mystics would chant the holy phrase *Ja Hu* for days on end until the whole building in which they sat began to shake. As a child, Suleyman had once looked through a keyhole at the ceremony and seen his own father in a trance state. He got such a shock that – though he remained an orthodox Sunni Muslim and even became a *haci* as a result of making the pilgrimage to Mecca – he had no time for any of the dervish or mystic orders (the *tarikatlar*). He looked askance at anything that could be considered radical, extremist or fundamentalist in any form. He also held it against his father that he had died young, leaving a widow to bring up a family of six sons on her own. His father had been blond-haired and blue-eyed, of that particular cerulean blue, which is not as rare as might be expected in Middle Anatolia.

My father-in-law was usually scathing about light-coloured people, saying that they had no stamina and melted like candles in the summer heat. As well as his own father, he had in mind his wife, a Bosnian with the ash-blonde hair so typical of that part of the world, when he said this.

In spite of which he took to me enormously. Quite a demon in his youth, he had mellowed considerably by the time we met. He was in his own words *kurt kocayince,* 'an old wolf', which refers to the proverb *'Kurt kocayinca kopeklerin maskarasi olurmus'* ('When the wolf gets old and thin he becomes the laughing-stock of the dogs'). In some ways I was a kind of honorary man for him. He would call me out of the kitchen, saying *'Benim gelin mutfacta avratlarin icinde ne yapior?'* ('What is my daughter-in-law doing in the kitchen amongst the womenfolk?'), using in ironic manner the old-fashioned word *avrat* for woman, which might be better translated as 'female slave'. Likewise he didn't like to see me reading books, thinking it was a waste of time – time which would be much better spent in pleasant conversation with himself.

So we would spend hours talking to each other. When it was time for him to say his prayers, he went into the next room with his prayer rug, said them and then came in again and we continued the conversation where we had just left off. In the afternoons I would make him his *gelin kahvesi,* the special coffee made by the lily-white hands of the new bride, and he would drink it with great pleasure and we would continue speaking about everything under the sun. He never once suggested that I should convert, though once he set out to teach me the Arabic alphabet so that I could read the holy book *Koran-i-Kerim.* After three days of wrestling with *ayin, kayin* and I don't know what else, I proved to be a total *eejit,* and he decided that conversion was a grace obviously not vouchsafed me by Allah. I was fine as I was, one of the 'people of the book', *kitaplilardan*. As the *Incil*, or New Testament, and the *Tevrah*, or Torah, are considered holy books in Islam, the idea of conversion never rose again. After a few years I think I became in his eyes an honorary Muslim as well as an honorary man, and we got on together like the proverbial house on fire.

I remember one day one of his cronies named Berber Huseyn called by. I made *gelin kahvesi* in the usual small cups, and as they sat there sipping it I was an 'ear-guest' at their conversation, as the lovely Turkish expression for eavesdropping has it:

'She is very nice, for a heathen,' says Berber Huseyn.
'Indeed and she is, but you know those heathens aren't all bad people at all,' says Suleyman Dede.
'Oh, don't I know well. I have two sons in Germany amongst the heathens, and according to them, you couldn't find a straighter or more honest people on this earth.'
'If it weren't for the drink.'
'Yes, the alcoholic drink makes animals out of them. Animals entirely.'
'Yes, it is a real pity about the drink.'

This would have been amusing in itself even if it hadn't reminded me of similar conversations about Turkey I was to have in Irish with Thomas Murphy, my aunt's husband, and his cronies in a pub in the Gaeltacht:

'And you mean to tell me that the Muslims don't take drink at all?'
'No. They think that drinking is a mortal sin. It is against their religion.'
'God, that's hard. They must be a very straight people.'
'They are indeed.'
'And tell me one thing if you tell me no more; is it true that Muslims have more than one wife?'
'Yes, sometimes they can have more than one wife. Their

religion allows them to have anything up to four.'
   'Four wives. That's awful. They must make right animals of
themselves to be even thinking of having four wives.'

Same difference. *Plus ça change.* This is the sort of thing that
has always made me aware of the fact that so many things,
whether ideas of dirt and pollution, or of inward and outward,
edible and inedible, sacred and secular, are just lines that are
drawn on the chaos of the world in a way that is highly cul-
ture-bound and pretty arbitrary, if not downright gratuitous.
All cultures draw these lines; it's just that they draw them at
slightly different places. Living *a la Turca* for five years at an
early age made me something akin to an anthropologist. It
was sharpened by feeling myself at home in a language so
entirely different from Irish, and paradoxically, helped me
focus more than ever on Irish. Being outside an English-speak-
ing world for so long also made me aware of my other mother-
language. This all came to me from learning Turkish.

   The language that Suleyman Dede taught me was a Turk-
ish that was colloquial, slightly old-fashioned and basically
Middle Anatolian, rather than the more precious language
spoken in Istanbul – just like Gaeltacht Irish, a language with
a large stock of proverbs and formulaic phrases. Suleyman
Dede's Turkish is located somewhere between the written
and the spoken, perhaps with more emphasis on the spoken.
This is best illustrated by its marked reliance on context.
Who says what and to whom is very important, because of
the construction of the language, where a single word may
have an autonomous function to an extent unknown to us:
for instance the well-known example, often used to me
'Irlandalilastiramadiklarimizdanmisiniz?' ('Are you one of
those whom we have not been able to turn into an Irish per-
son?') Unlike the sometimes amazingly long words in Ger-
man, which are really chains of words, this is one single word

with the function and meaning of a whole long sentence.

In spite of the huge differences in syntax, however, I recognized something in the language that made me feel very much at home. Like the Gaeltacht Irish I had learned as a small child, the appropriate use of a key word from a well-known story or from a proverb can either clinch an argument or cause general hilarity. All one has to mention are the words *ahu gozler* or *sirma scalar*, 'almond eyes' or 'golden hair', and everybody knows you are referring to the apotropeaic over-praising of the dead, from the proverb *'Kor olur ahu gozler olur, kerl olur, simra sacli olur'* ('When the blind man dies they say he had almond eyes; when the bald man dies they say he had golden hair'). This is a good example of a Turkish proverb in that it contains the highly characteristic parallelism and balanced structure of two complementary clauses. Also the two verbs *olur* 'to be' and *olur* 'to die', have an alliterative and euphonic charm almost too strong to resist.

Then there is the whole range of colloquial language which stems from the stories associated with Nasreddin Hodja. According to the most reliable sources Nasreddin Hodja was born in 1208 in the Anatolian village of Hortu. He has become the delightful and inimitable personification of Turkish humour. He has also become a bit of an international celebrity, and his stories have been translated into many languages, including Russian and Chinese. His fame at home is assured, and, like the case of Homer, many towns in Anatolia vie for the exclusive honour of being his birthplace. The Hodja stories have been passed down chiefly by word of mouth and a wide knowledge of Nasreddin Hodja stories can be taken for granted among all Turks. He is the archetypal Turkish Everyman, and his down-to-earth humour and the sagacity of his repartee are redolent of the best of Turkish culture. His stories are so renowned that usually you only have to mention a key phrase from a story in the appropriate place in conversation to raise a laugh. By a process of metonymy, the audience supplies the rest of the story. And if someone doesn't get it, this is as good an opportunity as any to tell the story all over again from the start. *'Bir varmis, bir yokmus, Bir gun Nasreddin Hodja ...'* ('Once upon a time, Nasreddin Hodja was walking along the road when ...')

Many stories about Nasreddin Hodja require some basic knowledge of Turkish life. One such story might very well be understood by an older generation of Irish people for whom *DV* or *Deo Volente*, 'By the Will of God', would be a phrase that was written in every letter and that tripped readily off the tongue. In this story Nasreddin Hodja looks up at the sky one evening and says to his wife:

> 'Tomorrow morning, if the weather is fine, I will go out and work in my vineyard. If it is not fine, I will stay in and work at home.' 'Oh Nasreddin Hodja,' says his wife, 'you mustn't forget to say *inshallah* (by the will of God).' 'Woman,' he says, 'it has nothing to do with the will of God. Either the day will be fine or it won't be fine.'
>
> Next morning, when he woke up, the day was fine so he hopped up on his donkey and set off for the vineyard. But on the way he was set upon by robbers. They stole from him and beat him and then loaded up his donkey and him and made them carry the loads all day long. Very late that night his wife heard a very feeble knock at the door. *'Kim o?* (Who is there?),' she asked. *'Benim,'* said a very weak voice, which she recognized as her husband's. *'Benim, inshallah* (It is I, by the will of God).' He had learned his lesson the hard way.

During my five years in Turkey, I came under many literary influences. According to Chinese sources, Turkish literature began in the second century BC, but the first extant records are those of the Orhon cuneiforms, generally dated to the eighth century AD. As the Turks moved westward, different branches of the language came into existence. The most important is Caghatay, which evolved its own literature quite separately from Ottoman. There is also Oghuz, the forerunner of modern Turkish. The most notable work produced was *Dede Korkut Kitabi* (*The Book of Dede Korkut*), which, like the early Irish sagas, has a prose narrative punctuated by superb poetry insets. Ottoman literature began in the early thirteenth century, with poets such as Yunus Emre and Esrefoghlu soon founding a mystic tradition of considerable value in Islamic culture. A riveting sample of this mystic tradition voiced seven centuries ago comes in the following stanza from Yunus Emre's poem entitled 'Askin aldi benden beni' ('Your love has wrested me away from me'):

> *Askin aldi benden beni*
> *Bana seni gerek seni*
> *Ben yanarim dun u gunu*
> *Bana seni gerek seni.*

> *Your love has wrested me away from me*
> *You're the one I need, you're the one I crave*
> *Day and night I burn, gripped by agony,*
> *You're the one I need, you're the one I crave.*

> (Trans. Halaman)

This tradition of syllabic folk poetry, much of it marked by a mystic quality, was always sung to the poet's own accompaniment on the stringed instrument called the *baghlama* or *saz*. It continued as a live tradition down until the 1970s and competitions for extempore composition of folk poetry are still held.

Persian forms began to exercise an influence on Ottoman poets, who gradually adopted and used them to create a new Turkish language now known as *Osmanli*. Poetry inspired by

Persian forms began in the mid-sixteenth century, reaching its peak perhaps in the work of Nedim, the most prominent and most Turkish poet of the *Lale Devri* or Age of Tulips, which, like the subsequent period in Dutch history devoted to the same flower, was an age of excess and effeteness. Westernization started in the late nineteenth century, and the work of Ahmed Hasim and his contemporaries combines Persian metre with themes prompted by the French symbolists. The emergence of modern Turkey produced poetry far more aware of its local, popular roots. Poets turned to take up the syllabic metres of folk poetry, and the old Osmanli literary style gave way to the more direct language characteristic of most Western poetry.

In both Persian and Arabic, the literary language is poles apart from the colloquial language, but in Turkish, because of the extremely robust and widespread tradition of folk poetry, the language as it exists since the reforms of the 1920s is not so polarized. The most famous folk poet of recent times is Ashik Veysel from Sivas province. Here is an extract from 'Kara Toprak' ('The Black Earth'), perhaps his most famous composition:

> *Dost dost diye nicesine sarildim*
> *Benim sadik yarim kara topraktir*
> *Benhude dolandim yar, bosa yoruldum*
> *Benim sadik yarim kara topraktir.*

> *I embraced so many, thinking them a friend*
> *My true love is the black earth*
> *In vain I wandered, exhausted myself for naught*
> *My true love is the black earth.*

The kind of poetry composed by Ashik Veysel became possible not only because of the depths of the folk tradition in

Turkey, but also because of the work of several major Turk-
ish poets of the twentieth century, especially Nazim Hikmet,
Oktay Rifat and Orhan Veli. Two other main strains of poetry
also affected me during my half-decade in turkey: the mystic
tradition of Mevlana Djellal a-Din Rumi and the Osmanli
tradition, written in Persian forms, mostly as *gazel* or *rubai,*
as the Turkish pronunciations of those forms go. Of particu-
lar interest to me at the time were the poems of Mevlana
Djellal a-Din Rumi, so much so that I used to go by bus to
Konya every December on the treacherous snowy roads, to
watch the dancing dervishes of his religious order perform
the *Sema* or 'dance' of the whirling dervishes. In one poem he
writes:

> *Come, come whoever you are*
> *Wonderer, worshipper, lover or leaving*
> *It doesn't matter.*
> *Ours is not a caravan of despair.*
> *Come, even if you have broken your vow*
> *a thousand times.*
> *Come, yet again, come, come.*

> *(Trans. Annemarie Schimmel)*

I took enormous pleasure in my exposure to Turkish litera-
ture. Imagine my amazement and delight when a few years
ago 'Toircheas I', a three-stanza poem of mine, was translated
into one short and three long Turkish sentences, each sen-
tence taking up nearly a whole stanza. Similarly, another
poem, 'Ceis na Teangan', was translated into two very com-
plicated sentences. These poems and fifteen or so others were
translated during a week-long seminar on one of the Princes'
Islands, Heybeli Adi, by a group led by the noted poet and
translator Cevat Capan. After listening to the different possi-

ble suggestions, Cevat Capan would keep his pen poised in mid-air until he was satisfied. Then, as I watched in amazement, he would come out with one perfectly enunciated, complicated, long agglutinative sentence of such elegant structure that it left me spellbound. I could appreciate enormously the verbal virtuosity involved but could never hope to match it myself.

Living an almost hermetically sealed Turkish lifestyle for five years was the greatest inducement I could possibly have had for writing in Irish. Outside the English-language *mentalité* I felt freed to deal with Irish on its own terms. Free of the conflict between my two mother languages that I often feel when in an English-speaking environment. The five years I spent in Turkey contributed greatly to my ending up as a poet writing in Irish. Strangely enough, losing myself in the delights of my new environment, in the carpets and kilims, in the handicrafts of all kinds, in Turkish classical music and calligraphy, I came to appreciate my own language all the more acutely.

To this day I am enamoured of Turkey, the cradle of so many different civilizations and nations – Hittite, Urartian, Sumerian, Armenian, Lycian, Lydian, Bythian, Gallatian – and among my favourites, the great cities of the Ionic Greeks. Not to mention later invaders such as Romans, Byzantines, Arabs, Turks of all shapes and forms, ending in the Great Imperial culture of the Ottomans and in the twentieth century, the founding of Turkish republic. The layer upon layer of peoples and cultures is astounding. I feel that if I am vouchsafed even a very long life I will never get to the end of it.

When I wrote the poem with which I will finish, I was informed by the best authorities that I was visiting the only known *Plutonium*, or temple of Pluto, known to have existed in the ancient world. Since then I have discovered that a few

others have been uncovered, including one at ancient Nyssa,
just up the road. Next summer I must go and visit it and
maybe it will give me another poem. Of course, one of the
main reasons for writing the poem at all was that I was so
tickled by the two different meanings of 'Plutonium': the
very old and the very new, all in the one word. Which to me
goes to the very centre of the paradox that is Turkey.

Plútóiniam

a tugtar air
iseatóp dainséarach radaighníomach
is ar theampall Dia Ifrinn.

Tá's agam, bhíos ann.
I Hieropolis, an chathair bheannaithe,
láimh le Pamukkale na Tuirce,

tá an teampall, nó an poll
faoin dtalamh, an t-aon cheann
a mhaireann ón sean-am.
Níl cead isteach ann.

'Dikkat, girilmez.
Tehlikeli gaz var'
a fógraítear dúinn go dóite.

Ba leor dan domhsa.
Thugas as na bonnaibh é
chomh maith is a bhí sé ionam

á rá gurb olc an áit
a thug mo chosa mé

is a conách san orm!

Fós, in aimsir Strabo
bhí sagairt ann – na Galli –
imithe chomh mór san i dtaithí

ar na scamall nimhe go siúlaidís timpeall
beag beann ar a n-impleachtaí
is na daoine ag titim ina bpleistí
fuar marbh ar gach aon taobh dóibh.

Ba mhór an power é.
Ba mhór an chabhair é
chun greim docht daingean an uafáis
a dh'agairt ar an bpobal áitiúil.

É seo go léir dearmhadta
is imithe as mo cheann
gur chuala casaoid íogaiir
mo dhuine muinteartha
san ospidéal meabharghalair.

'Áit Phrotastúnach é seo'.
'Cá bhfios duit?' 'An tslí
a bheannaíonn siad duit
nó ná beannaíonn siad.'

Catshúil faichilleach tháirsi aniar –
Tá siad ag iarraidh mé a chasadh,
tá's agat. Teastaíonn uaithu
go dtabharfainn diúltú deom' chreideamh'.

An bhean bhocht.
Do leath mo bhéal orm
Is dhein dhá mhórúilí groí
dem shúile.

Nó níl sé fíor
is ní raibh sé riamh
le linn a marthain féin
nó le linn saol dhá ghlúin
a chuaigh roimpí.

Ach d'fhíor dó tráth
le linn an Ghorta Mhóir
nuair a bhí an 'Irish Missionary Society'
go láidir i mbun gnímh
go háirithe i gCeann Trá.

Seo radachur núicléach na Staire
ní foláir. Fuíoll maraitheach
an drochshaoil is Ré na Súpanna.

Éiríonn sé aníos i gcónaí
is de shíor
ón duibheagán do-aitheanta
atá istigh ionainn.

Gal bréan an ocrais,
an deatach nimhe
ón bPlútóiniam, teampall
uafar Dia Ifrinn.

Plutonium

is what they call
a dangerous radioactive isotope,
also the name of the temple of the Infernal Gods.

I know, I've been there.
In Hieropolis, the holy city
near Pamukkale in Turkey,

The temple, or the hole,
Is underground, the only one
Remaining from the ancient days.
Entry is forbidden

The grave warning read:
'Dikket, girilmez. Tehlikeli gaz var'.
'No admission. Dangerous gases are found here. By
    Order.'

That was enough for me.
I fled away as fast
as my feet could carry me,

Damning the place
And my curiosity
And my feet that brought me there.

Still in Strabo's day
The eunuch priests, the Galli,
Were so practised in breathing the poisonous clouds

That they could walk freely

Nuala Ní Dhomhnaill

Not caring for the deathly atmosphere
While people fell down in flocks
Dead on every side.

It was a terrible power –
It was the power of terror
That kept the grip of dread
Firmly on the local people.

And I had forgotten it all,
Cleared it from my memory,
Until I heard a mad line
From one of my family
In the Mental Hospital.

'This is a Protestant place, you know.'
'How would you know?' 'It's the way
They say hello to you,
Or say nothing.'

A catlike glance, alert, over her shoulder –
'They want me to change over,
You see. That's what they want.
Me to deny my faith.'

Poor woman –
My mouth fell open,
My eyes were wide
As millstones.

There's no truth in it
Nor has there ever been
In her lifetime

Nor in the two
Generations before hers.

But it was true once
During the Great Famine
When the Irish Missionary Society
Was manfully at work
And in Ventry above all.

It's the radioactive rain
Of History. A deadly residue
Of starvation and Soupers.

It rises up always
Out of the ground
From underworld caves
Within us:

A cloud of hunger
A poisoned smoke
From Plutonium, the dreadful
Church of the Infernal Gods.

(Trans. Éiléan Ní Chuilleanáin)

An Chailleach agus an Spéirbhean agus an Saol Eile i gCoitinne

Léacht a tugadh i UCD sa bhliain 2006

Ní fadó ó shin do scríobhas dán

Primavera

D' athraigh gach aon ní nuair a ghaibh sí féin thar bráid.
Bhainfeadh sí deora áthais as na clocha glasa, deirim
*   leat.*
Na héanlaithe beaga a bhí go dtí seo faoi smál,
d' osclaíodar a scornach is thosnaigh ag píopáil
ar chuma feadóige stáin i láimh gheocaigh, amhail
Is gur chuma leo sa diabhal an raibh nó nach raibh
*   nóta acu.*
Bláthanna fiaine a bhí chomh cúthail, chomh humhal
Ag lorg bheith istigh go faichilleach ar chiumhaiseanna
na gceapach mbláth, táid anois go rábach, féach an fal-
*   caire fiain*
ag baint radharc na súl díom go hobann lena réiltíní
*   craorag.*

Bhíos-sa, leis, ag caoi go ciúin ar ghéag,
i bhfolach faoi dhuilleog fige, éalaithe i mo dhú dara,
ag cur suas stailce, púic orm chun an tsaoil
Thógfadh sé i bhfad níos mó ná meangadh gáire
ó aon spéirbhean chun mé a mhealladh as mo shliogán,
bhí an méid sin fógartha thall is abhus agam roimh ré.
Ach do dhein sí é, le haon searradh dá taobh,
le haon sméideadh meidhreach, caithiseach, thar a
   gualainn
do chorraigh sin a rútaí ionam, is d' fhág mé le míobhán
im' cheann, gan cos ná láimh fúm, ach mé corrthónach,
   guagach.

Bhí sé de cheart agam 'Anois teacht an Earraigh' a thabhairt air, ach ag an am chéanna bhíos ag cuimhneamh ar dhá phictiúr de chuid Botticelli – 'Primavera' agus 'Breith Bhénus'. D' fhág san gur 'Primavera' a thugas mar theideal ar an dán sa deireadh.

Ach tharlódh sé leis gur 'Spéirbhean' nó 'Cailleach/Spéirbhean' a bheinn tar éis a thabhairt ar an dán. Rud go mbeadh ciall leis, agus a thabharfadh siar isteach sa traidisiún Gaelach mé, idir an traidisiún liteartha agus traidisiún an bhéaloidis. Mar tá íomhá dúbailte seo na Spéirmhná agus na Caillí chomh seanda in Éirinn leis an litríocht féin. Sa traidisiún liteartha ní gá ach an scéal ón Sean-Ghaeilge a lua ina luíonn Niall Naoi nGiallach leis an seanchailleach atá i mbun an tobair. Deintear spéirbhean di ar an dtoirt. 'Mise an Flaitheas,' a deir sí agus deineann sí a thuar go mbeidh Niall agus sliocht a shleachta ina ríthe ar Éirinn.

Ní gá a lua anseo conas a chuaigh traidisiún na haislinge i gcion ar mhuintir na hÉireann thar na céadta blian. Is leis a bhaineann cuid des na hiarrachtaí filíochta is áille agus is tarraingtí dá bhfuil again – ó 'Gile na Gile' go 'Róisín Dubh', go 'Úirchill an Chreagáin', agus is boichte go mór a bheadh litríocht na Gaeilge ina éagmais. Fiú amháin litríocht an Bhéarla in Éirinn, cá mbeadh sé gan 'Oh My Dark Rosaleen' agus: 'Did you see an old woman going down the road?' 'I didn't, but I saw a young girl and she had the walk of a queen,' gan trácht fiú ar shamplaí eile den rud chéanna ar nós na brídeoige a léimeann ar mhuin an phríomh-charachtair sa dráma *Northern Star* de chuid Stewart Parker. Tharla go rabhas sa siopa gruaige áitiúil uair go raibh an dráma sin ar siúl i mBaile Átha Cliath. Bhíos ag cúléisteacht ar mo chomharsain a bhí ag biadán ar seo is ar siúd. Thosnaigh bean amháin ag caint ar an dráma a bhí feicthe aici an oíche roimh ré. 'And as soon as I saw that jilted bride I knew who she was,' a dúirt sí. 'She was Ireland.'

Ach is sa traidisiún béaloidis is mó a chuireas riamh mo shuim agus is ar bhéalaibh daoine a thángas trasna íomhá na Caillí ar dtúis. De réir dealraimh, bhí seanbhean thiar i nDún Chaoin darb ainm Mór agus bhí mórán scéalta fúithi fós sa tsiúl agus mise ag fás suas. Bhí sí ag bruíon de shíor lena fear, Donncha Dí, agus lá amháin bhris ar an bhfoighne aige agus ghuigh sé go mbeadh faid agus leithead Éireann idir é agus í. Deineadh san ar an bpointe boise agus ardaíodh tríd an aer é agus leandáladh síos é san áit gurb ainm Doncha Dí i gCo. an Dúin agus tá sé ann ó shoin. Blianta fada ina dhiaidh san bhíos ag éisteacht le Breandán Feirtéar, ar Raidió na Gaeltachta, faid is a bhí sé ag cur agallaimh ar Hannah Daly, iarmháistreás poist Dhún Chaoin. Bhíodar ag caint ar scéal seo Mhóir agus ar cad a tharla dá fear. 'Agus,' arsa Hannah, nár chuir aon nath sa scéal, 'bhí daoine lasmuigh de thigh Challaghan sa Daingean tráthnóna Sathairn a chonaic ag gabháilt soir é agus paca ar a dhroim.' Amhail dá mba inné nó inniu a tharla sé. Chaitheas gáire. Ní thabharfadh aon ní aon sásamh dom go bhféadfainn dán a chumadh chun an líne sin a chur ann. Rud a dheineas, leis, tamall ina dhiaidh san:

Clabhsúr

... is ansan
Lá
Do bhailibh an dia leis.

D' éirigh ar maidin le fáinne an lae ghléigil,
rug ar a rásúr, a scuab fiacal is ar thravelling bag
is thug dos na bonnaibh é.
Bhí daoine lasmuigh de thigh Challaghan sa Daingean
tráthnóna Sathairn a chonaic ag gabháilt soir é
agus paca ar a dhrom.

Chualasa leis, mar a bheadh i dtaibhreamh,
é ag gabháilt thar bráid,
a scol amhráin is a phort feadaíola aige
faoi mar a bheadh obónna i dtaobh thíos den stáitse
'is é an dia Hercules, a ghráigh Anthony,
Atá á fhágaint' –

Anois táim folamh, is an poll seo i mo lár
Is n' fheadar cé líonfaidh é
Nó cad leis? Dá mb' áil liom é a leanúint
ins an mbóithrín achrannach...
Ach ó, is fada fairsing í Éire
is tá iallach mo bhróg gan snaidhm.

Ar ndóigh, nuair a bhíos ag cuimhneamh ar scéal seo Mhóir, tháinig scéal eile a bhaineas léi chun mo chuimhne agus d' úsáideas an scéal sin chomh maith. De réir an scéil seo, tháinig uaigneas agus cumha ar Mhóir i ndiaidh Dhonncha agus thug sí faoi taisteal suas go híochtar na hÉireann ag tri-all air. D' fhág sí a tigh féin i nDún Chaoin agus nuair a tháinig sí go barr an Chlasaigh agus go bhfeaca sí paróiste leathan-aoibhinn Fionntrá ag leathadh roimpi amach, do tháinig lagmhisneach uirthi. 'Ó, is fada fairsing í Éire,' ar sise, agus do chas sí ar a sáil abhaile di fhéin. Tá scéal eile a bhaineann leis an eachtra áirithe seo. Nuair a bhí sí ag casadh abhaile tháinig glaoch nádúrtha uirthi agus do dhein sí a mún taobh le bóthar an chlasaigh, agus bhí a mún chomh cumhachtach sin gur dhein sé an dá chlais mhór ar dhá thaobh an bhóthair as a n-ainmnítear ó shoin é. Thomas Murphy, fear m' aintín, bhíodh 'Leá bumbóire,' nó, 'leá múin Móire,' mar nath nó mallacht aige, leath mar mhagadh, agus ní bhíodh aon mheas aige ort mura rabhais ábalta ciall na bhfocal a dhéanamh amach dó, agus an scéal seo a insint.

Sampla is ea é seo do chomh láidir is chomh tábhachtach is a bhí íomhá na Caillí i meon na ndaoine agus i ndúchas an bhéaloidis. Tá seo fíor go speisialta i gcás na logainmneacha agus an dinnseanchais. Ba liosta le háireamh an méid baile fearann is móin is ard is tullach is loch a ainmnítear ón gCailleach nó a luaitear léi. Téann sé i bhfad siar roimh ré na gCeilteach, fiú. Mar a deir Gearóid Ó Crualaoich ina leabhar *The Book of the Cailleach*:

> Old Europe was intensified in Ireland, where an abiding sense of a supreme, sovereign, female, cosmic agency appears to have operated on the incoming culture to a degree that resulted in a continuing, powerful sensibility to the presence in the landscape of such divine, female agency – a sensibility that has remained at the heart of Irish ancestral cosmology and mythological legend.

Tuigtear dom go raibh suim agam féin riamh is choíche san íomhá áirithe seo. Tá sé le tabhairt faoi ndeara ins na céad dánta a scríobhas go leomhfainn 'dánta' agus ní 'dréachtaí bhéarsaíochta' a thabhairt orthu:

An Chailleach agus an Spéirbhean agus an Saol Eile i gCoitinne

Teist Dhonncha Dí ar Mhór

Do sheas sí lomnocht
sa doircheacht,
a bosa fuara–iasc gealúr–
ar mo ghuailne,
a cromáin– tine ghealáin
faoi dhá ré a broinne.

Thumas mo cheann
i bhfeamnach a gruaige;
bhí tonn ghoirt na sáile
am' bhualadh, am' shuathadh;
ár gcapaill bhána ag donnú
ina bhfrancaigh mhóra.
Gach aon ní ina chorcra.

Nuair a dhúisíos ar maidin bhí tinneas cinn orm.
Thugas faoi ndeara
go raibh gainní an liathbhuí ag clúdach a colainne.
Bhí fiacla lofa an duibheagáin
ag drannadh orm.
Sea, thógas mo chip is mo mheanaithe
is theicheas liom.

Nílim críochnaithe léi mar théama, fós, ach oiread, mar gach uair a thagaim treasna ar ruainne éigin den gcailleach, músclaíonn sí dánta ionam. Seo ceann cuíosach nua:

Eithne Uathach

an chéad bhean a luaitear
i mórshaothar Chéitinn
'Foras Feasa ar Éirin'

> *d' itheadh sí leanaí*
>
> *óir 'do bhí ar daltachas*
> *ag Déisibh Mumhan:*
> *agus do hoileadh leo*
> *ar fheoil naoín í',*
>
> *chun gur luaithede*
> *a bheadh sí in-nuachair*
> *de bharr gur tairngríodh*
> *go bhfaighidís talamh*
> *ón bhfear a phósfadh sí.*
>
> *Seans go bhfuil sí fós á dhéanamh.*
> *Nó cad a déarfá*
> *le Seán Savage, Mairéad Farrell*
> *agus Dan McCann*

Cúpla bliain ó shoin nuair a thug an scríbhneoir is foilsitheoir Micheál Ó Conghaile Léacht Uí Chadhain san ollscoil seo dúirt sé go raibh sé idir dhá chomhairle faoi.

B'fhearr leis go mór, a dúirt sé, gearrscéal a scríobh nó tabhairt faoi cheann ar a laghad, fiú mura gcríochnófaí choíche é.

Táimse díreach ar an dálta chéanna. Gach uair a shuínn síos le hiarracht a thabhairt faoin léacht seo a scríobh, is ea a thosnaínn ag scríobh dáin. Rud nach gearánta dhom ar shlí, mar is maith is eol dom nach ceart eiteachas a thabhairt don mBé, pé uair a thagann sí id threo. B' fhéidir go mbeifeá tamall maith eile ag lorg inspioráide is nach dtiocfadh sí. Ach mar sin féin tá léacht le tabhairt...

Mar is léir ón méid atá scríte agam go dtí seo bhí suim mhór riamh agam sa bhéaloideas, cé ná féadfainn ag an am san ainm chomh hardnósach leis sin a thabhairt air. Ní raibh ann ach scéalta beaga a bhí fite fuaite mar dhlúth agus inneach tríd an gcaint agus mé i mo dheoraí beag cúig bliana d' aois thiar i dtigh m'aintín Máire i gCathair an Treanntaigh i bparóiste Fionntrá i lár na gcaogaidí.

Rudaí beaga a tharlaíodh ó lá go lá go luaití seanscéal leo nó tagairt éigin neamh-ghnáthach. Ar nós an lae, cúpla bliain ina dhiaidh sin, is mé i mo chailín óg, go rabhas ag siúl suas bóthar na Cathrach agus gúna síoda orm a bhí déanta de dhá stráice stuife a bhí fuaite le chéile agam agus fáithim curtha faoina mbun thíos – an t-aon iarracht fuála riamh a dheineas, agus an ceann deireanach. 'Ó,' arsa John Sé, col ceathrair lem' Dhaid críonna, a bhuail liom ar an mbóthar, 'Is maith liom do ghúna.' 'Sea,' arsa mise le teann mórtais, 'síoda is ea é.' 'Nach maith atá a fhios agam é,' arsa John Sé, 'tháinig an méid sin síoda isteach sa bhfaill sin thiar ar a dtugann siad Faill a' tSíoda, go raibh muintir an pharóiste ag ceangail na n-ainmhithe leis: "Bhí laincisí síoda faoi chaoire na Cathrach," mar a dúirt an file,' – abairt a d' fhanfadh im' cheann go deo agus a léimfeadh amach chugam nuair a bheadh dán ar bun agam blianta fada ina dhiaidh sin.

Ní hamháin san ach bhí fear m' aintín, Tomás Ó Murchú nó Thomas Murphy mar ab fhearr aithne air, ar an dtinteán agam. Fear é seo go raibh an-eolas ar stair an pharóiste aige, ní hamháin san ach ar sheanchas na seacht sean-pharóistí laistiar den Daingean. Chuala oíche ina dhiaidh sin é i dtigh Dhónail Uí Chatháin, an tráth go raibh Oireachtas na nGael á thionól ag Breandán Mac Gearailt ar an mBuailtín. Bhí Máirtín Ó Cadhain sa chomhluadar. Thárla áiteamh idir Tomás agus Art Ó Beoláin maidir le suíomh agus tógaint sáipéal na Carraige.

> 'Tá sí tógtha ar an gCarraig,' arsa Art.
> 'Níl, ná an diabhal,' arsa Thomas, 'ach ar an mBóthar Buí.'
> 'Tá sí tógtha ar an gCarraig,' arsa Art arís.

'Cé dúirt leatsa é?' arsa Thomas.

'Nach bhfuil sé léite agam. Tá sé scríte sa leabhar.'

'Ó,' arsa Thomas, 'an té a bhreac an leabhar sin, do bhreac sé an diabhal d' éitheach!'

'Níl aon teora,' arsa Máirtín Ó Cadhain, 'níl aon teora leis an gcainteoir dúchais ceart.'

Timpeall an ama sin do thugas cóip don leabhar *Romantic Hidden Kerry* do Thomás. Cúpla lá ina dhiaidh sin do chuas á fhiosrú. 'Bhuel, a Thomáis, cad é do mheas ar an leabhar?' 'Níl sé olc,' a dúirt sé, 'téann sé siar dhá chéad bliain. Níl san olc ach raghainnse a ceathair duit.'

Ní áibhéal ar fad a bhí ann mar bhí a fhios aige gur piléar gunna mhóir ó árthach amuigh ar Bhá an Daingin a bhain an ceann de chaisleán na dTreanntach a bhí ar an mbaile, in ionad é á leagadh ó bhád a bhí istigh i gcuan Fionntrá, mar ba dhóchúla le duine. Ní raibh oiread is cloch os cionn cloiche den gcaisleán sin ar an bhfód leis na céadta bliain. Seans maith gur in aimsir Dhún an Óir, nó ar a dhéanaí le linn chogadh na gCroiméalaíteach a cuireadh deireadh leis an gcúirt. Ní raibh éinne de chine na dTreanntach ar leithinis Chorca Dhuibhne le fada, cé go bhfuil trí bhaile fearainn i bparóiste Fionntrá ainmnithe uatha is go bhfuil an t-ainm coitianta go leor i gCiarraí thuaidh. Murab ionann is a gcomh-Normannaigh, na Feirtéirigh, na Rísigh, na Gearaltaigh agus muintir Hussey, ní raibh siad buan sa leathinis.

D' fhéadfadh Tomás dul siar seacht nglúin ina shinsear féin, bhí a n-ainmneacha go léir aige agus mórán eolais i dtaobh a saol. Deireadh sé gur rugadh a athair críonna féin ar an gCuan Uachtar, baile a tháinig saor ón mbleaist ar na prátaí i rith an Ghorta Mhóir. Ba bheag an mhaitheas dos na tionóntaí é, mar glanadh an baile agus dhá bhaile eile a bhí ar an gCuan, an Cuan Íochtar agus an Chúilín Bhán, sa bhliain 1867 ag athmháistir de chuid Lord Ventry, Corcaíoch darbh ainm Léithí. Deireadh Thomas i gcónaí go raibh a athair críonna dhá bhliain déag nuair a cuireadh amach as an gCuan iad. Chuaigh mórán des na tionóntaí go Meiriceá nó siar go Fán nó isteach ar an Oileán Tiar nó scaipeadh ar fuaid na dúthaí iad. Tháinig cuid acu ar an gCathair. 'Conas gur éirigh leo seilbh a fháil ar an áit anseo ar an gCathair?' arsa mise. 'Nuair a bhí an áit bán,' ar seisean, 'bhí na héinne bailithe leo.'

Bhí a fhios aige conas a aistríodh an sáipéal i bparóiste Fionntrá óna shean-ionad thiar ar oirthear an pharóiste, mar a bhfuil an scoil anois ann, go láthair ar an Imleach Shlat a bhí tugtha saor in aisce ag Muintir Shé an Imligh. A uncail críonna Mícheál, a cailleadh go tragóideach díreach tar éis dó a dhul go Meiriceá, dob é an duine deireanach a cuireadh faoi ghuí an phobail sa sean-sáipéal, agus a aintín an chéad duine a baisteadh ins an sáipéal nua. Bhí eolas aige ar mo mhuintir féinig, eolas nárbh fhearr leat a chloisint, uaireanta. 'Léan an phuis is na súile cruthóige', a thugadh sé ar mo shin-seanmháthair, Léan Ní Chearna, lena rabhas in ainm is bheith dealraitheach. Nuair a bhíos ag cur suime breise sa Ghaolainn agus mé im' chailín óg is mó a thógas síos an seanchas seo go léir uaidh, ach is sia siar ná san go mór a théann mo chuimhní air siúd agus ar chuid eile des na seanphlandaí. Bhí aighneas agus gearrchaint a ndóthain acu, agus níorbh aon nath acu an teaspach a bhaint díot go tapaidh dá mb' áil leo é. 'Leá bumbóire', nó 'Leá múin Móire ort,' an guí a bhíodh acu go minic, nó an mhallacht, ba chirte a rá agus bhí: 'Cá bhfios duitse, ní hamhlaidh go bhfuil Fios Fátha an Aoinscéil agat', mar nath leis acu.

Ach téann mo chuimhní orthu i bhfad níos sia siar ná san, go dtí an tréimhse a chaitheas thiar faróthu is mé i mo dhílleachta beag cúig bliana d' aois anall ó Shasana. Is cuimhin liom ag an tréimhse sin go raibh Johnny Long is a mhac Maidhc i mbun na feirme béal dorais is go raibh Jacksaí Sé is a dheirfiúir Neil sa tigh os a gcionn suas ar an mbaile. Bhí tigh John Sé i mbarr an bhaile is bhí de bhua ag an gcaidéal nó an puimp a bhí acusan ina gclós ná triomaíodh sé riamh sa tsamhradh. Sheasaíodh gach fear díobh anairde ar mhullach a bhuaile féin agus bhíodh sé ag caitheamh gearrchaint is aighnis leis uaidh leis an bhfear eile. Ní cuimhin liom aon abairt dá ndúradar ach is cuimhin liom go maith chomh filiúil, dea-mheabhrach is a bhí an chaint acu. An aon ionadh más ea nuair a chuas i mbun mo chéad dánta gur ar an leibhéal seo teangan a thairgíos:

Móir Chráite

Tá Móir go dlúth faoi ghlas
ina meabhairín bheag fhéin; – 3" / 4" / 2"
ábhar liath is bán –

dearg (a bhíonn na créachta
a bháthann leath na gcuileanna
faid is a dheineann an leath eile a mbiaiste
ar feoil na n-imeall).

'Éistíg', in ainm Dé,' ar sise leis na préacháin
is cabairí an Daingin a thagann san iarnóin
ag suathadh a mbolg.

'Tá na héinne dúnta isteach
ina ifreann féinín féin.'
Scaipeann na mionéin
nuair a chuireann sí scrabhadh scraith
lastuas dóibh.

Bhí daoine eile ar an mbaile ag an am go raibh bua iontach teangan acu. I dteannta a bheith ina gcainteoirí dúchais bhíodar ina gcainteoirí maithe. An fear ba Ghaelaí ar fad acu, Tomás Mháiréad (Ó Sé), bhí sé caillte ón mbliain 1956, bliain díreach sara thángas-sa ar an gCathair. Ba é an duine deireanach ar aonteanga a bhí sa pharóiste é. Bhí sé de theist air nach raibh aon Bhéarla aige. Ní dóigh liom gur chreideas an scéal sin riamh ar fad ar fad. 'Conas nach raibh aon Bhéarla aige agus é ina chónaí ar an mbaile seo, áit a raibh 'coastguards' le breis is céad bliain?' 'Nó ní thaithíodh sé iad. Ní théadh sé ina measc.' B' fhéidir go raibh smut maith don bpolaitíocht i gceist chomh maith. Bhí sé orthu siúd a bhí ag an gcéad chruinniú poiblí don Land League i rith Chogadh na Talún, cruinniú a tionóladh i naomhóga i lár an chuain (200 éigin acu) nuair nach dtabharfadh Lord Ventry cead é a thionóladh ar an dtalamh. 'Na Parnells' a tugtaí ar a mhuintir le fada an lá. Ach mura raibh sé siúd ann, bhí mórán eile acu ann, Fitzie is John Sé is Jacksaí is a dheirfiúr Neil, is Joeín, is Annie Sheehy is a deartháir Jackie, is Johnny Long is a mhac Maidhc Long na Cathrach. Bhíodar ann go rábach, is má deirim arís é, go dea-chainteach.

Ach tharla rudaí eile i mo shaol agus bhailíos liom as an dtír chomh luath in Éirinn agus a bhíos ábalta air. Tar éis seacht mbliana a chaitheamh thar lear, go háirithe san Ísiltír agus sa Tuirc, tuigeadh dom gurb é an rud is mó a theastaigh uaim sa tsaol ná filleadh ar Éirinn agus luí go lánaimsireach leis an scríbhneoireacht, dá bhféadfainn in aon chor é. Chuireas isteach ar bhursaireacht ón gComhairle Ealaíon agus fuaireas é, rud a thug mé féin agus mo bheirt clainne abhaile liom agus chuireas fúm i dtigh samhraidh mo mhuintire i gCathair an Treanntaigh. Na 'Turcaís Bhána' a thugtaí ar na leanaí mar bhíodar chomh fionn san. 'Niúla agus na Turcaís Bhána' a bhí mar nath sa tsiúl ag an am. Bhíos ag gabháilt do mhórán rudaí ag an am, úrscéal a chuaigh sa bhfraoch orm, cnuasach gearrscéalta a chríochnaíos ach nár

Nuala Ní Dhomhnaill

foilsíodh riamh, ach thar aon ní eile do luíos leis an bhfilíocht. Ní raibh m' fhear céile fillte orainn fós agus bhíos an-uaigneach ansan sa tigh i m'aonar, agus na leanaí ina gcodladh, mé ag féachaint amach ar thráigh Fionntrá agus an taoide tráite. Má bhí féin is i dtéarmaí an bhéaloideasa a chuireas mé féin in úil, ag tarrac chugam 'persona' na Maighdine Mara:

> Má tá eireaball éisc féin orm
> Nílim gan dathúlacht éigin.
> Tá mo ghruaig fada is buí
> is tá loinnir óm' ghainní
> ná chífeá riamh ar mhná míntíre.
> Dath na gcloch an tsúil acu
> ach féach go cúramach isteach
> im' mhogaillse
> is chífir an burdán fearna
> is róinte groí
> ag macnas
> im mhac imreasan.
>
> Ní gan phian
> a thángas aníos
> ar thalamh.
> Do bhriseas
> an slabhra réamhordaithe,
> do mhalairtíos snámh
> ar luail cosa
> ag priocadh liom
> ar nós na gcuirliún.
> Creid uaim gur grá, ní Dia
> a dhein é a ordú.

> *D' imís*
> *is thógais uaim mo chaipín draíochta.*
> *Níl sé chomh furasta orm teacht air*
> *is a bhí sa scéal*
> *i measc cearachail an díona.*
> *Tá' s agam;*
> *dheineas tochailt síos go dtí an gaíon*
> *is níl aon rian do.*
> *Theip an taoide orainn chomh maith*
> *is tá francach ag cogaint na gréine*

(An Mhaighdean Mhara)

Timpeall an ama chéanna is ea do chuir Seán Ó Tuama in aithne do Joe Daly agus don mBab Feirtéar mé. Théinn ar a dtuairisc go minic agus bhíodar an-mhaith ar fad dom. An-chuideachta ar fad ab ea iad, an Bhab ina tigh féin, tine ghreadhnach síos agus cupaí tae ar siúl agus Joe lena bhean Peig ina dtigh féin nó i dtigh Dhónail Uí Chatháin ar an mBuailtín. Is cuimhin liom ag an am gur thógas roinnt téipeanna den mBab ag insint scéalta agus go seinnfinn dom féin iad sa leaba go dtí go dtitfeadh mo chodladh orm. Ní haon áibhéil a rá gur thángas go mór faoina n-anáil. Ní hamháin gur thug siad teidil agus scéalta frámacha mo chéad dá leabhar filíochta dom ach do mhúineadar dom chomh maith conas mé féin a chur in iúil trí chúinsí mo bheatha féin a athrú agus an t-amhábhar mothála a chlaochló, chun go ndéanfaí dó rud níos uilí ná tarlachain bheaga phearsanta mo shaoil féin, nó rudaí ró-phearsanta, a bhainfeadh lem' shaol féin amháin. Do chabhraigh na scéalta liom an fhírinne a insint ach sceabha a chur fúithi, faoi mar a mhol Emily Dickinson tráth: 'Tell the truth, but tell it slant', agus rudaí a rá ná beadh ar mo chumas a rá amach díreach.

Sampla don gcur chuige seo is ea an dán, 'Féar Suaithinseach', teidealdán mo tharna chnuasaigh. An chéad uair a dheineas é a thaifeadadh, thug an Bhab leagan dom ar bhunaíos an dán air. Ní fada a bhí an téip déanta, áfach, nuair a scrios mo dheirfiúr é trí phopcheol a thaifeadadh anuas air, mar dhea is gur téip folamh ab ea é mar nach raibh air ach caint!

Chuas thar n-ais go dtí an mBab agus fuaireas leagan agus leagan eile ach bhíodar go léir imithe ón leagan ar a raibh an dán bunaithe. Mar a tharlaíonn sé níor inis sí riamh arís mar is céad-chuimhin liomsa é; a rá go mbeireadh an sagart 'go haiclí' ar an gcomaoin naofa. Theastaigh an nath áirithe san uaim thar aon insint eile. An leagan a d' úsáideas sa deireadh ná leagan a fuaireas ón Ollamh Bo Almquist, leagan a bhí tógtha ar téip agus ansan athscríte ag an Dochtúir Ríonach Uí Ógáin.

Faoin am a tharla sé seo bhí athruithe móra eile tarlaithe i mo shaol. Bhíomair tar éis trí bliana a chaitheamh i gCorca Dhuibhne. Bhí bliain acu-san go raibh m' fhear céile ag obair i mBaile Átha Cliath, ag filleadh ar Chorca Dhuibhne gach re deireadh seachtaine. Thuigeamar go raibh an turas ró-chruaidh air agus go gcaithaimíst bogadh linn go Baile Átha Cliath. Ba stracadh uafásach dom é an áit thiar a fhágaint agus ar feadh i bhfad bhíos an-uaigneach i ndiaidh na Gaeltachta. Bhí Raidió na Gaeltachta ar siúl agam de shíor, ar ndóigh, agus ar feadh roinnt blianta ina dhiaidh sin do dheininn smut de chlár le Maidhc Sé ar an stair áitiúil, go háirithe ón méid a bhíodh á léamh agam sa Roinn le Béaloideas. Ach sé Joe Daly a threoraigh mo chosa i dtreo na Roinne an chéad lá. Dúirt sé liom dul isteach ann, go ndéanfadh sé maitheas dom, agus ar seisean liom, 'Féach a bhfeicfir'.

Ar dtúis chuas ar thuairisc mo mhuintire féin. Thosnaíos ar ndóigh le Thomas Murphy. Más ea, bhí sé ann. Bhí trí scéal bailithe uaidh. Scéal ar gheall ar an iontas ba mhó, scéal ar an mbuachaill agus na pictiúirí beannaithe agus tosach scéil áirithe, 'An Luch is an Dreoilín'. Bhí Joe tar éis a rá liom go mbeadh an scéal sin ann. Scéal is ea é atá sa *Seanchaí Muimhneach*, agus a bhailigh Pádraig Ó Siochfradha, nó 'An Seabhac' mar ab fhearr aithne air, i dtús an chéid. Faoin am a raibh Joe ag bailiú ins na triochaidí is na daichidí ní raibh sé fanta níos mó i gcuimhne nó i mbéal na ndaoine. Bhí cuid den scéal fachta aige thall is abhus ach ní raibh tús an scéil ag éinne. Tháinig sé ó dheas go Cathair a' Treanntaigh d' aon ghnó chun tús an scéil a bhailiú mar go raibh sé cloiste aige go mb' fhéidir go raibh sé ann. Bhí sé ag Thomas. De réir an chur síos atá i dtús an scéil, is óna mháthair a chuala sé an scéal, fiche éigin bliain roimhe sin. Sé an cur síos atá air féin ná gur mac feirmeora é agus go raibh sé a hocht mbliana fichead d' aois. Bhí san fíor mar ní raibh an talamh fachta fós aige óna athair.

Ach sé an t-athair céanna Peats Ó Murchú an tseoid is mó gur thángas air. Bhí mórán cloiste agam riamh faoi Pheats, mar duine an-dheisbhéalach ab ea é agus bhí abairtíní dá chuid fós á n-aithris ag daoine le mo linnse. Mar shampla, rugadh a mhac Tomás, oíche sneachtaigh sa tslí go dtugaidís ina diaidh sin 'Tomáisín an tSneachta' air. Lá arna mháireach go moch ar maidin d' imigh Peats de shiúl cos thar Mhám na Gaoithe suas is bóthar na Leataithe i leith, ar a shlí ó thuaidh go dtí Cathair Deargáin, arbh as dá bhean, Cáit Foley. Lá sneachtaidh ab ea é, Lá Nollaig Bheag, agus bhí mo Neain ina gearrchaile beag i Leataoibh Meánach ag crústadh liathróidí sneachta ar a cairde. Buaileadh bleid air. 'Aon scéal nua, a Pheats?' 'Tá,' arsa é sin, 'mac ó aréir agam, ábhar fathaigh. Cnámha capaill óig faoi, is ní bhfaighidh sé aon fhuacht go brách.'

B' fhíor dó sa tarna cuid don gcaint mar bhí a shláinte go maith ag Thomas riamh agus do ghaibh sé gan aon mháchail trí Fliú Mór na bliana' 1918, nuair a tógadh trí cinn de chónraí – dhá uncail agus deartháir leis – amach as an dtigh in aon choicíos amháin. Ní raibh an fháidhiúlacht chéanna ag

roinnt leis an gcéad chuid den abairt, áfach, mar cé go raibh
sé tapaidh, aiclí go dtína sheanaois, ba fhada é ó thoirt
fathaigh, sa tslí is go raibh meas mór aige i gcónaí ar an
scrothaíocht. 'Níl aon teora leis,' a deireadh sé. Is beag a shíl
sí, a deireadh mo Neain i gcónaí ina dhiaidh sin, go bhfásfadh
sí féin suas, go mbeadh leanbh iníne aici, is go bpósfadh an
iníon sin leanbh na hóiche sin aréir.

Ráiteachas eile leis a bhí fanta i gcuimhne na ndaoine ná
an straidhn a bhí air le fear éigin a chuaigh ag áiteamh leis ag
aonach an Daingin. 'Ar sin d' éirí in airde,' ar seisean, 'ar
fhear atá i dtaoibh le dhá seana-raga, seachas fear go bhfuil
fear hocht mbó aige, i gCathair,' ag tagairt dó féin agus an-
amhras aige as féin.

Ach ní go dtí go bhfaca mé an stuif ar fad a bhí bailithe ag
Joe Daly uaidh a thuigeas cad é chomh maith de sheanchaí a
bhí i bPeaid. Bhí na scéalta fada Fiannaíochta aige, scéal ar
Bhalar Bhéimneach, scéal ar Fhionn is Rí Athadonáis. Ní
hamháin sin ach bhí na cóirithe catha aige. Cóiriú catha an
ghaiscígh, cóiriú catha an árthaigh, cóiriú catha na farraige.
Ar feadh tamaill ansan do thógas na cóirithe catha sa cheann:

'Cioca ab fhearr leat,' arsan fathach, 'iomrascáil cruaidh ceal-
gánta nó gabháilt de chlaimhte géara glasa i mbun is i mbarr
easnaíocha a chéile?' 'Is fearr liom iomrascáil cruaidh cealgánta
mar is í a thaithíos ar na faichibh fairis na leanaí uaisle.' 'Seo ar
a chéile iad, bhuaileadar lámh in uachtar is lámh in íochtar is
lámh i mbuaic na hiomrascála ar a chéile is an té a thiocfadh ó
íochtar an domhain go huachtar an domhain ag féachaint ar dhá
iomrascálaí is orthu araon ba chóir teacht ag féachaint. Do
dheinidís talamh bog don dtalamh cruaidh agus talamh cruaidh
don dtalamh bog, ísleáin dos na hardáin is ardáin dos na
hísleáin. Thairgídís toibreacha fíoruisce tré chroí na gcloch
nglas is trín screabhlach cruaidh aníos is na fóidíní gabhaidh a
imíodh óna gcosa, bhainidís trí fhiacla as an gcailleach a bhíodh
ina suí i gcathair Londan ag deargadh a pípe, agus ní stadadh na
trí fhiacla sin trí bhogaithe is trí sléibhte go leagaidís trí chúirt
a bheadh sa Domhain Toir.

Thógas é seo go léir sa cheann. Ghaibh sórt éigin buile mé. Ghaibheas ó sheanchaí go seanchaí ag féachaint ar na leaganacha deifriúla den gcóiriú catha. Is ag Peats a' tSaoir ac' Loinsigh ó Bhaile an tSléibhe is fearr a bhí na cóirithe catha. Bhí sé tar éis scéalta a thabhairt don mbailitheoir Meiriceánach, Jeremiah Curtin, agus é ina fhear óg, thíos in Ard a' Bhóthair. I nGaeilge is ea a thug sé na scéalta uaidh agus is amhlaidh a chuir a athair Béarla orthu do Churtin. Ach ní raibh Peats féin aon phioc sásta leis an leagan Béarla a cuireadh orthu. Nuair a bhí sé á dtabhairt amach san Edifón don mbailitheoir Seán Ó Dúbhda ina dhiaidh sin dúirt sé: 'Bhíos ag insint scéalta do Churtin agus a bhean a bhí ag scríobh agus bhí m' athair ag cur Béarla ar an nGaolainn di. Agus cheannaigh buachaill, mac feirmeora, do cheannaigh sé ceann des na leabhra sin agus bhí mo scéalta-se thíos ann agus ní shamhlófá, ní raibh sé á chur síos in aon tslí ceart ná cóir ann mar bhíodar. Ní raibh an cóiriú catha in aon chor ann. Ní fhéadfaidís an cóiriú catha a scríobh chuige!'

An aon iontas ina dhiaidh san má bhí na dánta a bhí á scríobh agam ag an am lán den gcóiriú catha de shaghsanna deifriúla. Sé a tháinig chun m'aigne is leanbh ar deol agam, is mé ag iarraidh cur síos a dhéanamh ar an sórt domhain inar mhair an leanbh nuabheirthe ag an am, domhan lán de radharcanna agus de fhuaimeanna nach raibh sí fós ábalta ar a idirdhealú óna chéile, domhan úd na fuaime réamhshiombalaí, nó an *chora* mar a thugann an teoiricí feimineach ón bhFrainc, Julia Khristaeva, air:

Ag Cothú Linbh

An eol duit an lá ón oíche,
go bhfuil mochthráigh mhór
ag fógairt rabharta,

> *go bhfuil na báid*
> *go doimhin sa bhfarraige*
> *mar a bhfuil éisc is rónta*
> *is míolta móra*
> *ag teacht ar bhois is ar bhais*
> *is ar sheacht maidí rámha orthu,*
> *go bhfuil do bháidín ag snámh*
> *óró sa chuan*
> *leis na lupadáin lapadáin*
> *muranáin maranáin*
> *í go slím sleamhain*
> *ó thóin go ceann*
> *ag cur grean na farraige*
> *in uachtar*
> *is cúr na farraige*
> *in íochtar?*

Bhí dánta eile lán des na cóirithe catha chomh maith, dánta ar nós 'An Rás'. Séard a tharla anseo ná gur theastaigh uaim cur síos a dhéanamh ar fhlosc agus faobhar ruaill buile nó babhta fiain tiomána suas faoin dtír. Cóiriú catha an ghaiscígh a thairgíos chugam féin chun é seo a chur in iúil.

> *Faoi mar a bheadh leon cuthaigh nó tarbh fásaigh*
> *nó ceann de mhuca allta na Fiannaíochta,*
> *nó an gaiscíoch ag léimt faoi dhéin an fhathaigh*
> *faoina chírín singilíneach síoda,*
> *tiomáinim an chairt ar dalladh*
> *trí bhailte beaga lár na hÉireann.*
> *Beirim ar an ghaoth romham,*
> *is ní bheireann an ghaoth atá i mo dhiaidh orm.*

> *Mar a bheadh saighead as bogha, piléar as gunna*
> *nó seabhac rua trí scata mionéan lá Márta*

scaipim na mílte slí taobh thiar dom.
Tá uimhreacha ar na fógraí bóthair
is ní thuigim an mílte iad nó kiloméadair.
Aonach, Ros Cré, Móinteach Mílic,
N' fheadar ar ghaibheas nó nár ghaibheas tríothu.
Níl iontu faoin am seo ach teorainní luais
Is moill ar an mbóthar go dtí thú.

Trí ghleannta sléibhte móinte bogaithe
scinnim ar séirse ón iarthar,
d' aon seáp amháin reatha i do threo
d' aon fháscadh ruthaig i do chuibhreann.
Deinim ardáin des na hísleáin, ísleáin des na hardáin
talamh bog de thalamh cruaidh is talamh cruaidh de
     thalamh bog,
imíonn gnéithe uile seo na léarscáile as mo chuimhne,
ní fhanann ann ach gíoscán coscán is drithle soilse.

Timpeall an ama chéanna thángas ar leabhar *Italian Folk-
tales*, roghnaithe agus athinste ag Italo Calvino. Seo aistriúchán
Béarla ar chnuasach síscéalta a bhí aistrithe go hIodáilis ar
dtúis ag Italo Calvino ó theangacha éagsúla na hIodáile. Thó-
gas an-cheann don méid a bhí le rá aige sa réamhrá i dtaobh
cad a tharla dó féin nuair a chuaigh sé greamaithe i ndomhan
seo na síscéal:

> Domhsa ba léim caorach san aigéan é. Aigéan ina raibh mórán
> daoine romhamsa cheana tar éis a thumadh, thar 150 éigin bli-
> ain, ní lé dúil i nuaíocht nó sa rud neamhghnáthach ann féin,
> ach le creideamh doimhin go raibh eilimint dúrúnda éigin ina
> luí ar an ngrinneall, eilimint nár mhór a tharrtháil ar son na
> teangan.

Ón méid a scrígh sé tuigeadh dom nárbh galar éinne amháin
an galar a bhí orm féin.

Do léimeas isteach sa domhan fó-thoinn seo gan oiread na fríde de dhúthracht intleachtúil ar son aon ní spontánaigh nó fréamhaithe nó bunaidh. Ba údar mór míshuaimhnis agam é bheith tumtha in eilimint éagruthach, eilimint a bhí chomh mall malltriallach san leis an oideas béil, eilimint nach bhféadfaí smacht coinsiasach a imirt air.

Bhíos féin faoin am seo imithe ós na cóirithe catha agus na scéalta Fiannaíochta go dtí na síscéalta agus go dtí scéalaithe eile, Tomás (Mhárthain) Mac Gearailt, Tadhg Ó Guithín, Seán' ac Gearailt ó Mhárthan a bhí pósta ar na Gorta Dubha. ('Danger' a bhí mar leasainm air seo). Peig Sayers agus a mac Maidhc (File) Ó Guithín, Domhnaill Ó Mainín ó Chill Uraidh (Domhnaillín an Deataigh) a thug an scéal is faide a scríobh sé riamh do Joe Daly, scéal a thóg dhá oíche dhéag é a scríobh síos. Ansan bhí Seán Ó Grífín ó Chathair Boilg ann. An fear deireanach acu seo ní raibh aon ainm in airde air mar scéalaí i measc an phobail mar ní bhíodh sé ag insint scéalta go poiblí toisc iarracht don luaithbhéalaíocht a bheith air. Ach bhí a shaol caite aige istigh i dtigh Pheats' ac Loinnsigh, ag éisteacht leis go beacht agus ag tabhairt gach aon scéal acu leis, 'An Gadaí Dubh', 'Balor Béimneach', 'Cuid, Céad agus Céatach', 'Feirmeoir Aodhaire na hAimsire', etc. Faoin am go raibh Joe Daly ag bailiú scéalta bhí Peats ar shlí na fírinne ach d' aimsigh sé Seán Ó Grífín agus fuair na scéalta ar fad uaidh. Tá na scéalta sin go hiontach. Arís níorbh aon díobháil, b'fhéidir, éisteacht le Italo Calvino agus é ag trácht ar an ábhar céanna:

De réir mar a thugas faoin obair, ag tógaint ceann i gcónaí den ábhar a bhí ar fáil, á rangú agus á chatalógú, do ghaibh sórt buile mé, díocas thar meon agus gan cur suas, chun teacht ar gach sórt leagain agus malairt leagain de mhóitífeanna áirithe. Bhí sé mar a bheadh fiabhras orm a ghaibh lastuas díom. Bhraitheas go raibh paisiún orm faoi mar a bheadh ar fheithideolaí, sa tslí is go mbeinn lán tsásta iomlán dá raibh scríte ag Proust a thabhairt

suas ar aon leagan amháin eile den scéal úd 'Cac óir, a asailín'.
[An leagan Gaeilge den scéal seo is forleithne ná an ceann darb
ainm 'Cac airgead, a chapaillín bháin'.]

Ba shásamh mór aigne dhom é go raibh scríbhneoir eile tar éis
gabháilt tríd an sórt buile a bhí orm féin. Ní hamháin san ach
teacht amach ar an dtaobh eile. Óir ba é an tréimhse seo a
chaith sé ar snámh in aigéan dosháraithe seo an bhéaloidis a
chuir athrú mór foirme ar scríbhneoireacht Italo Calvino. D'
fhág sé an réalachas laistiar dó agus thug aghaidh ar an rud go
dtugtar anois 'meitificsean' air, mar shampla ina úrscéal ion-
tach, *Once on a Winter's Night a Traveller*. Bhain sé cuid don
mhearbhall díom é a fheiscint ag cur síos ar ar rud céanna a bhí
tarlaithe domhsa. Bhí sé chomh cóngarach san do m' eispéireas
féin gur dhóigh liom gur bhain sé na focail as mo bhéal:

> Ar feadh dhá bhliain do mhaireas i gcoillte agus i gcaisleáin faoi
> dhraíocht, mé am stracadh idir fonn machnaimh agus fonn
> gníomhaíochta … I rith an dá bhliain seo thóg an domhan
> mórthimpeall orm gnéithe den saol sí air féin agus gach rud a
> tharla ba dhraíocht nó biorán suain éigin nó claochlú de shaghas
> amháin nó de shaghas eile faoi ndear é … D' oscail neadracha
> nathrach faoi bhonn mo chos agus chomh hobann céanna dhein
> sruthanna bainne is meala dhóibh. Do dhein tuismitheoirí
> míthrócaireacha do ríthe a cheapfá go dtí sin a bheith gan
> cháim. Do tháinig ríochtaí a bhí faoi gheasaibh thar n-ais ina
> mbeathaidh. Tuigeadh dom go raibh rialacha dearmadta saol an
> bhéaloidis ag titim tóin thar cheann amach as an mboiscín
> draíochta a bhí oscailte agam.

Agus arís, a deir sé:

> Anois nó go bhfuil an leabhar críochnaithe agam, tuigtear dom
> nach rámhaillaíocht nó speabhraídí a bhí orm dearbhú glan a
> dhéanamh ar rud go raibh amhras láidir agam air cheana féin, sé
> sin, go bhfuil an fhírinne ag roinnt le scéalta sí.

Bhíos-sa tagaithe ar an dtuairim chéanna go neamhspleách,
agus mo dhánta athraithe ó bhonn dá bharr.

De réir mar a bhíos ag taighdeadh liom bhí mo shuim ag athrú ó rud go rud. Tar éis bheith ag gabháilt des na cóirithe catha agus des na móitífeanna idirnáisiúnta thosnaíos ag cur suime ins na scéalaithe, agus go háirithe ins na scéalaithe ban, daoine ar nós Peig Sayers, Cáit Ruiséal agus ach go háirithe Máire Ruiséal. Is dóigh liom gur thiteas i ngrá le Máire Ruiséal. Ní mar a chéile an cur chuige a bhí aici in aon chor agus a bhí ag Peig Sayers. Tá rud éigin geall le barócach ag baint le Peig, tá castaíocha beaga reitrice ag roinnt léi. Is maith léi focail dheacra nó 'carraigreacha' agus cuireann focal go minic scéal i gcuimhne dhi. Abraimis nuair a luaitear na prátaí ar a dtugtar 'minions' deir sí: 'Bliain na minions ab ea é nuair a bhí m'athair istigh age baile. Tháinig bean Ultach isteach 'on tigh chuige agus...' away léi.

Tá nósmhaireacht scéalaíochta ana-dhíreach ag Máire Ruiséal, cé go bhfuil cóiriú catha na scéalaíochta aici chomh maith le duine: 'Agus bhí drúcht agus deireanaí an tráthnóna agus na hoíche ag teacht uirthi, agus an madra gearra ag dul ar scáth na copóige, an chopóg ag teicheadh uaidh, agus an madra rua ag dul ina phluaisín féin, ní nach locht ar an madra macánta.'

Tá aon áit amháin i lár scéil a thaithníonn go mór liom, áit a labhrann sí i leataoibh le Joe Daly: 'Bhí clann an rí amuigh ar an... Joe, an féidir liom an focal Béarla a úsáid anseo?' 'Abair leat,' arsa Joe. 'Bhí clann an rí amuigh ar an bpiazza...'

Táim an-shásta a fheiscint gur roghnaigh Éilís Ní Dhuibhne scéal le Máire Ruiséal don gcaibidil ar an dTraidisiún Béil, sa chúigiú himleabhar de dhíolaim *The Field Day Anthology*. Tugann sí scéal darb ainm Scéal an Ghabhairín Bháin, sampla iontach de 'síscéal banúil' nó 'feminine fairytale'. Leagan is ea é den seanscéal 'Psyche agus Amor'. Ag trácht ar an méid a deir Vladimir Propp i dtaobh an scéil seo ina aiste *Historical Roots of Russian Fairy Tales*, deir Calvino:

Although the customs of millennia are disregarded, the plot of
the story still reflects the spirit of those laws and describes
every love thwarted and forbidden by law, convention or social
disparity. That is why it has been possible, from prehistory to
the present, to preserve, not as a fixed formula but as a flowing
element, the sensuality so often underlying this love, evident in
the ecstasy and frenzy of mysterious nocturnal embraces.

Tá an grá collaí seo le braith ar leagan Mháire Ruiséal den
scéal agus, ar chuma scéalaíocht Pheig Sayers, tá oscailteacht
aigne ann i dtaobh nádúir an duine ná beifeá ag súil leis,
b'fhéidir, ón léamh coitianta a deintear ar an mbanscéalaí
mar dhealbh náisiúnta:

Do chuadar isteach i gcúirt bhreá. Do labhair sé léi ansan:
'Mhuise, sea anois,' ar seisean, 'cé acu is fearr leatsa anois,' ar
seisean, 'mise bheith mar ghabhar istoíche is mar fhear isló nó
mar fhear istoíche agus mar ghabhar isló?' 'Ó go deimhin,' ar
sise, 'is fearr liom cuideachta na hoíche – tú bheith mar fhear
istoíche agus id ghabhar isló.' Mar sin do bhí.

Thugas faoi ndeara de réir mar a chuas isteach sa Roinn le
Béaloideas gur athraigh mo shuim. Le déanaí is ins na píosaí
beaga seanchais is mó a chuirim spéis, na scéalta beaga
neafaiseacha a thit amach do dhaoine. Sítheach Bhaile
Eaglasta ag cur síos ar cé méid tigh a leagadh ins gach baile
fearainn le linn an Droch-Shaoil. Peats Dhónail (Ó Cíobháin)
na Muirígh ag caint ar iascach nó ar Thomás na bPúcaí, gaol
dom fhéin. Bhí scéal amháin aige i dtaobh Thomáis agus
caithfead é a bhréagnú. Bhí triúr ban óg ag gabháilt aniar ag an
am chéanna ar an Leataoibh Meánach. Bhí fios ag Tomás na
bPúcaí, agus dúirt sé go mbeadh púir mhór ar an mbaile ach
ní déarfadh sé cioca duine des na mná óga a scuabfaí. Mar a
tharla ba í an bhean ba mhó go raibh gaol aige léi a scuabadh,
bean mic a dheirféir. Cailleadh í don bhfiabhras aerach tar éis
di leanbh iníne a thabhairt ar an saol. 'Agus,' arsa Peats Dhó-
nail, 'cailleadh an bhean óg go luath ina dhiaidh sin, agus

cailleadh an iníon chomh maith.' Bhuel, níor cailleadh an iníon. Conas go bhfuil a fhios agam san? Mar ba í mo mháthair chríonna í, agus mura mbeadh sí siúd tar éis maireachtaint, ní bheinnse anseo anois.

Scéal eile a bhain le mo mhuintir féin a d'úsáideas mar réamhrá le mo chnuasach deireanach, *Cead Aighnis*:

Trí Anam an Duine

> Bhíos istigh sa leabaidh am' chodhladh theas i mBaile Móir agus pé rud a thug Eoghainín Finton amach chonaic sé ag gabháil amach as an dtigh mé. Ghlaoigh sé ar a bhean, Léan Ní Chearna. 'Hanamain diabhal, a Léan,' ar seisean, 'tá stróc nó rud éigin ar Sheán! Féach taobh aon tí síos é. Téir amach,' ar seisean 'agus glaoigh air.' Ach chonaic sé a' casadh aríst mé agus ag dul isteach 'on tigh. Ach níor ghlaoigh Léan in aon chor orm. Ach bhíodar á rá liom lárna mháireach agus ní chreidfinn in aon Eoghainín mara mbeadh Léan á rá. Dúrt leis nár fhágas an leaba ó chuas inti gur fhágas ar maidin í, ach mé im chodladh go sámh. 'Bíonn a leithéid i gceist,' arsa Léan, 'agus do chuimhníos-sa air. Dá nglaofainnse an uair sin air,' arsa Léan, 'd' fhanfadh sé ann go deo.'
>
> Ach táim á chlos riamh go bhfuil an duine ina thrí chuid. Tá an t-anam anála ann, an t-anam mothála agus an t-anam síoraíochta. Fanfaidh an t-anam síoraíochta ionat go dtí go gcaillfear tú. N' fheadar ab é an t-anam anála nó an t-anam mothála liomsa a bhí lasmuigh agus mé im' chodladh. N' fheadar é sin.'

(ó bhéalaithris Sheáin Uí Chíobháin, RBÉ ls 965, lch. 63)

Ach chun filleadh ar an scéal a bhí agam i dtús na cainte seo, i dtaobh laincisí síoda a bheith ar chaoire na Cathrach', bhíos istigh sa Roinn le Béaloideas an lá cheana agus thángas de sheans ar eolas breise ina thaobh. Tuigeadh domhsa riamh gur eachtra miotaseolaíochta a bhí i gceist leis seo. Sampla suaithinseach ab ea é dar liom do chumas filíochta na muintire agus don gcumas iontach samhlaíochta a bhí riamh le braith go láidir i gCorca Dhuibhne. Níor taibhsíodh riamh dom go raibh

aon bhonn stairiúil air, ach féach go bhfuil. Bád mór seoil darb
ainm an *Lady Nelson* ab ea é a raiceáladh ar an Sceilg agus í lán
de phíopaí fíona i dteannta an tsíoda. Is i ndiaidh an long seo a
raiceáil ann a thógadar an teach solais sa Sceilg:

> Oíche cheoigh ab ea é agus bhí an captaen a' rá go rabhadar trí
> léig ó aon talamh. Bhí cuid den gcriú ar a mhalairt de thuairim,
> agus an ceart acu mar ní fada nó gur bhuail sí an Sceilg. Briseadh
> agus báthadh agus bascadh a raibh innti ach triúr a chuaigh in
> airde ar smut adhmaid. Tháinig a dó nó trí de laethanta ceoigh is
> báisteach aniar is aneas is bhí na píopaí fíona ag gluaiseacht
> aniar. Bhíodh báid ag dul á gcuardach. Bhí Cuan Fionntrá lán de
> bháid agus Cathair a' Treanntaigh. Bhí fear darb ainm Scainlin
> agus bád aige is a chriú siar sa bhá ag lorg an fhíona nuair a
> chonaiceadar an raic i bhfad uathu is na fir anáirde air. Beirt a bhí
> ann nuair a shroiseadar iad. Bhí fear eile tamaillín beag roimis
> sin taréis titim san uisce le codladh. Thógadar an bheirt is do
> shábháileadar iad. Sin ar tháinig saor. Chuireadar crann is dhá
> sheol chun Scainlin is a chriú mar bhuíochas ina dhiaidh sin.

Tá súil agam go bhfuilim tar éis léaspairt éigin a thabhairt
díbh, ar cad é chomh tábhachtach domhsa is atá béaloideas
na hÉireann agus bailiúcháin an Choimisiún Béaloideasa, ach
go háirithe. Is dóigh liom go n-oibríonn sé ar dhá leibhéal,
leibhéal na Gaeilge ar dtúis, áit a gcuireann sé i gcuimhne
dhom an dlús is an neafaise teangan a chuala á chaitheamh
thar bhuailtí ó dhuine go duine is mé im leanbh. Ansan
oibríonn sé ar leibhéal na samhlaíochta, nuair a thugann
móitífeanna na scéalta agus fiú na píosaí beaga seanchais atá
scaipthe anso is ansúd ar fuaid na lámhscríbhinne samhlaoidí
iontacha dom gur féidir liom bheith ag imirt leo, ag spraoi
agus ag gleáchas, á gcaitheamh san aer is ag breith orthu arís.
Agus ar ndóigh sé an spraoi sin ceann des na riachtanachtaí
is tábhachtaí in obair chruthaitheach.

Tá rud amháin eile a theastaíonn uaim a lua sara dtagam
do dheireadh mo chuid cainte anocht, agus baineann sé sin le
teideal na cainte, 'neacha neamhbheo agus nithe nach bhfuil

ann'. Bhuel, go dtí le déanaí do thabharfainn an leabhar go raibh a leithéid de theideal ar cheann des na rannaíocha atá sa chatalóg ginearálta sa Roinn le Béaloideas Éireann, seo catalóg a bhí déanta amach ag ceann do bhunaitheoiri na roinne, an bailitheoir Seán Ó Súilleabháin. Ach mo léir, nuair a chuas á chuardach i gcomhair na cainte seo ní fhéadfainn í a fháil. Do chuardaíos is do chuardaíos is ní bhfuaireas aon rian do in aon chor, rud a thugann i gceist go bhfuil seans maith nach raibh sé riamh ann agus gur speabhraídí a bhí ormsa ina thaobh ó thus deiridh. Thárlódh sé.

Ba mhaith liom an focal deireanach a thabhairt do Ghearóid Ó Crualaoich ó *Leabhar na Caillí*, *The Book of the Cailleach, Stories of the Wise-Woman Healer*. Tá píosa den gcaibidil 'Traidisiún agus Teoiric' a léimeann chun mo shúile ar an bpointe boise mar gurb é atá á rá ag Gearóid ná an méid a bhíos ag iarraidh a chur in iúil sa léacht seo:

> The texts of the oral narrative presented in this book and the commentaries offered with them bear witness, hopefully, to the way that traditional material, frequently seen as outmoded, naïve, parochially-bound, can constitute a rich imaginative resource for our own times and our own circumstances in a world where the local and the global are intermeshing at an increased rate for greater numbers and in ways not previously imagined.

Agus sin tús agus deireadh mo scéil – an chuma ina bhfuil acmhainn iontach againn in oideas béil na hÉireann, pioctha ó lámhscríbhinní na Roinne anseo, nó ó ghnáthchaint scéalaithe maithe, ar chuma an dá dhlúthdhiosca ón mBab Feirtéar a tháinig amach anuraidh agus go raibh ráchairt chomh mór san orthu, gur dóigh liom go bhfuil siad díolta amach faoi dhó.

Níl suim ar bith agamsa réimsí teangan ná eiseamláirí litríochta a thabhairt isteach sa Ghaeilge – per se – cé go raghaidh mé ar thóir foclóir eolaíochta, fisice nó ceimice, má tá gá agam leis, mar shampla nuair a theastaíonn uaim cur síos ar an bhfeiniméan nádúrtha san An Chaor Aduaidh a chonnac uair gur thugas turas ar Fairbanks Alasca. Ach an rud a theastaíonn uaimse a dhéanamh thar aon ní eile ná rud éigin a chur ar fáil trí bhíthin acmhainní nádúrtha na teangan nach raibh sa bhfilíocht roimhe sin, in aon teanga. Is chuige sin a bhím ag póirseáil liom sa Roinn le Béaloideas, agus lé cúnamh na ndéithe agus na ndeamhan, na neacha neamhbheo agus na nithe nach bhfuil ann, beidh mé á dhéanamh an dá lá is an fhaid a mhairfidh mé.

DEIREADH AN LÉACHTA ANSEO. A BHUÍ LE DIA.

The Hag, the Fair Maid and the Otherworld

I wrote a poem recently.

Primavera

D' athraigh gach aon ní nuair a ghaibh sí féin thar
    bráid.
Bhainfeadh sí deora áthais as na clocha glasa, deirim
    leat.
Na héanlaithe beaga a bhí go dtí seo faoi smál,
d' osclaíodar a scornach is thosnaigh ag píopáil
ar chuma feadóige stáin i láimh gheocaigh, amhail
Is gur chuma leo sa diabhal an raibh nó nach raibh
    nóta acu.
Bláthanna fiaine a bhí chomh cúthail, chomh humhal
Ag lorg bheith istigh go faichilleach ar chiumhaiseanna
na gceapach mbláth, táid anois go rábach, féach an fal-
    caire fiain
ag baint radharc na súl díom go hobann lena réiltíní
    craorag.

Bhíos-sa, leis, ag caoi go ciúin ar ghéag,
i bhfolach faoi dhuilleog fige, éalaithe i mo dhú dara,
ag cur suas stailce, púic orm chun an tsaoil
Thógfadh sé i bhfad níos mó ná meangadh gáire
ó aon spéirbhean chun mé a mhealladh as mo shliogán,
bhí an méid sin fógartha thall is abhus agam roimh ré.
Ach do dhein sí é, le haon searradh dá taobh,
le haon sméideadh meidhreach, caithiseach, thar a
*   gualainn*
do chorraigh sin a rútaí ionam, is d' fhág mé le míobhán
im' cheann, gan cos ná láimh fúm, ach mé corrthónach,
*   guagach.*

I should have called it 'Anois teacht an Earraigh' (the name of Raftery's poem on spring), but at the same time I was thinking of two paintings by Botticelli – 'Spring' and 'The Birth of Venus'. And so, in the end I, called the poem 'Primavera'.

I could have equally called it 'Fair Maid' or 'Hag/Fair Maid'. It would make sense and would bring me back into the Gaelic tradition, both the literary and the folkloric. This double image of the fair maiden and the hag are as old in Ireland as the literature itself. As to the literary tradition, one needs but mention the story from Old Irish in which Niall of the Nine Hostages lies with the old hag at the bottom of the well and she is instantly transformed into a fair maid. 'I am Sovereignty,' she says, and she prophesizes that Niall and his descendents will be kings of Ireland.

In the *aisling* we find some of the most beautiful and compelling poems in the canon – from 'Gile na Gile' to 'Róisín Dubh', to 'Úirchill an Chreagáin' – and Irish literature would be much the poorer without them. Indeed, where would English literature in Ireland be without 'Oh my Dark Rosaleen' and: 'Did you see an old woman going down the road?' 'I didn't, but I saw a young girl and she had the walk of a queen,' not to mention other examples of the same thing such as the bride who leaps on the back of the main character in Stewart Parker's play *Northern Star*. I happened to be at the local hairdresser when that play was staged in Dublin, overhearing my neighbours as they chatted about this and that. One of the women began to talk about the play she had seen the night before; 'And as soon as I saw that jilted bride I knew who she was,' she said. 'She was Ireland.'

But it was the old tradition that I was more interested in and it was from the mouths of people that I first came across the image of the hag. There was an old woman once by the name of Mór in Dún Chaoin and there were loads of stories about her as I was growing up. She constantly quarrelled with her husband Donncha Dí, and one day he lost patience with her and prayed for the length and breadth of Ireland between them. This happened in the twinkle of an eye and he was taken up into the air and landed up in Donaghadee in County Down – and he's been there ever since. Years later I was listening to Breandán Feirtéar on Raidió na Gaeltachta interviewing Hannah Daly, former postmistress of Dún Chaoin. They were discussing Mór and what had happened to her husband and then Hannah said nonchalantly; 'There were some people outside Callaghan's on a Saturday evening and they saw him going east with a bundle on his back.' As though it only happened yesterday or today. I had to laugh. Nothing would satisfy me but to write a poem in which that line occurred and this I did some time afterwards:

Clabhsúr

... *is ansan*
Lá

Do bhailibh an dia leis.

D' éirigh ar maidin le fáinne an lae ghléigil,
rug ar a rásúr, a scuab fiacal is ar thravelling bag
is thug dos na bonnaibh é.
Bhí daoine lasmuigh de thigh Challaghan sa Daingean
tráthnóna Sathairn a chonaic ag gabháilt soir é
agus paca ar a dhrom.

Chualasa leis, mar a bheadh i dtaibhreamh,
é ag gabháilt thar bráid,
a scol amhráin is a phort feadaíola aige
faoi mar a bheadh obónna i dtaobh thíos den stáitse
'is é an dia Hercules, a ghráigh Anthony,
Atá á fhágaint' –

Anois táim folamh, is an poll seo i mo lár
Is n' fheadar cé líonfaidh é
Nó cad leis? Dá mb' áil liom é a leanúint
ins an mbóithrín achrannach...
Ach ó, is fada fairsing í Éire
is tá iallach mo bhróg gan snaidhm.

Of course when I was thinking about the Mór story, I remembered another one about her and used that as well. According to this tale Mór became lonesome after Donncha and she travelled to the top – or the bottom – of Ireland looking for him. She left her own house in Dún Chaoin, and when she came to Barr an Chlasaigh and saw the wide and beautiful parish of Ventry extending before her, she became afraid: 'Oh, the length and breadth of Ireland!' she said, and turned back home. There is another story concerning this adventure. On the road home nature called and she did a piss by the side of the ditch. It was such a powerful stream that it formed two grooves on both sides of the road, which give it its place-name today. My aunt's husband, Thomas Murphy, used '*Leá bumbóire*' or '*Leá múin Móire*' as an expression or as a curse, tongue in cheek, and he'd have no respect for you if you weren't able to understand the saying, or tell the story that went with it.

This is an example of the significance attached to the image of the hag in the mind of the people and in the nature of their folklore. It is especially true in the case of place-names and their lore. We'd be here all week listing townlands and lowlands and highlands and lakes named after the hag or associated with her. This tradition is older than the Celtic era, it must be said. Gearóid Ó Crualoich states in his *The Book of the Cailleach*:

> Old Europe was intensified in Ireland, where an abiding sense of a supreme, sovereign, female, cosmic agency appears to have operated on the incoming culture to a degree that resulted in a continuing, powerful sensibility to the presence in the land-scape of such divine, female agency – a sensibility that has remained at the heart of Irish ancestral cosmology and mytho-logical legend.

I have always been interested in this particular image. One can see it in the first poems I wrote, poems that I can call poems other than compositions in verse:

Teist Dhonncha Dí ar Mhór

Do sheas sí lomnocht
sa doircheacht,
a bosa fuara – iasc gealúr –
ar mo ghuailne,
a cromáin – tine ghealáin

faoi dhá ré a broinne.

Thumas mo cheann
i bhfeamnach a gruaige;
bhí tonn ghoirt na sáile
am' bhualadh, am' shuathadh;
ár gcapaill bhána ag donnú
ina bhfrancaigh mhóra.
Gach aon ní ina chorcra.

Nuair a dhúisíos ar maidin bhí tinneas cinn orm.
Thugas faoi ndeara
go raibh gainní an liathbhuí ag clúdach a colainne.
Bhí fiacla lofa an duibheagáin
ag drannadh orm.
Sea, thógas mo chip is mo mheanaithe
is theicheas liom.

Every time I come across a trace of the hag, she sparks off a poem in me. This is a relatively recent example:

Eithne Uathach

an chéad bhean a luaitear
i mórshaothar Chéitinn
'Foras Feasa ar Éirin'
d' itheadh sí leanaí

óir 'do bhí ar daltachas
ag Déisibh Mumhan:
agus do hoileadh leo
ar fheoil naoín í',

chun gur luaithede

145

> *a bheadh sí in-nuachair*
> *de bharr gur tairngríodh*
> *go bhfaighidís talamh*
> *ón bhfear a phósfadh sí.*
>
> *Seans go bhfuil sí fós á dhéanamh.*
> *Nó cad a déarfá*
> *le Seán Savage, Mairéad Farrell*
> *agus Dan McCann*

A couple of years ago when the writer and publisher Micheál Ó Conghaile gave the Ó Cadhain Lecture here in UCD, he said he was in two minds about it. He'd much prefer, he said, to write a short story, or attempt one – even if it never got finished. I am in the same situation. Every time I sat down to write this lecture, I started writing a poem instead. Nothing to complain about – we should never refuse the Muse when she comes our way. You could be waiting quite a while for inspiration to come and it might not come at all.

I have always been fascinated by folklore, though I wouldn't always have called it by such a lofty name. What were they but little stories stitched into the everyday narratives around me, a five-year-old exile, back in my aunty Máire's house in Cathair an Treanntaigh in the parish of Ventry in the mid-fifties. Little things that happened from day to day, an old story or an unusual reference attached to them. Like the day a few years later when I as a young girl was walking up the Cathair Road in a silk dress made of two pieces of material that were stitched together with a hem below – the first and only bit of sewing I ever did. 'Oh,' said John Sé, a cousin of my grandfather's who met me on the road, 'I like your dress.' 'Yes,' says I with great pride, ''tis silk.' 'Don't I know it well,' says John Sé, 'there was so much

silk in the place they call Silk Cliff that the people of the
parish were tying their animals with it: "The sheep of the
Cathair had fetters of silk", as the poet said.' A sentence that
will stay in my head forever and that would leap out at me
years later when I was writing a poem.

Not only that but my aunt's husband, Tomás Ó Murchú,
or Thomas Murphy as he was better known, was by the fire-
side with me. He was a man with a vast knowledge of the
parish and of the lore of the seven old parishes west of Din-
gle. I heard him one night in Donall Ó Catháin's pub when
Breandán Mac Gearailt convened Oireachtas na nGael in Bal-
lyferriter. Máirtín Ó Cadhain was in the company. Tomás
and Art Ó Beoláin differed about the location and the con-
struction of the Carraig chapel:

'It's built on Carraig,' says Art.
    'The divil it is,' says Tomás, 'it's built on Bóthar Buí.'
    'It's built on Carraig,' says Art again.
    'Who told you that?' says Tomás.
    'Haven't I read it? It's written in the book.'
    'Oh,' says Tomás, 'whoever wrote that book he put down a
divil of lies in it!'
    'You can't beat him,' says Máirtín Ó Cadhain, 'you can't
beat the proper native speaker.'

Around that time I gave a copy of the book *Romantic Hidden
Kerry* to Tomás. A couple of days later I went enquiring.
'Well, Tomás, what's your opinion of the book?' 'It's not bad,'
he says, 'it goes back two hundred years. Not bad – but I'd go
the four for you.'

This was no great exaggeration because he knew that it
was big guns from a ship in Dingle Bay, and not in Ventry Har-
bour as one might expect, that knocked the top off the town
castle, Caisleán na dTreanntach. There wasn't a stone upon
stone of that castle to be seen in a hundred years. It's likely
that it was in the time of Dún an Óir, or at the latest during

the Cromwellite wars that the court fell. There hadn't been any of the Treanntaigh in the Dingle Peninsula in a long, long time – although they gave their names to three townlands in the parish of Ventry and the name is still common enough in North Kerry. They didn't flourish as much as their fellow Normans in the peninsula, the Ferriters, the Rices, the Gear-altaighs and the Husseys.

Tomás could go back to seven generations of his people. He had all their names and knew much about their lives. He claimed his grandfather was born in Cuan Uachtar, a village saved from the potato blight of the Great Famine. Much good it did to the tenants, because the village and two other vil-lages in the harbour, Cuan Íochtar and Cúilín Bhán, were cleared in 1867 by Lord Ventry's steward, a Cork man by the name of Leahy. Tomás always said that his grandfather was twelve years of age when they left. Many of the tenants went to America or to Fán or to the Oileán Tiar (in the Blaskets) or were scattered throughout the district. Some of them came to Cathair. 'How did they manage to settle down in Cathair?' says I. 'Wasn't the place deserted,' says he, 'everyone had gone away.'

He knew how the chapel in the parish of Ventry was transferred from its old site in the eastern part of the parish, where the school now is, to the site in Imleach Shlat, given away for nothing by Muintir Shé of Imleach. His grand-uncle Micheál, who tragically died after going to America, was the last person prayed for in the old chapel and his aunt was the first to be baptized in the new one. He knew a lot about my own people, stuff you wouldn't want to hear sometimes. 'Léan with the puss on her and the cross eye,' he called my great-grandmother, Léan Ní Chearna. It was when I was becoming more interested in Irish as a young girl that I began to take down much of this lore from him, but my memories

of him, and of many others, go back further still. They had
the sharp tongues and wouldn't blink before cutting you
down a bit if they wanted to: '*Leá bumbóire*' or '*Leá múin
Móire to you*' was a frequent expression, or curse I should
say, and another: 'What would you know, it's not that you
have the origins of all stories.'

But my memories stretch back further than that to the
period I spent with them as a five-year-old 'orphan' over from
England. I remember the time when Johnny Long and his son
Maidhc were farming next door, and Jacksaí Sé and his sister
Neil were up beyond them in the village. John Sé's house was
at the top of the village and the pump in their yard was
famous for never drying out in the summer. Each man of
them would stand on his own little hill throwing all sorts of
daggered phrases at the next man. I can't recall a single sen-
tence now but I remember the speech as being eloquent and
poetic. Little wonder then that when I first began to write
poetry I drew my linguistic resources from them:

Móir Chráite

*Tá Móir go dlúth faoi ghlas
ina meabhairín bheag fhéin; – 3" / 4" / 2"
ábhar liath is bán –*

*dearg (a bhíonn na créachta
a bháthann leath na gcuileanna
faid is a dheineann an leath eile a mbiaiste
ar feoil na n-imeall).*

*'Éistíg', in ainm Dé,' ar sise leis na préacháin
is cabairí an Daingin a thagann san iarnóin
ag suathadh a mbolg.*

'Tá na héinne dúnta isteach
ina ifreann féinín féin.'
Scaipeann na mionéin
nuair a chuireann sí scrabhadh scraith
lastuas dóibh.

There were others in the village who had the great talk. Not only were they native speakers, they were the finest of speakers too. The most Gaelic of them all, Tomás Mhairéad (Ó Sé) died in 1956, a year exactly before my arrival. He was the last monoglot. They say he had no English. I don't know if I ever believed that entirely. 'How could he have no English living here with all the coastguards around for more than a hundred years?' 'He kept away from them. He didn't mix with them.' There might have been a bit of politics involved as well. He was one of those who attended the first public meeting of the Land League during the Land War, a meeting held in 200 or so *navogues* (curraghs) in the middle of the harbour when Lord Ventry wouldn't allow the meeting on land. His people were known as the Parnells for many a day. But if he wasn't there for me there were many more who were: Fitzie, John Sé, Jacksaí and his sister Neil, Joeín and Annie Sheehy and her brother Jackie, Johnny Long and his son Maidhc Long na Cathrach. They were there in plenty, and they were honey-tongued.

Other things were happening in my life and I got the hell out of Ireland as quickly as I could. After spending seven years abroad, mostly in the Netherlands and Turkey, I knew that what I most wanted in the world was to return to Ireland and start writing full time. I applied for and received a bursary from the Arts Council. This allowed me to come home with my two children and settle in my people's summer house in Cathair an Treanntaigh. My children were so fair that we were known as 'Nuala and the White Turkeys'. I was trying my hand at everything; a novel in which I got bogged down, a selection of short stories that was finished but never published, but, above all, I sank myself into poetry. My husband hadn't arrived yet and I was very lonely in the house on my own with the children asleep looking out over Ventry Strand and the ebbed tide. It was in folkloric terms that I expressed myself and invoked the persona of a mermaid:

Má tá eireaball éisc féin orm
Nílim gan dathúlacht éigin.
Tá mo ghruaig fada is buí
is tá loinnir óm' ghainní
ná chífeá riamh ar mhná míntíre.
Dath na gcloch an tsúil acu
ach féach go cúramach isteach
im' mhogaillse
is chífir an burdán fearna
is róinte groí
ag macnas
im mhac imreasan.

Ní gan phian
a thángas aníos
ar thalamh.
Do bhriseas
an slabhra réamhordaithe,
do mhalairtíos snámh
ar luail cosa
ag priocadh liom
ar nós na gcuirliún.
Creid uaim gur grá, ní Dia
a dhein é a ordú.

> *D' imís*
> *is thógais uaim mo chaipín draíochta.*
> *Níl sé chomh furasta orm teacht air*
> *is a bhí sa scéal*
> *i measc cearachail an díona.*
> *Tá' s agam;*
> *dheineas tochailt síos go dtí an gaíon*
> *is níl aon rian do.*
> *Theip an taoide orainn chomh maith*
> *is tá francach ag cogaint na gréine*

(An Mhaighdean Mhara)

Around the same time Seán Ó Tuama introduced me to Joe Daly and Bab Feirtéar. I'd visit them often and they were very good to me. They were great company. Bab in her house, a grand fire in the hearth, cups of tea going round, and Joe and his wife Peig in their house or in Daniel's pub in Ballyferriter. I remember taping some stories from Bab and I'd play them to myself in bed until sleep came. It's no exaggeration to say that they influenced me greatly. Not only did they supply me with titles and narrative frameworks for my first two books of poems, they also taught me how to make something more universal out of the raw emotions and changing circumstances of my own life. The lore helped me to tell stories with a slant, as Emily Dickinson once recommended: 'Tell the truth, but tell it slant', and to say things that could not be expressed directly.

An example of this approach is the title poem of my second volume, 'Féar Suaithinseach'. The first time I taped Bab, she gave me a version of the story on which I based my poem. It wasn't long on tape, however, before my sister destroyed it by taping pop music over it – she had mistaken it for a blank tape because there was nothing on it but speech.

I went back to Bab and got another and then another version, but the version on which the poem was based was gone. As it happens, she never told it again the way I first remembered it; the way the priest would handle the communion so deftly. That was the expression I needed above all other tellings. The version I eventually used was the one I was given by Professor Bo Almquist, a taped version later transcribed by Dr Ríonach Uí Ógáin. By this time other great changes were happening in my life. We had spent three years in Corca Dhuibhne. For one of these years my husband had been working in Dublin, visiting us every second weekend. We knew that the journey was too hard for him and that we would have to move to Dublin. It was horrible to be torn away from the western world and for a long time I missed the Gaeltacht sorely. I had Raidió na Gaeltachta on all the time, and for many years afterwards I contributed an insert on Maidhc Sé's programme about local history, especially from my gleanings in the Department of Folklore. It was Joe Daly who pointed me towards the Department in the first place. He told me to go in, that it would do me good, and, he said to me, 'See what you see.'

Firstly I traced my own people, beginning of course with Thomas Murphy – and yes, he was there. He had contributed three stories. One story was a great wonder, the story of the boy and the holy pictures, and the beginning of a story called 'The Mouse and the Wren'. Joe had told me that the story would be there. It's a story to be found in *Seanchaí Muimhneach*, collected by Pádraig Ó Siochfhradha, or 'An Seabhac' as he was known, at the beginning of the century. By the time Joe started collecting in the 1930s and 1940s, it was no longer in the memories or on the lips of the people. He picked up fragments of the story here and there, but no one had its beginning. He came down to Cathair an Treanntaigh to find it because he had heard it might be there. Thomas had it. According to the description at the beginning of the story he had heard it from his mother twenty-odd years before. He describes himself as the son of a farmer, twenty-eight years of age. That was true, since he had not yet been given the land from his father.

But the father himself, Peats Ó Murchú, was the biggest jewel I discovered. I had always heard a good deal about Peats, as someone who was a very fine speaker, and in my own time people used many of his phrases. For example, his son Tomás was born on a night of snow so they called him ever afterwards 'Tomáisín an tSneachta' (Little Tom of the Snow). The day after his birth Peats went walking past Mám na Gaoithe and up Bóthar na Leataithe on his way north to Cathair Deargáin where his wife Cáit Foley came from. It was a snowy day, the Feast of the Epiphany, and my granny, a young girl in Leataoibh Meánach, was throwing snowballs at her friends. He was greeted with 'Any news, Peats?' 'I have,' said he, 'a son last night, the makings of a giant. He has the bones of a young horse and never will he get a cold.'

He was right about the second half because Tomás always had good health and he came through the Great Flu of 1918 without a bother when three coffins – two uncles and a brother – were taken out of the house within a fortnight. The first part of the prophecy wasn't up to much, however, because although he was supple and active into his old age he was far from being a giant. He always admired a good physique: 'Nothing like it,' he'd say. My granny always said she little thought when she was growing up that she would have a daughter who would marry the child of that snowy night.

Another expression that stayed in people's minds was the agitation on Peats when he was bargaining with a man at a fair in Dingle. 'Such pride from a man,' said he, 'with only two worthless beasts compared to the man with eight cows in a city,' referring of course to himself.

But it was only when I saw all that Joe Daly had collected from Peats that I understood what a fine *seanchaí* we had in him. He had the long stories of the Fenian Lays, the story of Balor Béimneach, the story of Fionn and King Athadonas. Not only that but he had the battle rhetoric as well: the battle rhetoric of the warrior, the battle rhetoric of the vessel, the battle rhetoric of the sea. For a while I was very taken with the battle rhetoric:

> 'Which would you prefer,' said the giant, 'hard piercing wrestling or the clash of sharp steel swords on each other's ribs?' 'I'd prefer the hard piercing wrestling because it is such that I practised on the greens with the sons of noblemen.' And they set to it with downward blows and upward blows and with wrestling holds at one another and he who would come from the bottom of the world to the top of the world to view two wrestlers, it is these two he should be watching and the hard ground softened under them and the soft ground hardened and hollows became hills and hills became hollows. From the grey stones beneath them they drew up wells of pure water and through the hard sods scattering here there, and everywhere beneath their feet, they would extract three teeth from the hag that sits over in the city of London and she reddening her pipe, and those three teeth would not stop in their course through mountain and moor before they toppled three courts yonder in the Eastern world.

I took it all in. It became a bit of a frenzy. I went from one *seanchaí* to another, checking different versions of the battle rhetoric. Peats a' tSaoir 'ac Loinsigh from Baile an tSléibhe had the best of them. He had given stories to the American collector Jeremiah Curtin as a young man below in Ard a' Bhóthair. He told the stories in Irish and his father put English on them for Curtin. But Peats wasn't in the least bit satisfied with the English version. When he was reciting them again into an ediphone for the collector Seán Ó Dubhda, he said; 'I was telling stories for Curtin and his wife was writing them down and my father was putting English on the Irish for her and a boy, a farmer's son, didn't he buy one of those books and my stories were in it and you wouldn't believe it, he wasn't putting them down in any proper way at all. The battle rhetoric wasn't in it at all. They weren't able to write the battle rhetoric at all, at all!'

Is it any wonder that the poems I was writing at the time are full of all sorts of battle rhetoric? It is what came to mind as I was nursing a child and trying to describe the type of world a newborn baby comes into, a world full of sights and sounds that she could not distinguish from one another, that world of pre-symbolic sound or the *chora* as the feminist theorist from France, Julia Kristeva, calls it:

Ag Cothú Linbh

An eol duit an lá ón oíche,
go bhfuil mochthráigh mhór
ag fógairt rabharta,
go bhfuil na báid
go doimhin sa bhfarraige
mar a bhfuil éisc is rónta
is míolta móra
ag teacht ar bhois is ar bhais
*   is ar sheacht maidí rámha orthu,*
go bhfuil do bháidín ag snámh
óró sa chuan
leis na lupadáin lapadáin
muranáin maranáin
í go slím sleamhain

ó thóin go ceann
ag cur grean na farraige
in uachtar
is cúr na farraige
in íochtar?

There were other poems of the battle rhetoric as well, such as
'An Rás'. What happened here is that I wanted to describe the
wild dash of a cart race up the country. It was the battle
rhetoric of the hero that I used to give that great spin to it:

Faoi mar a bheadh leon cuthaigh nó tarbh fásaigh
nó ceann de mhuca allta na Fiannaíochta,
nó an gaiscíoch ag léimt faoi dhéin an fhathaigh
faoina chírín singilíneach síoda,
tiomáinim an chairt ar dalladh
trí bhailte beaga lár na hÉireann.
Beirim ar an ghaoth romham,
is ní bheireann an ghaoth atá i mo dhiaidh orm.

Mar a bheadh saighead as bogha, piléar as gunna
nó seabhac rua trí scata mionéan lá Márta
scaipim na mílte slí taobh thiar dom.
Tá uimhreacha ar na fógraí bóthair
is ní thuigim an mílte iad nó kiloméadair.
Aonach, Ros Cré, Móinteach Mílic,
N' fheadar ar ghaibheas nó nár ghaibheas tríothu.
Níl iontu faoin am seo ach teorainní luais
Is moill ar an mbóthar go dtí thú.
Trí ghleannta sléibhte móinte bogaithe
scinnim ar séirse ón iarthar,
d' aon seáp amháin reatha i do threo
d' aon fháscadh ruthaig i do chuibhreann.
Deinim ardáin des na hísleáin, ísleáin des na hardáin

157

Nuala Ní Dhomhnaill

> talamh bog de thalamh cruaidh is talamh cruaidh de
>   thalamh bog,
> imíonn gnéithe uile seo na léarscáile as mo chuimhne,
> ní fhanann ann ach gíoscán coscán is drithle soilse.

Around the same time I came across the book *Italian Folk-tales*, selected and retold by Italo Calvino. This is an English translation of a collection of fairytales translated initially into Italian by Italo Calvino from the various languages of Italy. I took particular notice of what he had to say in the introduction about what happened to him when he became embroiled in the world of the fairytale:

> ... it was a leap in the dark, a plunge into an unknown sea into which others before me, over the course of 150 years, had flung themselves, not out of any desire for the unusual, but because of a deep-rooted conviction that some essential, mysterious element lying in the ocean depths must be salvaged to ensure the survival of the race ...

From what he had written, I knew that I was not the only one who had come down with this disease. Calvino says:

> I, however, plunged into that submarine world totally unequipped, without even a tankful of intellectual enthusiasm for anything spontaneous and primitive. I was subjected to all the discomforts of immersion in an almost formless element which, like the sluggish and passive oral tradition, could never be brought under conscious control.

I myself had moved on from battle rhetoric and Fenian lays to fairytales and to other storytellers; Tomás (Mhárthain) Mac Gearailt, Tadhg Ó Guithín, Seán 'ac Gearailt from Márthain who had married into the Gorta Dubha (nicknamed 'Danger'), Peig Sayers and her son Maidhc (File) Ó Guithín, Domhnall Ó Mainín from Cill Uraidh (Domhnaillín an Deataigh), from whom Joe Daly took the longest story ever, a story that took twelve nights to write down. Then there was

Seán O Grifín from Cathair Boilg – he did not have a reputation as a storyteller in the community because he didn't recite stories in public, his speech being indistinct. But he had spent his life inside the house of Peats 'ac Loinnsigh, carefully listening to every story and remembering them: 'An Gadaí Dubh', 'Balor Béimneach', 'Cuid, Céad agus Ceatach', 'Feirmeoir Aodhaire na hAimsire', and so on. By the time Joe Daly was collecting stories, Peats had gone to his eternal reward, but he discovered Seán Ó Grifín and got all the stories from him. Those stories are wonderful. Italo Calvino discourses on the same subject:

> Meanwhile, as I started to work, to take stock of the material available, to classify the stories into a catalog which kept expanding, I was gradually possessed by a kind of mania, an insatiable hunger for more and more versions and variants. Collating, categorizing, comparing became a fever. I could feel myself succumbing to a passion akin to that of entomologists, which I thought characteristic of the scholars of the Folklore Fellows Communications of Helsinki, a passion which rapidly degenerated into a mania, as a result of which I would have given all of Proust in exchange for a new variant of the 'gold-dung donkey'. [The Irish version of this, *Cac airgead, a chapaillín bháin* or 'Shit money, little white horse', is a well-known variant.]

It gave me great satisfaction to know that another writer had experienced the same intoxication as I had. Not only that, but to have come through, because the period Calvino spent swimming in the unconquerable tide of folklore brought about great formal changes in his writing. He left realism behind and embraced metafiction, as in, for example, the wonderful novel, *Once on a Winter's Night a Traveller*. Describing what had happened to him was so close to my own experience that he took the words out of my mouth:

> For two years I have lived in woodlands and enchanted castles,

torn between contemplation and action ... and during these two years the world about me gradually took on the attributes of fairyland, where everything that happened was a spell or a metamorphosis, where individuals, plucked from the chiaroscuro of a state of mind, were carried away by predestined loves, or were bewitched... snake pits opened up and were transformed into rivers of milk; kings who had been thought kindly turned out to be brutal parents; silent, bewitched kingdoms suddenly came back to life. I had the impression that the lost rules which govern the world of folklore were tumbling out of the magic box I had opened.

And again he says:

Now that the book is finished, I know that this was not a hallucination; a sort of professional malady, but the confirmation of something I had already suspected – folktales are real.

I had come to the same conclusion independently and my poems changed fundamentally as a consequence.

As I continued searching, my interests jumped from one thing to another. Having been immersed in battle rhetoric and international motifs, I now became interested in the storytellers themselves, especially women storytellers, the likes of Peig Sayers, Cáit Ruiseal and Máire Ruiséal in particular. I think I fell in love with Máire Ruiséal. Her approach was much different to that of Peig Sayers. Peig is almost baroque with her little rhetorical flourishes. She likes difficult words and a word can often trigger off a story in her memory. For instance when mention is made of the potatoes known as 'minions', she says, 'It was the year of the minions when my father was at home. A wild woman came into the house and ...' off she goes on her narrative. Máire Ruiséal's narrative custom was much more direct though she has as much rhetoric as anybody else: 'And the dew of late evening descended on her and night fell and the terrier was going under the dockleaf and the dockleaf was fleeing it and the fox was going into its own little den and who would blame him.'

There's one place in the middle of the story when she talks aside to Joe Daly: 'The King's children were out on the ... Joe, can I use an English word here?' 'Keep going,' says Joe. 'The King's children were out on the piazza ...'

I'm delighted that Eilís Ní Dhuibhne selected a tale from Máire Ruiséal for the chapter on Oral Tradition in the fifth volume of *The Field Day Anthology*. The story is 'Scéal an Ghabhairín Bháin' ('The Story of the White Kid Goat'), a fine example of the so-called feminine fairytale. It is a version of the ancient tale, 'Psyche and Amor'. Calvino says of it, in the context of an essay by Vladimir Propp in *Historical Roots of Russian Fairy Tales:*

> Although the customs of millennia are disregarded, the plot of the story still reflects the spirit of those laws and describes every love thwarted and forbidden by law, convention or social disparity. That is why it has been possible, from prehistory to the present, to preserve, not as a fixed formula but as a flowing element, the sensuality so often underlying this love, evident in the ecstasy and frenzy of mysterious nocturnal embraces.

The sensual aspect of love is palpable in Máire Ruiséal's version of the story and, as with the storytelling of Peig Sayers, there is an openness of mind in it about human nature, which one might, perhaps, not expect from the general stereotype of the female storyteller as a pillar of society:

> They entered a fine court. He spoke to her then: 'Wisha, now tell me then,' says he, 'which would you prefer, for me to be a goat at night and a man by day or a man by day and a goat at night?' 'Oh to be sure,' says she, 'I prefer nocturnal company – for you to be a man at night and a goat by day.' And that's the way it was.

I noticed as I visited the Department of Folklore that my interests had changed. Recently I have become more drawn to little bits of local lore, innocent wee stories about people. A certain Sítheach from Baile Eaglasta describing how many houses fell in every townland during the Great Famine. Peats Dhónaill (Ó Cíobháin) from Muiríoch talking about fishing or about Tomás na bPúcaí, a relation of mine. He had a story about Tomás and I'm afraid I have to contradict it. Three young women came from the east to Leataoibh Meánach. Tomás na bPúcaí had second sight and he said the village would be under a great pall, but he wouldn't say which of the young women would be taken away. As it happened, it was the woman he was most closely related to, the wife of his sister's son. She died of the puerperal mania bringing a daughter into the world and, says Peats Dhónaill, 'She died shortly afterwards and the daughter died as well.' Well, the daughter didn't die. She was my grandmother and if she hadn't lived I wouldn't be here now.

Another story belonging to my own people I used as an introduction to my last volume, *Cead Aighnis:*

A Person's Three Souls

I was in bed, asleep, down in Baile Móir, when something brought Eoghainín Finton outside, and he saw me emerging from the house. He called his wife, Léan Ní Chearna. 'Your soul from the devil, Léan,' says he, 'Seán has had a stroke or something! Look at him there by the side of the house. Go out,' says he, 'and call on him.' But he saw me turning again and going back into the house – Léan never called on me. They were telling me this the following day and I wouldn't believe Eoghainín, except that Léan was saying it too. I told him I hadn't left the bed since the time I got into it until the morning, and that I had slept soundly. 'Such things exist,' says Léan, 'and I remembered it. Had I called on him that time,' says Léan, 'he'd be stuck there forever.'

But I've always heard the person to have three parts. There's the soul of the breath, the soul of feeling and the eternal soul. The eternal soul will stay in you until you die. I don't know was

it the soul of breath or the soul of feeling in me that was outside
while I was asleep, that I don't know.

(From the telling of Seán Ó Cíobháin, Department of Folklore,
Ms 965, p. 63)

But to return to the story at the beginning of my talk, about
'fetters of silk on the sheep of Cathair', I was at the Depart-
ment of Folklore the other day and happened to discover
some more information about it. I always understood it to be
a mythological event. It was a remarkable example, or so I
thought, of the poetical mind of the people and of the strong
imagination always associated with the people of Corca
Dhuibhne. I never imagined it to have any historical basis,
but it has. The *Lady Nelson* was a big sailing ship that was
wrecked on the Skellig, and she was laden with pipes of wine
and silk. It was after this ship was wrecked that they built
the lighthouse on Skellig:

> It was a foggy night and the captain was saying that they were
> three leagues from land. Some of the crew were of another mind
> and right they were, because it wasn't long before the ship hit the
> Skellig. They all drowned except three of them who got up on
> some floating wood. Two or three days of fog and rain went by
> and the pipes of wine were washing up on land. Boats were out
> looking for them. Ventry Harbour and Cathair a' Treanntaigh
> were full of boats. There was a man called Scanlon who had a
> boat and a crew in the bay looking for the wine, when they saw
> the flotsam and jetsam and the men atop. There were only two
> left when they reached them. A little while before, the third man
> had fallen into the water, heavy with sleep. They took the two
> survivors on board. No more were saved. Later, the two men sent
> Scanlon and his crew a mast and two sails out of gratitude.

I hope I have thrown some light on the importance that Irish
folklore holds for me, and on the importance of the Folklore
Commission's collection. I believe folklore works on two lev-
els, firstly on the level of Irish in which I am reminded of the

compactness of the everyday language I heard as a child from mouth to mouth in the farmyards. It also works on the level of the imagination when the motifs of the stories – and even the bits of lore scattered throughout the manuscripts – create wonderful images with which one can play, throwing them up in the air and catching them again. And of course that play is one of the most necessary ingredients when it comes to creative writing.

The essence of my lecture has to do with beings not alive, and things that aren't there. Well, until recently I could have sworn that this was the name of a section in the general catalogue of the Department of Folklore in Ireland, a catalogue created by one of the founders of the department, the collector Seán Ó Súilleabháin. Alas, when I went looking for it – for the purposes of this talk – I couldn't find it. I searched and searched, but there wasn't a trace of it, so maybe there is good reason to believe that it was never there in the first place and I had only dreamt it all along.

I would like to leave the last word to Gearóid Ó Crualaoich from *The Book of the Cailleach, Stories of the Wise-Woman Healer*, a section from the chapter 'Tradition and Theory', because Gearóid says what I am trying to convey in this lecture:

> The texts of the oral narrative presented in this book and the commentaries offered with them bear witness, hopefully, to the way that tradition material, frequently seen as outmoded, naïve, parochially-bound, can constitute a rich imaginative resource for our own times and our own circumstances in a world where the local and the global are intermeshing at an increased rate for greater numbers and in ways not previously imagined.

We have a fantastic resource in the oral tradition of Ireland, taken here from the Department's manuscripts and from the ordinary speech of storytellers such as Bab Feirtéar and her two CDs, issued in 2006, which are enjoying such a success that I believe they have sold out twice.

I am not particularly interested in bringing linguistic ranges or literary exemplars into Irish *per se*, though I will consult science, physics or chemistry dictionaries if, for example, I need to describe natural phenomena such as the Northern Lights, which I once saw on a trip to Fairbanks, Alaska. What I would like to do above everything else is to use the natural resources of the language, resources not previously found in the poetry, in any language. That's why I go rummaging in the Department of Folklore and with the help of gods and demons, of beings not alive and things that aren't there, I'll be doing it as long as I am around.

HERE ENDS THE LECTURE. THANKS BE TO GOD

Paul Durcan
Photograph courtesy of Whitespace Publishing Group Ltd

Cronin's Cantos

95

We went to Brighton in our Little Nine,
The open touring model Leslie bought
On what was called H.P. A gorgeous day,
The sky was somehow deep, you know, like heaven,
I thought the bubbling tar might melt the tyres
And Leslie laughed, called me a silly juggins.
He was a lovely driver, doing forty
Once we were free of Staines. It's tommy rot
To tell us now that people weren't happy.
We had our own nice house, a Tudor villa,
Which was the new thing then, a vacuum cleaner,
Dance music on the wireless, lovely murders.
Of course the war was still to come, that Hitler,
But it all seemed somehow new then, somehow modern.

In literary Dublin in the early winter months of 1963 – for there did exist then such a blood-and-guts encampment as 'literary Dublin' (it has of course long vanished from the River Liffey's banks) – there were rumours and whispers concerning the possibly imminent return to Dublin from Spain of a man called Cronin. Literary Dublin encompassed a small slope, running up from the Liffey on the north shore of Trinity College to the Grand Canal on the south shore of University College. At night in the pubs around the camp fires, mutterings and speculation, innuendo and foreboding went on about this man called Cronin.

All that winter, it was always night; I remember no daylight. Personages were as much shadows as substances, and you could as much intimate them as discern them. Patrick Kavanagh, John Jordan, James Liddy and Harry Kernoff were in McDaids, Brendan Behan and John Ryan were in the Bailey, Sean O'Sullivan was in Neary's, Ronnnie Drew and Luke Kelly were in O'Donoghues, Leland Bardwell was in O'Dwyers, Macdara Woods was in Bartley Dunnes, Michael Longley and Derek Mahon and Brendan Kennelly were in O'Neills, and Michael Hartnett and myself were everywhere.

> Has Cronin arrived?
> He has.
> He has not.

I was eighteen years old, setting out on the road to be a poet and nothing but a poet, so help me Dostoyevsky. I had spent my adolescent years reading up about Moscow and now I had set foot on the road to Moscow. Little did I know, in no way could I have foreseen, that that was how I would spend the rest of my life, tramping the road to Moscow. I could not figure out at all clearly why this Cronin man was the cause of such apprehension and expectation. Some said that he was a Communist. Others that he was a poet. He was a tyrant, an upstart, a saint, a genius. The wet dark nights were rife with suspense. What would he look like, I wondered, this intellectual pirate who was about to swoop in from the sea? I thought I had read every contemporary Irish poet and yet I had never seen, much less read a line by Cronin. I felt like Jack Hawkins in The Admiral Benbow waiting on the cliffs to catch sight of the figurehead of the schooner of doom or ecstasy, salvation or damnation, Dr Livesey invisible at my shoulder.

And then he was there. He was here. Six feet away from me. At midnight in the basement flat of Leland Bardwell. 33 Lower Leeson Street. Amongst the writers and the ex-revolutionaries and all the rest of the Bohemian flotsam and jetsam with their brown bags of stout and the odd naggin of whiskey. I didn't have to be told it was Cronin. In dress and style as well as in person, he was completely different from everyone else in that dungeon. A slight, dark, handsome man of about forty and middle height. Spanish-looking. His slightly pugilistic, slightly amatory posture was as if he had just stepped out the stage door at the back of the bullfight arena. Norman Mailer disguised as El Cordobes. A light corduroy suit, white shirt and tie, black beret, a cigarette in one hand, a bottle in the other, conversing fiercely with those nearest to him, conducting life-and-death arguments, yet suddenly collapsing in mirth, only to rise and sink the banderilla into his neighbour's shoulder blade. Politics, history, poetry, war, horse racing, boxing, Liberty, Equality, Fraternity; and Injustice.

In the weeks and months that followed over the next two years I was to find myself often in the company of Anthony Cronin. Naturally I was never introduced to him. I was a boy of eighteen on the edge of the crowd but it seemed to me that he treated me as he treated everyone else – as an equal companion. Angry, impatient, idealistic intellectual he was, but equally he was gentle. What the young e.e. cummings wrote about walking Paris streets at night with the older Ezra Pound would also be true of how I perceived Cronin in the early 1960s: 'He was more than wonderfully entertaining: he was magically gentle as only a great man can be towards some shyest child.' He was all soft edge as well as all hard edge. He had phenomenal memory, wit, knowledge and sense. And always, then as now, forty-two years later, that hovering glint of a smile and that shingle beach intake of breath prefiguring a three-stroke chuckle as he awaited his moment to expose the cant the rest of us were regurgitating. He had as rigorous and subtle a critical mind as T.S. Eliot but as audacious a footstep as Ezra Pound. Twenty years later in 1984, the legendary Steward of Annaghmakerrig, Bernard Loughlin, employed one word to describe Cronin: 'cniptious'.

A typical ordinary spring evening in 1963 comes to mind. It is about five in the afternoon in O'Dwyers public house on the corner of Lower Leeson Street and St Stephen's Green. Cronin is sitting with his back to the foam-window with a review copy of a new Alan Sillitoe novel on his lap. He is reviewing it for the TLS. This is how Cronin makes his living. Book-reviewing and most other forms of hack journalism. I have never met such a creature before. A fully qualified, fully harassed member of Grub Street. His glamorous, yellow-haired Mayo wife Thérèse is sitting beside him checking and sorting out other review books to help her husband. Out of the blue, Cronin quotes the American poet Hart Crane, the greatest American modernist poet of them all: a passage from the hobo section of Crane's epic poem *The Bridge*. Cronin utters the lines with a mixture of joy and outrage and laughter as if he were Danton or Baudelaire at the bar of the French Chamber of Deputies:

Behind

My father's cannery works I used to see
Rail-squatters ranged in nomad raillery,
The ancient men – wifeless or runaway

Hobo-trekkers that forever search
An empire wilderness of freight and rails.
Each seemed a child, like me, on a loose perch,
Holding to childhood like some termless play.
John, Jake or Charley, hopping the slow freight
– Memphis to Tallahassee – riding the rods,
Blind fists of nothing, humpty-dumpty clods.

Yet they touched something like a key perhaps.
From pole to pole across the hills, the states
– They know a body under the wide rain;
– Youngsters with eyes like fjords, old reprobates
– With racetrack jargon – dotting immensity
They lurk across her, knowing her yonder breast
Snow-silvered, sumac-stained or smoky blue –
Is past the valley sleepers, south or west,
– As I have trod the rumorous midnights, too,

And past the circuit of the lamp's thin flame
(O Nights that brought me to her body bare!)
Have dreamed beyond the print that bound her name,
Trains sounding the long blizzards out – I heard
Wail into distances I knew were hers.
Papooses crying on the wind's long mane
Screamed redskin dynasties that fled the brain,
– Dead echoes! But I knew her body there,
Time like a serpent down her shoulder, dark
And space, an eaglet's wing, laid on her hair.

Cronin then relates the story of Hart Crane's suicide and
how just before he leapt from the stern of the ss *Orizaba*
another passenger asked Crane how he was feeling and Hart
replied: 'Like a rat in a trap'. This leads into a story about

Paul Durcan

David Gascoyne visiting Herne Cottage in Sussex near Tennyson's house where the Cronins had lived in the 1950s. From Gascoyne, on then to George Barker and suddenly to John Cornford. Silence. Grief. The Spanish Civil War. Killed at twenty-one during the second battle of the Ebro. Cornford's poem to his girl back in England, Margot Heinemann. Cronin throws back his head defiantly and quotes the poem by heart again, by heart. All of it, all of it:

> *Heart of the heartless world,*
> *Dear heart, the thought of you*
> *Is the pain at my side,*
> *The shadow that chills my view.*
>
> *The wind rises in the evening,*
> *Reminds that autumn is near,*
> *I am afraid to lose you,*
> *I am afraid of my fear.*
>
> *On the last mile to Huesca,*
> *The last fence for our pride,*
> *Think so kindly, dear, that I*
> *Sense you at my side.*
>
> *And if bad luck should lay my strength*
> *Into the shallow grave,*
> *Remember all the good you can;*
> *Don't forget my love.*

Shillings, sixpences and three-penny bits are counted to procure a few more beers and someone mentions President John F. Kennedy who is due to fly into Dublin in a month or two whereupon Cronin names a name no one has ever heard of – Robert Duncan – and he begins to sing:

172

Hoover, Roosevelt, Truman, Eisenhower –
Where among these did the power reside
That moves the heart? What flower of the nation
Bride-sweet broke to the whole rapture?
Hoover, Coolidge, Harding, Wilson
hear the factories of human misery turning out
    commodities.
For whom are the holy matins of the heart ringing?
Noble men in the quiet of morning hear
Indians singing the continent's violent requiem.
Harding, Wilson, Taft, Roosevelt,
Idiots fumbling at the bride's door,
Hear the cries of men in meaningless debt and war.
Where among these did the spirit reside
That restores the land to productive order?

That was just an ordinary spring evening in O'Dwyers public house in the month of April 1963. And those of us who were lucky enough to be sitting there were being vouchsafed a rare kind of education. Cronin in O'Dwyers in the early 1960s was the classic Central European artist-intellectual and hedge schoolmaster practising Newman's idea of a university in the corner of a smoky bar. Cronin set me free. After Kavanagh, he put the final kybosh on the curse of flag-waving, tattooed Celtic poetry, fairies, wet turf and the treble-whammy whine of self-pity, retrophilia, and nostalgia.

Another evening in 1963, a summer's evening, Cronin is sitting the far side of O'Dwyers lounge bar, at least six or seven people around him when I enter. I sit on the edge and listen to Cronin debate with a young man from Lurgan, County Armagh called Michael Deeny (later in life to be manager of Horslips and a financial wizard in the City of London) the pros and cons of the Franco-Prussian war of 1870.

Young Deeny puts up a brave, spectacular show but Cronin's mastery of detailed fact and his eloquence would have trounced Socrates and he would have given A.J.P. Taylor a serious run for his money. It was evident that for Cronin there were no neat frontiers between work and leisure, poetry and history and philosophy and economics and art. He was mixing them all the time but fundamentally from a poet's point of view. To purify my metaphor, he was Norman Mailer disguised as Cassius Clay.

This was what made the poet Cronin different from any other poet in Ireland: his ferocious passion for ideas. Back then in 1963 and ever since. Ideas for Cronin were as much flesh and blood as sex. And now forty-two years later I can say that I have met only one other Irish writer of whom I could say the same in respect of the intellect being as visceral as the heart and that is John Moriarty and, amazingly and wonderfully, two more different artist-intellectuals you could not meet than Cronin and Moriarty. Polar opposites joined at the equatorial conscience by passion for thought and language that admits absolutely no compromise.

But still I had not read a line by Cronin. His one collection of poems entitled *Poems*, published in London by The Cresset Press in 1958, was out of print and unobtainable. It would not be until a long two years later and David Wright's Penguin anthology of poetry, *The Mid-Century*, published in 1965, that I or anyone of my generation would have revealed to us what a new and outstanding poet Cronin was. With what excitement of raw recognition I read Cronin's *Lines for a Painter*, *Elegy for the Nightbound*, and *Responsibilities*. In the following year, 1966, Penguin published Wright's companion anthology of *Longer Contemporary Poems*, in which alongside W.H. Auden's *Letter to Lord Byron*, Hugh MacDiarmid's *On A Raised Beach*, W.S. Graham's *The Nightfish-*

ing, Patrick Kavanagh's *The Great Hunger*, I read Anthony Cronin's *R.M.S. Titanic* and realized the huge, world-stage poetic stature of the man. Journalist, broadcaster, reviewer, controversialist, intellectual, activist, he was most certainly all of these; but never again would I mistake him for being anything other than that rare specimen, the original, radical, unique uncompromisable poet. What set Cronin apart was his absolutely uncompromising commitment to honesty in his writing as well as in his person, no matter what the cost.

Twenty years later, in February 1983, I found myself in snow-dumped, blizzard-blazing Moscow – the actual city in Russia in old Soviet Union time under Andropov – in the company of Anthony Cronin. I noticed again and again the shock on the faces of Party apparatchiks at the fact that Cronin was so much more obviously a true *tovarich* than any of themselves. Secondly, I recall the hardest and profoundest lesson I have ever received in the art of poetry. Sitting in the window seat of an Aeroflot airliner flying across the mountain peaks of the Caucasus from Armenia back to Moscow I remarked to Cronin who was in the aisle seat that the peaks below 'look like tents'. Cronin, with the stern, anxious, exasperated expression of a parent whose patience has been tested to the limit, remonstrated with me. 'Paul, will you please stop saying that things are *like* things. Either they *are* or they *are not*.'

In the snows of the Soviet Union in the winter of 1983, Cronin the Marxist idealist poet as plain and casual in his mode of dress as in his speech – a windcheater, a jumper, a cloth cap – was about as much out of place among the new generation of decadent party men and the new Gorbachev reformers as a veteran of the 1917 Revolution would have been; one of those veterans all of whom Stalin exterminated in the 1930s. In the Party rooms in Moscow in the winter of

1983 Cronin shone in the darkness like a brother of the radiant Bukharin.

149

> *Max Eastman wrote of meeting them on trains*
> *When under Lenin's leadership the country*
> *Was just emerging from the Civil War.*
> *Middle-aged men with philosophic foreheads,*
> *Motherly, grey-haired women with calm eyes,*
> *A younger woman, sensuous, beautiful.*
> *Who bore herself as if she had once walked*
> *Up to a cannon's mouth. You would enquire,*
> *He said, and you would find these were the veterans,*
> *Taught in infancy to love mankind,*
> *Master themselves, be free from sentiment,*
> *The high traditions of the terrorist movement.*
> *They had learned in youth a new mode from the*
>   *party,*
> *To think in practical terms, was how he put it.*

The second of April 1989 was a mild, calm, stationary spring day in Dublin. It was a Sunday, and just a little after eight o'clock in the daylight of eventide, a sixty-four year old poet began to read from a new book. There was a full but not complete audience in the function room of Buswell's Hotel, a modest Georgian inn, which stands opposite the gates to the parliament of the Republic of Ireland. Outside, except for two policemen, the streets were empty. The sort of mundane setting in which a tumultuous event occurs or a prophet gets born. The poet was Anthony Cronin and the new book was entitled *The End of the Modern World*. After the reading, I knew that not since the publication in 1928 of *The Tower* by W.B. Yeats had Irish history known such an occasion. For in

this new book-long poem of 161 sonnets Cronin had taken up
the same intellectual as well as artistic challenge as had his
fire-eating predecessor: he had attempted, dared to survey,
depict, analyse Western civilization from the Middle Ages to
the era of the Twin Towers of Manhattan.

Fifteen years later on 2 November 2004 in another Geor-
gian house around the corner on the west side of St Stephen's
Green on the occasion of the publication of his *Collected
Poems* Anthony Cronin read from his slightly enlarged,
slightly revised version of *The End of the Modern World*, the
number of sonnets having increased from the 161 of 1989 to
179. It was an occasion of momentous gentleness and to my
own mind came back a memory of the eighty-year-old Ezra
Pound's assignation with Mrs George Yeats in 1965 in the
Royal Hibernian Hotel in Dawson Street off the north side of
the Green. Grace; graceful; gracefully.

A sequence of 179 sonnets is Cronin's preferred designa-
tion of *The End of the Modern World*. But with respect I am
referring to it, first, as one long poem, all of a piece, and, sec-
ondly, as 'Cronin's Cantos'.

In embarking on this enormous long poem, Cronin set
himself the same problem as Ezra Pound had set himself dur-
ing the First World War. How to adumbrate in verse the his-
tory of Western civilization? Pound's solution was to begin
an open-ended work-in-progress in free verse called the *Can-
tos*. Somewhere Pound had written – probably more than
once – that the first task of the modern poet was to break the
dominance of the iambic pentameter line. But Cronin's solu-
tion, astonishingly, was not only to return to the iambic pen-
tameter line but to return to it in its most conventional
guise, the sonnet form.

Nor did Cronin choose the strait-jacket of the sonnet as
Robert Lowell and John Berryman when they performed

ego-manoeuvres and self-regarding monologues of solipsistic erudition and vanity gossip.

I believe that Cronin probably came to his solution via Auden and Kavanagh. In Cronin's early verse you can hear Auden plainly. But the unusual thing about Cronin is that, perhaps by wholly surrendering himself to Auden, he emerged with his own tone of voice intact; that tone of voice that comes off the page at you like no other *modern* Irish poet.

And then there was Kavanagh! In the early 1950s Kavanagh gave Cronin, as he gave anyone who cared to listen, permission to write verse about anything – anything – with the exception of 'Ireland'. 'The Irish Thing' as Kavanagh called it was a dead end, which indeed it was. Instead Kavanagh wrote a sonnet called 'The Hospital' and it's a long way from 'The Hospital' back to 'Bright star, would I were steadfast as thou art'.

The Hospital

A year ago I fell in love with the functional ward
Of a chest hospital: square cubicles in a row
Plain concrete, wash basins – an art lover's woe,
Not counting how the fellow in the next bed snored.
But nothing whatever is by love debarred,
The common and banal her heat can know.
The corridor led to a stairway and below
Was the inexhaustible adventure of a gravelled yard.

This is what love does to things: the Rialto Bridge,
The main gate that was bent by a heavy lorry,
The seat at the back of a shed that was a suntrap.
Naming these things is the love-act and its pledge;
For we must record love's mystery without claptrap,
Snatch out of time the passionate transitory.

I imagine that what Cronin discovered in the laboratory of his verse experiments was that Kavanagh's sonnet 'The Hospital' enabled the poet to include anything, no matter how banal, and yet still be in position to strike the singing line, viz, to create his own 'canto'. To me, one of the great achievements and great beauties of *The End Of The Modern World* is the juxtaposition of banal prose with the singing line. It's the prose basis of his poetry that makes Cronin's poetry such pure poetry.

But also, by employing the sonnet for his gigantic purpose, Cronin was opening up other possibilities of technical enhancement which have worked out perfectly. The sonnet frees Cronin from having to occupy the false position of narrative. The 179 sonnets as a whole constitute a tour-de-force technical accomplishment of collage technique, montage, intricate patchwork, cinematic editing; snapshots, headlines, quotations, bubbles, captions, slogans, advertisements. Paradoxically, of course, by eschewing narrative through his use of the sonnet, Cronin succeeds in achieving in verse an outstanding feat of storytelling. He tells the story of his own mind's adventures across the mountains and the seas of the history of Western man.

What follows here is a personal account of my sixteen years of reading, reading, reading *The End of the Modern World*. My account is as much about my own pleasure in reading the poem as it is about the poem itself.

As with any outstanding work of art, a Gothic cathedral, a Sibelius symphony, the architecture of Cronin's *The End of the Modern World* in its finished state seems outrageously simple, unbelievably simple. The 179 sonnets are divided into three sections or, musically speaking, three movements. Part 1 (Sonnets 1–48) begins with the birth of modern farming in the high Middle Ages and feudalism, and concludes with the French

Impressionists painting quickly with their women at Argenteuil on the Seine outside Paris on a Sunday afternoon. Along the way the poet introduces his major and minor themes that will recur throughout the other two sections. Early on the poet reports two famous works by Burne-Jones: 'The Arming of the Knights', a drawing in the Birmingham City Art Gallery and the extraordinary painting, 'King Cophetua and the Beggar Maid' in the Tate in London. These two archetypal works epitomize the Male Chivalry Dream or the Male Chivalry Myth of the Ideal Female, which Cronin sees at the heart of both medieval Europe and modern Hollywood. From Galahad to Clark Gable. This myth is a revolving glass in Cronin's mind throughout history as again and again he returns to the question of the relationship of man and woman.

Next, the Birth of Commerce and the Laws of Property and Tort, the sale of land and the concept in the Western world of the 'buyability' of everything.

But even at this early stage of the story nothing is seen in isolation. Good and Evil are inextricable. Cronin composes odes to great progress in architecture in the seventeenth and eighteenth centuries.

Then the first almighty political cataclysm of the modern era – the French Revolution. In one small single sonnet, an exquisite vignette of Cronin and the Italian poet Luciano Erba walking the grounds of the Schloss Leopold at the Salzburg Festival in 1951, discussing the French Revolution:

27

*But strike they did and threw a king's cropped head
As gage of battle to the kings of Europe,
Thus horrifying many gentle souls.
And Erba said, a far day to remember,*

Walking beside Max Reinhardt's urns and columns,
Two suns, the second broken on the water,
Schloss Leopold, the joy of the baroque,
A tracery across the darker side,
No Barbara that day; "Unhappiness
Came into Europe with that revolution
As mode where only misery had been."
Through thirty years quite clear, two poets in amber.
Now after all those years I find the answer:
No, not unhappiness but discontent.

Robert Emmet in three sonnets speaks with a candour not unlike Cronin's own direct mode of conversation:

30

"They dragged the Lord Chief Justice from his coach,
A mottled and blanched old man who loved his grand-
    child.
This has been held against me ever since
Alike by those who say, what is, is right,
And those who say what is should not remain
With unstained annals until it becomes
The true republic, Roman, rational.
My superbly folded stock and flowered waistcoat,
The justice and humanity of my cause,
My acquaintance with the works of Paine and Rousseau,
Worthless, in face of this. Yet this was progress.
Your other sad rebellions had been raised
For rural reasons. Mine at least were modern.
My mob was European, avant-garde.

Cronin and his comrade Brendan Behan visit the grave of Heine in the Père Lachaise cemetery in Paris or, rather, *happen* on the grave of Heine. They 'see' Heine's grave. Cronin is ever faithful to the process of drift and happenstance in life.

Cronin exposes the essence of the bourgeois lie of the Western world. Baudelaire understands that the basis of bourgeois civilization is prostitution:

44

The moral order of the bourgeois world,
Whose basis, as he knew, was prostitution.

And so to Lautrec and La Goulue in the Moulin Rouge and finally to the girls at Argenteuil, concluding Part 1:

48

Girls on the river, girls at Argenteuil,
Under the dappling trees in August light,
Skirts full and creamy like cloth waterfalls
Brushing the grass, each ankle an example
Of how athletic angels are, as eager
They stepped on land at one of Sunday's stages.
The light declined at last. The dance began
And music mingled with the wine in veins
Alive to summer and condemned to Monday.
Passion like night might follow light's decline
And be at odds with openness of glance,
Which should have lasted longer. We could ask
Was the whole day as easy as it seems,
Their comradeship unclouded like the moon?

Part II (Sonnets 49–97) brings us slap right bang back to the beginning of the whole human story – to the Garden of Eden:

49

What was it like in the Garden? Us naked as birch
    trees,
Their skin as native a sight as sheen of the river,
The curve of buttock but as the curve of bole,
No cloth occluding its shock or smooth synthetics,
To cling, suggest, to ruck and to reveal?
And psyches without disguise or covering either,
Everything natural, instinctive, happy,
No kinks, no hang-ups and no fetishes,
No thought about daring, or no thought at all.
It may have been a munch, but Baudelaire
Would not have been at home there, nor, in truth,
Might you, O hypocrite lecteur, less hyp-
Ocrite perhaps, more hip than them,
Those clear-eyed innocents in unshadowed groves.

There follows a generously critical, witty, yet slightly sympathetic account of Milton's lofty nonsense about the Original Item, the First Couple. Here are sonnets of virtuoso urbanity, choc-a-bloc with aphorisms to keep the reader thinking until the bell tolls in the garden and it is time to be whipped out the gates. The sexual question is approached again over a different course, the poles of the fences higher this time round. Freud, de Sade and most especially Ms Angela Carter are responded to:

Knowledge is power, yes, but power is knowledge.

Or

Of course most women were as ignorant
About themselves as any man could be.

But what is most thrilling of all is the actual writing itself – verse of such an order that the reader is lifted up on the waves of the energy of the poet's absolute fidelity both to his material and to his craft. Wit, humour, romance, verve, lucidity, élan, gusto; he has managed to get all of his own unique conversational, convivial human voice behind the verse and under the verse and in the verse. Sonnet 57, for example is simply pure poetic statement without any of the frills or evasions or tricks that most poets feel compelled to resort to:

57

The lower middle-classes still believed
There never could be much and that much worked for.
And even the romantics were quite certain
That money could not buy the things that mattered:
The steady grey-eyed gaze of understanding,
Time waiting on a leaf in autumn woods,
The envied love of enviable women.
One hardly needs to add that they missed out on
Much that was merely a short drive away,
A passing taxi or a routine flight.
Journey they must if lovers will have meetings.
Nor do the happy ask when they have landed,
Why money like the ocean drowns all guilt,
Why the shore smiles on those who have attained it.

To that last sonnet as to so much of Cronin's entire project, I would apply Ezra Pound's comment on Ford Madox Ford in Pound's 1914 essay *The Prose Tradition in Verse*: 'I find him significant and revolutionary because of his insistence upon clarity and precision, upon the prose tradition; in brief, upon efficient writing – even in verse.'

There follows a sequence on Vienna before World War One – that nightmare city of Karl Kraus, Klimt, Schiele, Adolph Loos. Two sonnets on Valentia Island are a prelude to a depiction of Picasso's 1907 painting 'Les Demoiselles d'Avignon' from MOMA in New York which is the middle painting of the three crucial paintings of the poem; the first being Burne-Jones's 'King Cophetua' and the third near the poem's end being Van Gogh's 'The Starry Night' (1889, also in MOMA). Of Picasso's preparatory sketches for 'Les Desmoiselles' the critic William Rubin suggests a progression 'from the narrative to the iconic'; the same should be also said of Cronin's poetic technique.

Enter Lenin, Matisse, Marinetti, Bleriot, as well as Picasso. In such close and natural proximity, such a galaxy seems unbearable and it is. World War One erupts and in Berlin the young historian Friedrich Meinicke bears witness:

74

In the summer twilight thousands filled the streets.
Embracing, weeping, eyes and faces shining.
And then as darkness fell there came the singing,
The old heart-breaking songs, the mighty, soaring
Es braust ein Ruf wie Donnerhall *and after*
The stern strong hymn of German Protestants,
Ein' feste Burg ist unser Gott. *I moved*
Slowly along the Wilhelmstrasse with them.
It was as if I floated with the crowds,
Forgetful now of self, immersed like them
In a great tide of Germanness, of oneness.
Although what was to come was terrible
That night seems still august, magnificent.
I shiver when I think of it today.

But at the war front the painter Fernand Leger experiences a total aesthetic liberation finding himself,

> ... *among real, intractable things.* (77)

Lenin's hysteria, Tatlin's and El Lissitzky's fantastic architectural plans, an ode to the automobile.

And now Cronin plucks out of his magic Bulgakovian handkerchief a snapshot of the painter Picabia of whom Ezra Pound once famously remarked: 'Picabia is the man who ties the knots in Picasso's tail.'

86

> *Picabia at the wheel of a Bugatti,*
> *The horn bulb to his painterly right hand*

We pause for a moment, for one sonnet, to put Romantic Ireland in her place before it's time for another ode to the city, which is pure Audenesque, yet pure Cronin. I estimate Cronin was sixty years old when he composed sonnet 92; only a poet in his prime could write with such authority, such confidence, all his powers under full sail:

92

> *Let the city open tonight, an unfolding flower*
> *Not yet full blown, glass petals tipped with promise,*
> *Let it greet its lovers with wide embracing tracks,*
> *Narrowing nearer to the nervous centre.*
> *Let the neon signs throw roses on shining pavements*
> *As the dusk of summer softens each separate vista.*
> *Let the tigerish hide of the quarter proclaim a fierce*
> *Energy in this decadence, this danger.*
> *Let all be famous, but everyone to be anonymous,*

Let all find their old friends, but stalk expectant
Through swathes of faces, seeking the lovely stranger.
Let the wicked streets be happy, the happy ones
*   wicked,*
Let us tremble, so great the depravity, lurid the darkness,
But come to the leafy gardens, finding the loved one.

Part III (Sonnets 98–179) begins in the family quarters of the precise, law-abiding, meticulous family man and Commandant of Auschwitz, Rudolf Hoss. We tread the cinder path,

... laid to the door of the officers' quarters
Of cinders cleared from the incinerators.

From the super-modern efficiency of Auschwitz we go straight to the Royal Festival Hall and the Hayward Gallery on London's South Bank. These are the viral connections of *The End of the Modern World.* It is Cronin's capacity to make such viral connections that lifts his great poem up into the realm of *The Waste Land.* Back once more, more ruthlessly than before, to the sexual question, Angela Carter (author of *The Sadean Woman*) and D.H. Lawrence.

And then at last we come to one of the very special glories of Cronin's opus: what those of us who have been reading the poem for the last sixteen years call 'the autobiographical sequence' or what Cronin himself in the body of the poem calls 'the Stella Gardens sequence' (Sonnets 116–122). In the heart of the Dublin docklands there is a small redbrick terrace enclave known only to the dock workers of Dublin and it is known as Stella Gardens and there in one of these tiny cottages in the 1970s Cronin with his wife and two young daughters, Iseult and Sarah, made their home. Without a hint of disingenuousness, coyness, false humility, pretentious slumming, mock irony, inverted snobbery or self-pity Cronin contrasts his working-class postage-stamp abode with W.B. Yeats's Tower at Thoor Ballylee:

116

There was supposed to be a Stella Gardens sequence
To put Yeats and his tower in their place,
For, after all, a visitor I had
Opined our little quarter had been built
For the aristocracy of labour – dockers,
Violent and bitter men perhaps when drinking.
The master bedroom measured twelve by six,
The other, square but smaller had no window
Since someone built the kitchen up against it.
The loo was out of doors. I don't complain.
In fact the Stella poems, like extensions
Projected, never started for the want
Of money, time and energy, were meant
To celebrate, as he did, rootedness.

Onwards, backwards to the zeitgeist of the 1960s, the eerie funeral of Robert Kennedy, the interior life of Elvis Presley. Only to arrive at Sonnet 131:

131

O lady of the moon whose profiled face
Halts our walk homeward underneath the trees,
Shine on unblessedness your blessing now,
Wed our desire with our desire to please.
Lonely Actaeon saw your bared, pale flesh
Through celluloid of water, silver bright,
And stood prolonging this unholy joy
Feasting on nerve ends in the moon's limelight.

You turned your back, autogamous as he,
But knew him gazing still on that expanse,
Turning to stasis what should be a dance.
Turning to wrong and sulkiness what should
Have touched with joy that whole nocturnal wood.

Approaching the climacteric of the poem, Cronin offers brutal, poignant depictions of modern England destroyed by Margaret Thatcher, the Russian Revolution and the life and work of Vincent Van Gogh:

147

And Arthur Scargill in his madness said;
"I see Jehovah in the wintry sun
Which looks to her like any golden guinea.
I see the lamb of God in England's fields."
And so on a bright day in England's winter
When Trafalgar Square lies dry and sharp and shadowed
We ask the right to work, close punk rock ranks
Beneath the heavy portico behind
Which shelter many splendid works of art
And underneath Lord Nelson who broke rules
But saved the bacon of the ruling class.
More moral than those rulers we reject
A life of idleness, a lack of aim,
Of purpose, effort, patriotic zeal.

Sonnet 152 begins:

Childe Roland to the dark tower came ...

We have hit the climacteric of the poem with twenty-two sonnets to go. Who is Childe Roland? Howard Hughes, possibly. Corporate man, certainly. Certes also the man against

Paul Durcan

whom Karl Kraus in Vienna in 1922 in his play *Last Days Of Mankind,* had warned; Kraus's thesis being, as summed up by Erich Heller in *The Disinherited Mind* (Penguin 1961, p. 218): 'Man has achieved a technical superiority over himself which threatens him with unavoidable disaster.' The Dark Tower might be the Hong Kong Stock Exchange or the International Financial Services Centre in Dublin but in the conclusion of Cronin's poem it is located actually in Manhattan. Whew! Bear in mind that these final sonnets were first published in 1989, twelve years before the attack on the Twin Towers. Who leered that poetry was not prophetic?

Childe Roland appears first as the mythical figure in Browning's poem of the same name who, having succeeded in his quest to find the Dark Tower does not enter, but instead, as Browning has him, says:

> *And yet*
> *Dauntless the slug-horn to my lips I set,*
> *And blew. 'Childe Roland to the Dark Tower came.'*

But Cronin's Childe Roland does not merely come, he penetrates:

152

> *Childe Roland to the dark tower came and climbed*
> *The massive steps in natural trepidation.*
> *But when the blonde beyond the blinding fountain*
> *Asked him his name and business, his composure*
> *Returned. He coolly showed his new ID*
> *And obeying bored directions took the bronze*
> *Lift to the fourteenth floor as he'd been told.*
> *He smiled quite naturally at them while he noted*
> *That Evil preferred its girls gaunt, doe-eyed, starving,*
> *And thought it would be nice to get to know*

The ones he met, while being quite aware
The person they responded to could never
Be himself. In the Dark Tower all tried
To be as was expected, not themselves.

We watch contrasting images of the corporate apparatchik sliding in and out the doors of his lunar megalometropolitan landscape and the honest English working man and bathos of the history of the British Labour Party.

The modern Roland's chic post-modern world of surgically hygienic, sterilized art museums is placed alongside a last snapshot of Vincent.

Childe Roland to the dark tower came and, having passed under the Tower of Auschwitz, penetrated deep into a void of art finance and corporate towers. We have come to the end of the modern world; we have come to the end of the poem of the same name:

179

Ask not what end, inquiring traveller,
Is served, what grim need to placate a god
Or worship him, what visions, definitions of
Our destiny, our purpose threw up these
Audacious towers to shine in evening light.
The sun, a crucible of nuclear rage,
Knows nothing of such ends: it thrummed out rays
Of heat until the ooze transformed itself.
Money's convulsions too are life-giving,
Neutral, imply no purpose in our hearts,
But blaze upon this rock to make Manhattan
Rise in resplendence, such a culmination
Of history seen at sunset from the harbour,
Meaningless, astonishing and simple.

Inevitably the outline I have presented is but a crude Cook's Tour through the poem. Better to consider again on the one hand the technique of the poem and on the other hand the grand themes of the book, which occur over and over, the great preoccupations and the ways they are so personally, immediately dealt with, yet with all the transfigurative grace that maybe only poetry can deliver.

There is the grand theme of the individual conscience in relation to society in history; the medieval warrior and his comitatus; the revolutionary leader and his chosen few; the avant-garde artist and his followers; man with woman and child; Childe Roland and his loyal band; the corporate magnate and his executives.

Most moving is Cronin's chronicle of modern English life. The poem is a direct response to the cry of William Blake:

> *I will not cease from mental fight*
> *Nor shall my sword sleep in my hand*
> *Till we have built Jerusalem*
> *In England's green and pleasant land.*

Apart from Mahon and the MacNeice of 'Autumn Journal' no other Irish poet has been so attuned to the English experience or has been able to write with such empathy about England, the English nation, and England's modern fate, not only on the large canvas of the civil war between Thatcher's Britain and Scargill's Britain but on the miniature household gods of domestic existence:

95

> *We went to Brighton in our Little Nine,*
> *The open touring model Leslie bought*
> *On what was called H.P. A gorgeous day,*
> *The sky was somehow deep, you know, like heaven,*

I thought the bubbling tar might melt the tyres
And Leslie laughed, called me a silly juggins.
He was a lovely driver, doing forty
Once we were free of Staines. It's tommy rot
To tell us now that people weren't happy.
We had our own nice house, a Tudor villa,
Which was the new thing then, a vacuum cleaner,
Dance music on the wireless, lovely murders.
Of course the war was still to come, that Hitler,
But it all seemed somehow new then, somehow modern.

As well as a tear or two, those lines bring smiles to our faces.
The comic note is achieved throughout the poem, the pure
anarchic note which few poets ever achieve:

159

When Patrick Kavanagh's mother took him to
The circus which had come to Inniskeen,
They saw among the other acts a man
Lifting enormous weights and staggering
Bow-legged around the ring, his biceps, eyeballs,
Bulging with fearful effort. After that
He lay down on a bed of pointed nails.
Attendants placed a plank across his chest.
Ten bashful local louts were then invited
To stand across it, their combined weight being
About half a ton. The poet observed
It seemed a hard way for a man to earn
His living; but his mother said it was
Better than working anyway, she thought.

I see and hear Cronin as an evolution of Leopold Bloom;
walker of the city; savourer of the minuscule and the vast.

Paul Durcan

Aesthetically as well as ethically, one of the most satisfying triumphs of the poem is the fact that Cronin adopts no persona and yet he manages to distinguish subtly for the reader which 'he' is being referred to at any one point. One might say that the entire poem is about a certain 'he' and yet there is that 'he' there and this 'he' here. Not to mention the 'he' who is Anthony Cronin. There is a marvellous sleight-of-hand in Cronin's technique and the reader feels like a child breathless at the ringside of a circus of magicians.

When an artwork makes a guest appearance in verse it invariably appears as ornament or conceit or toy or mere object but in Cronin when paintings occur, they occur as vital organs of the anatomy of the poem. Reading Cronin's great Argenteuil sonnet (48) we know that Cronin has swallowed whole 'The Luncheon of the Boating Party', Renoir's greatest and most revolutionary painting and any one of Monet's many 'La Grenouillère' paintings.

And yet although avant-garde art has always been a necessity to Cronin, there is nothing pictorial or descriptive in his own poetic technique. In Cronin's verse, the full force gale of modern art has blown away all the visual clichés of Irish poetry.

Who else has written poetry about money? Cash, loot, tin, cabbage, lucre, moolah in detergent boxes? Infamously, Ezra Pound descanted about 'usury'. But, certainly alone among Irish poets, Cronin addresses the subject of money as we treat money in our everyday lives, perhaps the subject closest to our acquisitive, fatty little arteries, and the sorts of lies and delusions, greed and double-speak with which we girdle round this taboo topic. Another triumph of these sonnets.

In 1996 Cronin subtitled his biography of Samuel Beckett 'The Last Modernist'. In fact it is Cronin himself who is the seriously last modernist; a modernist who unlike Eliot,

194

Pound and Beckett himself, has embraced modernity with all his soul, just as Hart Crane did in the 1920s. Throughout the poem there is the powerful current of Cronin's lyric passion for new engineering, new architecture, for wireless, cinema, airplanes and motor cars. Like Hart Crane, Cronin is the optimistic modernist, the lifelong born-again futurist. What Marinetti wrote in the first manifesto of Futurism in the *Figaro* in 1909 could just as easily have come from the lips of Cronin: 'a speeding automobile is more beautiful than the *Victory of Samothrace.*'

In the introduction to my commentary on *The End of the Modern World* I cited the *Cantos* of Ezra Pound and I did so with purposeful propriety. I stated that Cronin undertook the same project as Pound, to investigate the history of Western civilization and to tell the story of the tribe, i.e. to write an *epic* poem. Many of Cronin's preoccupations are the same as Pound's and in his own idiom he achieves the same tone of easiness, Kavanagh's dead slack string. If I were requested to provide an epigraph for *The End Of The Modern World* I would extract it from *The Pisan Cantos* of Ezra Pound:

> *What thou lovest well remains,*
>   *the rest is dross*
> *What thou lovest well shall not be reft from thee*
> *What thou lovest well is thy true heritage*
> *Whose world, or mine or theirs*
>   *or is it of none?*
> *First came the seen, then thus the palpable*
>   *Elysium, though it were in the halls of hell,*
> *What thou lovest well is thy true heritage*
> *What thou lov'st well shall not be reft from thee*

In 1974 in a foreword to a Gallery Press edition of the *Selected Poems of James Clarence Mangan* (ed. Michael Smith),

Anthony Cronin wrote apropos Mangan's poem 'The Name-less One': 'There is nothing rarer in poetry than a successful cry from the whole encircumscribed heart. This is one.' And so too is Cronin's own poem *The End Of The Modern World*: a sensational achievement when you consider its length and scope. He is the direct lineal descendant of Oliver Goldsmith as he is of Johnson, Blake, Clough, Browning, Scott, Steven-son, Tennyson, and Housman, T.S. Eliot and Ezra Pound, W.H. Auden and Patrick Kavanagh. The recent winner of the T.S. Eliot prize, George Szirtes, in an article in the *Irish Times* on 18 December 2004 concluded: 'Cronin is a major voice: he is Ireland's modern Dryden, a master of the public word in the public place.'

May it please the court, for your information: the text of *The End of the Modern World* is to be found in *Collected Poems*, Anthony Cronin, New Island Books, 2004, pp. 159–258. I have made no reference to the greater corpus of Cronin's life's work in poetry which includes at least five or six other major poems of the twentieth century, notably *R.M.S. Titanic*, first published in 1960 (London Literary Review X, volume I, number 2); suffice to say that the œuvre is a trea-sure trove which will gleam from chasms in the rocks under the cliffs where once the city centre was, long after almost all of our contemporary volumes of verse have mouldered into unidentifiable dust.

I rest my case.

Hartnett's Farwell

The poet Michael Hartnett was born in west County Limerick in 1941 and died in Dublin in October 1999 aged fifty-eight. The myth of Hartnett is of an existentialist leprechaun, an enchanting but fanatical imbiber piping his way to an early grave. I recognize traces of the man in these images but they constitute a caricature that is far removed from the man I knew for almost forty years.

The myth of his poetry is of a collection almost exclusively of short poems. Again I acknowledge a shadowy veracity but again it is a misrepresentation. Hartnett was the author of longer poems beginning with his 'Tao' in 1963, and continuing with 'Anatomy of a Cliché' in 1968, 'The Hag of Beare' in 1969, 'A Farewell to English' in 1975, 'The Retreat of Ita Cagney' in 1975, 'Cúlú Íde' in 1975, 'Maiden Street Ballad' in 1980, 'An Phurgóid' in 1982, 'An Lia Nocht' in 1985, 'Inchicore Haiku' in 1985, 'Mountains, Fall on Us' in 1992, and culminating in 1994 in three of the most outstanding longer poems by any poet in Irish literature, first *The Man who Wrote Yeats, the Man who Wrote Mozart*, secondly *Sibelius in Silence* and, thirdly, *He'll to the Moors*. In these three longer poems I recognize the sophisticated, iconoclastic, analytical, encyclopaedic, cosmopolitan, droll, ironic, tragi-comic poet I encountered in 1962. It is this Hartnett I want to consider and not the doomed hobgoblin of literary gossip. The Michael Hartnett I met in the early 1960s is well depicted by the words that the Finnish Swedish-language author Adolf Paul (1863–1942) used in his novel *A Book about a Man* (1891), to describe the young Sibelius in Berlin in the 1880s: 'He was a real natural genius, thoroughly individual. Without the slightest relationship to others.'

With my title 'Hartnett's Farewell' I am invoking 'O Riada's Farewell' which was the title given to the last record-ing of the composer Séan O Riada (1931–1971) released posthumously by Claddagh Records in 1972. O Riada was a kindred spirit of Hartnett's in his confrontation with the Irish language and the Gaelic inheritance. The two men, however, never met and O Riada was dead by the time Hartnett made his drastic decision in 1975 to relocate from Dublin to West Limerick just as O Riada initiated a comparably drastic relo-cation from Dublin to West Cork in 1963. It is improbable that Hartnett did not have O Riada's example in mind.

Of these three longer poems, it is on *Sibelius in Silence* that I want to concentrate. It is the single most engrossing, most suggestive and most beautifully crafted poem that Michael Hartnett ever wrote and yet, since its first publica-tion twelve years ago, I have encountered only one person who has read it, the poet Harry Clifton.

Sibelius in Silence, a poem of 195 lines, was inspired by Hartnett's lifelong preoccupation with the music and person of the Finnish composer Jean Sibelius (1865–1957). I recall Michael in 1962 in Dublin enthusing about Sibelius, espe-cially about the orchestral work known as 'Finlandia', which was first performed in November 1899 as a protest against the tyranny of the Russian Tsar Nicholas II and which was and, I think, remains Finland's unofficial national anthem. Sibelius's 'Finlandia' is to Finns what O Riada's *Mise Eire* used to be to many Irish people or Elgar's 'Pomp and Circumstance' to the British.

As a result of Michael's enthusiasm, I purchased an LP of 'Finlandia', one of the first LPs I ever purchased and the first LP I purchased of what was termed 'serious' or 'classical' music. Michael used to hum and whistle snatches of 'Finlandia'. It was as if Michael was playing the part of the speaker in Thomas Kinsella's poem, 'I wonder whether one expects / Flowing tie or expert sex', which was published in the year of Michael's arrival in Dublin 1962 in Kinsella's new volume, *Downstream*, a collection of poems admired by Michael:

> *I pat my wallet pocket, thinking*
> *I can spare an evening drinking;*
> *Humming as I catch the bus*
> *Something by Sibelius*

But Michael was not playing any part; he was being himself; a lover of music of all kinds ranging from Elvis Presley and Buddy Holly to Irish traditional music to Mozart, Tchaikovsky, Schumann and, above all, Sibelius.

It was fitting, therefore, that thirty years later, in 1992 after a lifetime of writing his own kind of music – a verbal music known as poetry – that Hartnett should attempt a kind of *summa theologica* in the form of assuming the voice of Sibelius. (*Summa theologica* is an apt analogy because Hartnett was a student of Thomas Aquinas, the Angelic Doctor. Hartnett was himself a logician and, indeed, a theo-logician, a theologian, as he demonstrated in his poem *He'll to the Moors*.) In *Sibelius in Silence*, Sibelius is speaking in the voice of Michael Hartnett. A process of triple-take is at work in the poem.

Nearing the end of his life, Sibelius (in the voice of Hart-nett) reflects on that life and on how it ended in thirty years of silence. In 1926 Sibelius published his symphonic tone poem 'Tapiola' and never published any music again until his death thirty-one years later in 1957. The poet Hartnett after the publication of *Sibelius in Silence* in 1994 was to write no more serious original poetry until his death in 1999.

In Hartnett's poem Sibelius reflects also on the history and prehistory of Finland and on his own dilemma of having being born a Swedish-speaking Finn in a Finland tyrannized by Tsarist Russia, who did not begin to learn and speak Finnish until the age of eight. In the poem we hear Sibelius brooding on the perennial conundrums of race, language and landscape; of the relationship of aboriginal peoples to later waves of immigration; of the tension between original inhab-itants and planters. Hartnett has Sibelius laconically observe: 'for even planters tend to meditation'.

All of these questions are the questions which dominated Hartnett's own life and which first found large expression in his infamous 'A Farewell to English', in 1975. I say 'infa-mous' for two reasons: first, it was misrepresented by the var-ious cultural, academic, media and political factions in the Ireland of the 1970s; and, secondly, it is not in the top flight of Hartnett's poetry in the sense that *Sibelius in Silence* is.

Two-thirds of the way into the poem Hartnett takes up the theme of alcohol; a subject which was at the centre of the lives and works of both Sibelius and Hartnett. The climax of the poem represents Sibelius conducting his own Fourth Symphony which of all Sibelius's works is the most crucial. The poem concludes with Sibelius's vehement, wise, Lear-like meditation on his thirty years of silence.

Sibelius in Silence
For Angela Liston

To have intricacies of lakes and forests,
harbours, hills, and inlets given –
and none of these with a name;
then to have posited nomads straggling
from the barricading Urals
bearing on their backs and horses
children, language, and utensils,
gods and legends;
then to have brought all these together,
yeast to the thawing mud –
this was to make in the Green Gold of the North
an ethnic and enduring bread.

They settled where their dead
were buried and gave names
to every hill and harbour,
names that might become unspoken
but would forever whisper 'Not yours'
to mapping strangers;
their dead became the land they lived on,
became the very lakes and corries,
the very myths and shadows that live
inside the birch and pine tree;
their dead sprung up in grains and berries
nourishing their offspring
that inhabited the cold expanses.
They sowed their gods in caves and hillsides,
gods that might become forgotten
but would forever whisper 'Go home'
to dreaming strangers.

Paul Durcan

After the land is first immersed
in language, gods, and legends,
sown with blood and bodies,
whatever strangers come and conquer
and stand upon the hills at evening
(for even planters tend to meditation)
they will sense they are not wanted here;
for the wind, the old, old voices
moulding ice and snowdrifts
into Arctic intimations of the shapes,
now quite unhuman, they possess
in a dead and parallel present,
will tell them:
'You are not ours, you are not wanted,'
and the lake, the pine, the birch tree,
the very slope and curve of mountain,
all will say the same:
'The name you call us by is not our name.'

Whoever comes and conquers –
from the first flake of fish eaten,
from the first crumb of bread taken
in this place –
blood in water and in ground
transubstantiates that race
and performs an altering justice;
its homeland becomes myth;
its very customs, clothing, accent
(if not language) change
and now are woven
from other soils and other souls
in this intricate biosphere.
It is not wanted here

nor loved at home;
it watches rivers wash
its labels from their banks
contemptuously to sea,
watches names it put on hills
detach themselves and doggedly slide down
a valley of unwanted nouns.
It sits inside its palisade
and sees its gods move out of reach
and fade
before the bright gods of the older race,
its children's mouths ringed purple
with their speech.
When I was young I did not know their language.
I visited the inns of Babel
where old and young drank mugs of syntax
that turned on tongues and hands to music,
where men at beer-ringed counters
told me heir melodious open secrets
and I held up identity papers
and said, 'I do belong: this is my country,'
and they let me join their ranks –
for part of me indeed throughout the centuries
had become this race's;
and although my origins still slunk
some thousand years away
in heavily guarded strong-rooms in my head
their edges had the tint,
had absorbed the purple hue
that revealed I ate
the berries that the conquered grew;
all this (papers, costume, customs,
fibre transformed and muscles

and my longing to belong)
was negated by my voice,
my traitor larynx
that then could never frame
their simplest proverb
or sing their simplest song –
but courtesy is not acceptance
so I left the friendly inns
and walked into the dark,
landmarks all around me
hinting at the road,
and a calvary of signposts
on which strange names were shown
that pointed out the way
but not the way home.

Blacker than the blackest swans are,
all my life their mythic figures
clothed in insistent rhythms
have pursued me and made me anxious,
called my name, and demanded answers:
and I listened. And I answered.
Music was my language, so I gave them my music;
and the land drank in my music.
Caught at school in webs of grammar
which still at night enmesh my face,
I had no tongue in the land I came from
but at first, at best, a stammer;
but the fluency I sought I found
in the speech that underlies my music.
The land took me in her embrace;
I wed the land and dreamed her freedom
somehow coalesced and marched maestoso

out through the hatchings of my music-sheets.
But the people heard the real programme:
the crescendi of shells in the air
and their climax in the streets.
'Alcohol's a cunning beast.
It fools the doctor and the priest,
it fools the clever and the sane –
but not the liver or the brain.'
Idle verses, so I thought,
that someone, doodling, idly makes.
But now blood breaks like snowflakes
from my brothers' nostrils
and my hand shakes.
I gave everything I could:
music, speeches, pat harangues;
intellectualised the fight
and, tremblando, wept adagios, wrung my hands –
in short, spilled every drink but blood.
Autumn breaks its rainbows
along the staggering trees
and my hand quivers.
Into my room across my music-sheets
sail black swans on blacker rivers.

They say my music weeps for the days
when my people ate the bark from trees
because all crops had failed.
Music disdains such theories:
I offer you here cold, pure water –
as against the ten-course tone-poems,
the indigestible Mahlerian feasts;
as against the cocktails' many hues,
all liquors crammed in one glass –

Paul Durcan

pure, cold water is what I offer.
Composed, I am conducting. It is my
fourth symphony, third movement and,
as my baton tries to make the music keep
to the key of C sharp minor,
vodka ebbs in tremors from my hand
and at the ragged corner of my eye
a raven flies through the concert hall
and I find a self saying to myself,
'It was the deer that stripped the trees,
not the people at all.'
Two flutes grapple with an ice-cold note
until the 'cello takes command.
As the audience's hiss escapes
splinters of birch-bark stick in my throat.

And now, because I made such strict demands
upon my art, I must dismiss such music as intrudes
on me as I conceal my shaking hands.
no loss indeed – it's now quite trivial and crude;
no more legends come out of the northern lands,
no more Virgins of the Air, no more black swans,
no more seamless symphonies project themselves.
I take down a book of poetry from my shelves
to share with my children's children the old store
of verses that this green-gold land reveres
(I speak their native language fluently
but when excited lapse into my planters' tongue).
You may think thirty years of silence far too long
but some composers now about should have learnt
    from me
that silence would have graced the world far more
than their gutting and dismembering of song.

And that which was part of me has not left me yet –
however etherialised, I still know when it's there.
I get up at odd hours of the night
or snap from a doze deep in a chair;
I shuffle to the radio, switch on the set,
and pluck, as I did before, Finlandia out of the air.

In his title *Sibelius in Silence* Hartnett is saying, I think, that the art of poetry is about concentration striving to become contemplation.

The eloquence and yet the simplicity of the introductory three-verse paragraphs are among the most beautiful lines Hartnett ever wrote. To my ear they equal what T.S. Eliot in the same vein attempted in *Four Quartets*. (Eliot was the first and greatest English-language influence in Hartnett's writing life, followed by Ezra Pound, with, in the background, William Yeats).

The viewpoint of the opening lines is godlike. The tone of voice, together with its statement, is of God holding out the globe of the world in the palm of his hand and considering the galactic orb as if it were a mathematical theorem or a puzzle for a chess master; and, indeed, Hartnett was an excellent practitioner of chess and he had that kind of abstract, logical cast of mind that Sibelius also had.

To have intricacies of lakes and forests,
harbours, hills, and inlets given –
and none of these with a name;
then to have posited nomads straggling
from the barricading Urals
bearing on their backs and horses
children, language, and utensils,
gods and legends;
then to have brought all these together,

> *yeast to the thawing mud –*
> *this was to make in the Green Gold of the North*
> *an ethnic and enduring bread.*

But while the angle is godlike and the voice is Sibelius, the vocabulary is Hartnettian: words and phrases such as 'intricacies', 'posited', 'yeast', 'ethnic and enduring bread', 'nomads straggling' and 'the barricading Urals' are peculiar to Hartnett.

Writing with the authority of the master poet, Hartnett is able to introduce one of his central themes as early as the third line: 'and none of these with a name'. For Hartnett, the key to human existence is the strange music of human language and the strange human need to name places. Heidegger liked to invoke Hölderlin's sentence 'Linguistically man dwelleth on earth.' In the third line Hartnett is reiterating that basic insight of Hölderlin's and Heidegger's. (In the early 1960s, Hartnett read as much of Heidegger as he could find in English translation.)

Note also the phrase in the fourth line 'nomads straggling'. Hartnett does not speak of, say, 'Mesolithic hunter-gatherers migrating'; an illustration of the difference between the art of poetry and the scientific discipline of archaeology. The poet Hartnett, striving for as linguistically profound a precision as is poetically possible, is saying that man in his origins was a nomad who straggled, not a typology that migrated.

In the second paragraph Hartnett presents cemeteries as the first settlements of Finland. Simultaneously he is depicting also the prehistory of Ireland. (One of Hartnett's own personal holy places was the prehistoric settlement of Lough Gur in County Limerick, twenty-five miles north north-east of Hartnett's hometown of Newcastle West.)

Hartnett establishes an absolute anthropological datum,

which is that a human being's first language is the language of place names. For Hartnett, the tradition of the *dindsenchas* is not only a practice in Gaelic poetry but a universal human norm. Hartnett in his person and poetry was the embodiment of Estyn Evans's pronouncement that 'geography is ultimately more important than genes'. Born into an English-speaking small-town working-class family in County Limerick in 1941 Hartnett heard the ancient landscape of Ireland, Eire, Banbha, Fodhla speak to him across intervals of thousands of years and the language of the landscape might have been Gaelic but possibly might have predated Gaelic, some remote, unknown species of Indo-European. Sibelius, born into a Swedish-speaking district of Finland in 1865 heard the ancient Finnish words and perhaps even older words.

Depicting how human settlement grows out of burial grounds, Hartnett delves into a metaphor of the Eucharistic character of death – how the living eat the dead:

> *their dead sprung up in grains and berries*
> *nourishing their offspring*

Since World War Two we have become accustomed to commentators such as Edward Said or Terry Eagleton analysing the dominant role of the coloniser in the relationship between colonialism and native populations. In the fourth paragraph of the poem Hartnett takes up this theme but holds up for our inspection a reverse process in which he perceives the native population as the dominant partner in the relationship. Hartnett depicts how 'blood and water' of the indigenous dead 'transubstantiates' the coloniser and, in a felicitous phrase, 'performs an altering justice'. (Note the ease with which Hartnett can introduce a technical theological term such as 'transubstantiates'; it is necessary to remember always that although he was not a conventional church-goer, Hartnett was steeped in Christian theology, liturgy and mysticism; not only was it, spiritually speaking, his mother tongue but it was also one of his abiding intellectual preoccupations as illustrated most dramatically in the third of the three major longer poems of his farewell period – *He'll to the Moors* – and also in his translations into Gaelic Irish of the poetry of St John of the Cross.)

Hartnett, the master of the extended metaphor, proceeds to depict the body physic of the landscape of Finland rejecting the serum of the invading languages of Swedish and Russian. When I read this passage, I am reminded of the play *Translations* and Brian Friel's English cartographers in all their ignorant naivety mapping and re-naming in English the Gaelic landscape of County Donegal:

> It is not wanted here
> nor loved at home;
> it watches rivers wash
> its labels from their banks
> contemptuously to sea,
> watches names it put on hills
> detach themselves and doggedly slide down
> a valley of unwanted nouns.
> It sits inside its palisade
> and sees its gods move out of reach
> and fade
> before the bright gods of the older race,
> its children's mouths ringed purple
> with their speech.

From the landscape of Finland Hartnett transports the Sibelian voice to the hinterland of his native town of Newcastle West in County Limerick and his childhood and young manhood in and around the public houses of remote and exotic and obscure locations such as Strand and Killeedy and Camas. We see the young Hartnett of the 1940s and the 1950s at the feet of his Gaelic-speaking grandmother and her cronies and other anonymous elders of the tribe who lurk in dark corners like presences out of a Jack B. Yeats painting. These are the borderlands of Slieve Luachra, the world of Padraig O'Keeffe, the fabled fiddler. The boy Hartnett, born into a small-town working-class English-speaking family longs to belong to the ancient, rural, Gaelic-speaking, aristo-cratic tribe but again and again he is betrayed and embar-rassed by what he terms his 'traitor larynx':

> *When I was young I did not know their language.*
> *I visited the inns of Babel*
> *where old and young drank mugs of syntax*
> *that turned on tongues and hands to music,*
> *where men at beer-ringed counters*
> *told me their melodious open secrets*
> *and I held up identity papers*
> *and said, 'I do belong; this is my country,'*
> *and they let me join their ranks –*
> *for part of me indeed throughout the centuries*
> *had become this race's;*

Following on that typical Hartnett play on conventional imagery – his 'inns of Babel' instead of 'towers of Babel' – there occurs a water-marked Hartnettian aphorism that had been reccurring in his verse since its beginnings in the late 1950s: 'but courtesy is not acceptance'. No matter how many hours and years he spends in the inns of Babel and Strand and Newcastle West he remains outcast:

> *so I left the friendly inns*
> *and walked into the dark,*

> landmarks all around me
> hinting at the road,
> and a calvary of signposts
> on which strange names were shown
> that pointed out the way
> but not the way home.

A shocking, yet simple image – 'a calvary of signposts'.

The signposts of rural Ireland in the last half century have been ten-foot poles with beak-shaped white plates bearing black characters of place names. Hartnett is preparing us for the black swans that introduce his next paragraph, the black swans that haunted Sibelius's life and work:

> Blacker than the blackest swans are
> all my life their mythic figures
> clothed in insistent rhythms
> have pursued me and made me anxious,
> called my name, and demanded answers:
> and I listened. And I answered.

Hartnett's line 'Blacker than the blackest swans are' is an almost direct transcription from an entry for 22 November 1917 in Sibelius's diary as quoted by Erik Tawaststjerna in volume three of Tawaststjerna's definitive biography of Sibelius: 'Saw a swan today. It was rocked by the waves at the edge of the ice ... There are moments in life when everything is blacker than black – darker than night.' Since his youth and his discovery of the legends of the Finnish national epic the *Kalevala*, (the *Kalevala* or 'Land of Heroes' was compiled and published by Elias Lonnrot in 1849 as part of the pan-European rediscovery of national folklore and it played the same role in the evolution of Finnish political independence as the Cuchullain cycle along with the Children of Lir and other myths played in Irish history.) Sibelius had been obsessed by the legend of the black swans of Tuonela in Rune XIV of the *Kalevala* and as early as 1893 he wrote one of his most celebrated compositions, the tone poem entitled 'The Swan of Tuonela'. Tuonela is the kingdom of death and around its perimeter circles the fast-flowing black waters of the river of Tuonela on which rides eternally the Black Swan of the Kingdom of Death. The hero Lemminkainen sets out to shoot dead with a crossbow the black swan as a gift for his bride but instead is shot dead himself by a herdsman of Pohjola.

Music was my language, so I gave them my music;

To conform to the iambic pentameter line most poets would have omitted the second possessive adjective 'my' but Hartnett has the nerve to go for the grace note and so, against the rules, he inserts the second possessive adjective 'my' so you get 'Music was my language, so I gave them my music'.

Hartnett's dramaturgy is analogous to the invention at the heart of Friel's *Translations*. Just as in *Translations* we are confronted by actors playing nineteenth-century Donegal peasants who are speaking Gaelic in English, so in Hartnett's poem he contrives to convince us that his language is music through the medium of the language of poetry; more subtly, we know that Hartnett's language is poetry and yet by his doubling as Sibelius, he is able to convince us that his language is music. Locking us into this double double-take, Hartnett then goes for broke with a triple-take by reverting in the next line to the autobiographical conceit of linguistic communication being his first language:

> *Caught at school in webs of grammar*
> *which still at night enmesh my face,*
> *I had no tongue in the land I came from*
> *but at first, at best, a stammer*

Pirouetting on the tightrope of his high wire act, Hartnett drags us up to yet another level – to the domain of the *dindsenchas*, a feature of Gaelic Irish poetry comparable to the topographical poetry of the *Kalevala* – and in so doing opens up us readers into the realms of *Mise Eire* and 'Finlandia':

> *The land took me in her embrace;*
> *I wed the land and dreamed her freedom*
> *somehow coalesced and marched maestoso*
> *out through the hatchings of my music-sheets.*
> *But the people heard the real programme:*
> *the crescendi of shells in the air*
> *and their climax in the streets.*

Simultaneously, we are in Dublin in 1916 outside the GPO, and in Helsinki in 1917 as the October Revolution in Russia prefigures civil war and revolution in Finland.

In the next paragraph or movement of Hartnett's poem – I say 'movement' because there is an obvious orchestral structure to the poem – Hartnett switches key and hammers out two heroic couplets to introduce the theme of the role of alcohol in the Finish composer's life as well as in his own life:

> *Alcohol's a cunning beast.*
> *It fools the doctor and the priest,*
> *it fools the clever and the sane –*
> *but not the liver or the brain.*

Whereupon, Hartnett drops the heroic couplet as abruptly as he initiated it and slows down to a free verse alternating rhymes with non-rhymes and short lines with longer lines as he paints a portrait of the terrifying black sobriety of the composer who made a quasi-Faustian pact with alcohol; Hartnett's metrical picture-making of a nosebleed as a snowstorm, and of forests falling down, and of the trembling of hands culminates in an apotheosis of black swans, the victory of death over life:

> *Idle verses, so I thought,*
> *that someone, doodling, idly makes.*
> *But now blood breaks like snowflakes*
> *from my brothers' nostrils*
> *and my hand shakes.*
> *I gave everything I could:*
> *music, speeches, pat harangues;*
> *intellectualised the fight*
> *and, tremblando, wept adagios, wrung my hands –*
> *in short, spilled every drink but blood.*
> *Autumn breaks its rainbows*
> *along the staggering trees*
> *and my hand quivers.*
> *Into my room across my music-sheets*
> *sail black swans on blacker rivers.*

Alcohol was as essential a concomitant of Sibelius's life and work as it was of Hartnett's life and work from 1980 to his death nineteen years later in 1999. Here is an entry from Sibelius's diary for 16 September 1916 when he was fifty-one years old, the same age as was Michael Hartnett when he wrote *Sibelius in Silence*:

> Went into town yesterday and the day before. Heavy drinking and afterwards much depression. Terrible this state. Particularly as my weakness for alcohol damages me in my own and others' eyes. At home here some furtive drinking to get my nerves in better condition.

Sibelius's biographer Erik Tawaststjerna records that in the following year of 1917 Sibelius's handwriting was affected by alcohol: 'His writing becomes rounder and broader, as are the diary entries themselves – repetitions, rhetorical questions and exclamation marks.'

In a diary entry in April 1919 Sibelius is alarmed by the tremor in his hands:

> It would be an easy thing for me to work if cheap and weak wines were ready to hand. These days I am drinking whisky and schnapps. My hands shake so much that I can't write.

His biographer comments: 'One wonders whether he in fact needed a regular intake of alcohol to steady his tremor! After his long period of temperance from 1908 to 1915 and further enforced abstinence during 1918, his drinking and tremor became something of a vicious circle; the drinking produced a tremor, which could then be stabilised only by further drink.'

In a diary entry for 11 February 1920 Sibelius writes:

> Scored *Valse Lyrique*. This orchestration has entailed enormous work, so much so that my hands tremble and I can't work at it without stopping from time to time. Only wine seems to steady me – and at present prices!

Two weeks later he writes:

> My hands no longer tremble. It feels strange to be able to write normally.

Towards the end of the year on 27 November 1920 he notes:

> Am curing myself with whisky and have already made considerable progress.

Five days later on 2 December 1920 he adds:

> Cheer up – death is around the corner.

Three years later on 11 November 1923 he writes:

> Alcohol, which I gave up, is now my most faithful companion. And the most understanding! Everything and everyone else have largely failed me.

In the following year, he writes:

> At nights I compose. No, at nights I sit at my desk with a bottle of whisky and try to work. Later, I wake, my head upon the score and my hand clasped round empty air. Aino (his wife) has removed the whisky while I sleep.

Four years further along the road, on 8 May 1927 he writes:

> In order to survive, I have to have alcohol. Wine or whisky.

Any or all of those diary entries by Sibelius could have been penned by Michael Hartnett in his own diary for the years 1980 to 1999. It is necessary for the understanding of Hartnett's poem *Sibelius in Silence* as well as for an understanding of his entire œuvre that we clarify Hartnett's view of the role of alcohol in art and life, for he had a definite and even more logical view of alcohol than Sibelius did.

In the early 1960s in Dublin Michael Hartnett spent a great deal of time in the pubs but he was different from all the other drinkers in that he was contemptuous of the culture of alcohol that ruled at that time, especially in the literary pubs. I remember being shocked in 1962 by the severity of his strictures. He acknowledged the ruthlessness of his attitude and warned me that it was morally necessary for his and my survival.

There were three types of drinker whom he condemned: firstly, the elder writer publicly in the grip of alcohol addiction. Hartnett felt that no poet worthy of the name should allow himself to become vulnerable to such an extent. Secondly, bohemian drinkers who regarded it as obligatory to offer up one's life on the altar of alcohol, and who preached a cult of alcohol. Thirdly, the lawyer-journalist-academic types who were so besotted with alcohol that no matter how witty their conversations and writings, their thinking was sodden with booze.

I was shocked because Hartnett's attitudes were so non-conformist. To take this stance in the early 1960s was to be a heretic and to stand outside everybody. I admired his independence of mind and the courage it required. He struck me as a kind of mid-twentieth-century reincarnation of the young James Joyce. His ruthless common sense could be mistaken for arrogance and his high standards for conceit. Hartnett knew his own mind as only the real poet does know it.

I say 'real' poet. I have met many writers of verse in my life but very few poets. Hartnett was a poet – a real poet. For him the writing of poetry was a vocation, an all-or-nothing calling.

Twenty years later in 1983 Hartnett's marriage, under attack from economic attrition and his own intellectual isolation, began to break up and with it his family home and life in the hills of Templeglantine in West Limerick. The end when it came, came suddenly and overnight at the end of 1984 he found himself alone, marooned and homeless in Dublin. I believe that being the ruthlessly logical artist that he was, he calculated that in order to survive as a poet in Dublin city he would be compelled to drink hard liquor in extreme and regular quantities. I believe he made a secret pact with himself in the privacy of his own soul. Knowing full well that the price would be an early death but believing that it was the only method of living whereby he would be able to continue writing poetry, Michael Hartnett dedicated the rest of his life to a black sobriety of a kind very similar to, only more extreme than that employed by Sibelius.

Hartnett and Sibelius were similar personalities. Robert Layton writes that Sibelius was a cordial *bon viveur* and connoisseur of food, drink and tobacco, constantly in financial difficulties, small in stature, who suffered from melancholia and yet was wonderful fun: 'spontaneous, warm, and immediate ... impulsive, instinctive, generous'. All of which is a precise evocation of the personality of Hartnett.

Having stated starkly the theme of alcohol Hartnett proceeds to the climax of the poem: a meditation by Sibelius as he beholds himself both composing and conducting his Fourth Symphony, the darkest, the most radical and most beautiful of all his works, known sometimes as the Barkbrod (the bark bread) Symphony because Sibelius had in mind famine times in the nineteenth century, when Finns used to grind birch tree bark and mix it with flour to make bread. The voices of Hartnett and Sibelius are interchangeable as he remarks at the beginning of the seventh paragraph:

> *They say my music weeps for the days*
> *when my people ate the bark from trees*
> *because all crops had failed.*
> *Music disdains such theories:*
> *I offer you here cold, pure water –*
> *as against the ten-course tone-poems,*
> *the indigestible Mahlerian feasts;*
> *as against the cocktails' many hues,*
> *all liquors crammed in one glass –*
> *pure, cold water is what I offer.*

Hartnett here is quoting from the composer's diary in which Sibelius recalls a visit to Germany:

> In Germany, they took me to hear some new music. I said, 'You are manufacturing cocktails of all colours. And here I come with pure cold water.' My music is molten ice. In its movement you may detect its frozen beginnings, in its sonorities you may detect its initial silence.

Panning across the œuvre of Sibelius, Hartnett zooms in on the notes that begin the third movement of the Fourth Symphony: two solo flutes playing so mutely, hesitantly as if not really playing but tentatively tuning up, frozen fingers struggling to warm up in a polar landscape against the rising winds of double-bass and cello, basset-horn and bassoon, viola and violins and brass. The Fourth Symphony but in particular the third movement epitomizes that epigrammatic concentration in form and content that both Sibelius and Hartnett always strove after. Throughout this great verse paragraph Hartnett has in mind the historic conversation in Helsinki in 1907 between Sibelius and Mahler, which Sibelius wrote up in his diary:

> When our conversation touched upon the symphony, I said that I admired its style and severity of form and the profound logic that created an inner connection between all the motifs...

Mahler protested against Sibelius's austerity. 'No, no', cried Mahler, 'the symphony must be like the world – it must contain everything.'

In the middle of this verse paragraph, Hartnett's verse line achieves what Kavanagh called 'the sonorous beat':

> *Composed, I am conducting. It is my*
> *fourth symphony, third movement and,*
> *as my baton tries to make the music keep*
> *to the key of C sharp minor*
> *vodka ebbs in tremors from my hand*
> *and at the ragged corner of my eye*
> *a raven flies through the concert hall*
> *and I find a self saying to myself,*
> *'It was the deer that stripped the trees,*
> *not the people at all.'*
> *Two flutes grapple with an ice-cold note*
> *until the 'cello takes command.*
> *As the audience's hiss escapes*
> *splinters of birch-bark stick in my throat.*

Hartnett's phrase 'the audience's hiss' illustrates how steeped he was in the primary sources of Sibelius's life. In the many books by Sibelius's foremost English language chronicler, Robert Layton, it is the word 'hiss' that is used to describe the audience's reaction to the January 1913 performance of the Fourth Symphony in Gothenburg.

The raven that flies through the concert hall is the raven of Edgar Allen Poe's poem 'The Raven', with which Sibelius was obsessed during the writing of the finale of the fourth movement of the Fourth Symphony, and in which the American gothic poet is sitting up alone in the small hours exactly as Michael Hartnett used do in his second-storey flat at 23 Upper Leeson Street and, as he portrays Sibelius in the poem, dozing in his armchair. The poet asks the raven if he will ever meet again his dead love Lenore: 'Quoth the Raven, "Nevermore".' The Raven of Poe's poem is that eternal oblivion of which each and every human being lives in dread:

> 'Be that word our sign of parting, bird or fiend!' I
>   shrieked, upstarting –
> 'Get thee back into the tempest and the Night's
>   Plutonian shore!
> Leave no black plume as a token of that lie thy soul
>   hath spoken!
> Leave my loneliness unbroken! – quit the bust above
>   my door!
> Take thy beak from out my heart, and take thy form
>   from off my door!'
>   Quoth the Raven, 'Nevermore.'

In 1908 Sibelius had been diagnosed with cancer of the throat and believed with good reason that he was facing certain death. Hartnett with his Sibelian-like technique of economy in verse underscores all of this with a confrontation with mythology: did the Finns of former times have recourse to eating the bark from birch trees? Or was it the deer who stripped the birches? By implication Hartnett is also questioning our own Irish mythologies of self-pity and self-delusion. But Hartnett, I think, is also hinting that it is he and Sibelius who ate the bark from trees. In the solitude and desolation of their art they were reduced to eating bark from trees; that was the price each paid.

But the ultimate price was silence and death. In the end, Hartnett's poem is about his conviction that the end of art is silence; that, as in Anthony Cronin's words apropos Beckett, 'the object of true, achieved and necessary utterance is silence.' (*The Last Modernist*, p. 376). Sibelius had written in his diary:

> What happens when music ceases? Silence. All the other arts aspire to the condition of music. What does music aspire to? Silence.

In the eighth and final paragraph or movement of the poem, Hartnett announces Sibelius's renunciation of his art:

> *And now, because I made such strict demands*
> *upon my art, I must dismiss such music as intrudes*
> *on me as I conceal my shaking hands.*
> *No loss indeed – it's now quite trivial and crude;*

What poet other than Hartnett would have such severe and stoic honesty to dismiss his own last verses as 'quite trivial and crude'? His brother-in-arms, Mahon, perhaps.

In a final chess-mate of triple-take metamorphosis, the poet Hartnett has the composer Sibelius take down from his shelves a book of the poetry of the *Kalevala* so that he can pass on these poems, not his music, to his grandchildren:

> *I take down a book of poetry from my shelves*
> *to share with my children's children the old store*

of verses that this green-gold land reveres
(I speak their native language fluently
but when excited lapse into my planters' tongue)

Once again I marvel at Hartnett's book-learning when in Robert Layton's volume entitled *Sibelius* (London 1965, revised edition 1992) in a footnote on p. 64 I read: 'According to Mrs Lauri Kirves, the composer's grand-daughter, Sibelius mostly spoke Finnish with the grandchildren, though in moments of excitement he would revert to Swedish.' (And I am even more astonished when I learn from Michael's partner Angela Liston that although Michael did own a copy of this particular volume by Layton, it was the 1978 edition, not the 1992 revised edition.)

Sibelius/Hartnett reproaches his younger contemporaries for the lack of substance in their verse:

You may think thirty years of silence far too long
but some composers now about should have learnt
  from me
that silence would have graced the world far more
than their gutting and dismembering of song.

Michael Hartnett rejected the mass production of superfluous verse; the poet's obligation, as he understood it, was to produce only utterance of necessity.

Hartnett's own theory of poetic practice was kindred to Sibelius's theory of musical composition. In his diary entry for 1 August 1912 Sibelius wrote:

I let the musical thought and its development in my mind determine matters of form. I'd compare a symphony to a river: the river is made up of countless streams all looking for an outlet: the innumerable tributaries, streams and brooks that form the river before it broadens majestically and flows into the sea. The movement of the water determines the shape of the river bed:

Paul Durcan

> the movement of the river water is the flow of the musical ideas and the river bed that they form is the symphonic structure. (*Sibelius*, Layton 1992, p. 5)

Sibelius in music like Hartnett in poetry had an avant-garde belief in the river-deep connection between improvisation and organic form.

The poem draws *diminuendo* to its close as in a late Friel play:

> *And that which was part of me has not left me yet –*
> *however etherialised, I still know when it's there.*
> *I get up at odd hours of the night*
> *or snap from a doze deep in a chair;*
> *I shuffle to the radio, switch on the set,*
> *and pluck, as I did before, Finlandia out of the air.*

Thus concludes one of the major poems in the Irish landscape of the last two hundred years. The tone of voice is pure Hartnettian and the vivid image is of the poet himself in the living room of his flat at 23 Upper Leeson Street half-asleep in the mid-hours of night, abruptly waking up and climbing to his feet, shuffling across the room and, as he says, plucking 'Finlandia' – or 'The Retreat of Ita Cagney' – from the air. Robert Layton's last words on the Fourth Symphony apply also to Hartnett's poem: 'There is a searching intensity here, a purity of utterance, and a vision and insight of rare quality.' (*Sibelius*, Layton 1992, p. 82)

It is exhilarating to observe also that even here at the closing of the poem Hartnett perseveres in sticking to the primary sources of Sibelius's life. These last lines are almost a direct transcription from a statement of Sibelius's wife Aino (quoted in David Burnett-James's book on Sibelius published in 1989 when Hartnett was composing his poem):

224

He was thought by his closest associates to be psychic – 'not dependent only on five senses,' as his secretary put it. His wife believed he was aware when one of his works was being broadcast anywhere in the world. 'He is sitting quietly reading a book or newspaper. Suddenly he becomes restless, goes to the radio, turns the knobs, and then one of his symphonies or tone-poems comes out of the air.' (p. 99)

But what about Hartnett's aside that precedes the final scene of the dozing composer?

> *And that which was part of me has not left me yet –*
> *however etherialised, I still know when it's there.*

What is still there? What is that part of Hartnett which has not left him yet? First, it is his faith in his calling as a poet and in the art of poetry. 'He was grounded in poetry. It kept his feet on the earth', wrote Anthony Cronin in the *Sunday Independent* four days after Hartnett's death. Secondly, it is his humanity, and that defiant belief that Hartnett had in man's common humanity and in its childlike essence. Over a lifetime's dedication to his art, Hartnett reiterated his credo in human and humane values and his repudiation of all the perversions of language, most especially the language of propaganda, euphemism and cliché. He understood his vocation in exactly the same terms as did Eliot and Mallarmé, 'to purify the dialect of the tribe'.

Yet *Sibelius in Silence* remains a tragic poem. Michael Hartnett had a 'tragic sense of life', to borrow the words of the title of one of the books that he cherished in his youth in the early 1960s, the Spanish classic wisdom-book *The Tragic Sense of Life* by Miguel de Unamuno.

Sibelius in Silence, along with its companion poems, *The Man who Wrote Yeats, the Man who Wrote Mozart,* and *He'll to the Moors* constitutes the last poetry of Michael Hartnett.

Paul Durcan

Apart from a few of what he termed 'strays' and his translations from the seventeenth- and eighteenth-century Gaelic Irish poetry of Haicead and O Rathaile, Michael Hartnett wrote no more poetry. On 13 October 1999 he died in St Vincent's Hospital in Dublin. He was laid to rest in the Calvary Cemetery in Newcastle West under a limestone cross carved by Cliodhna Cussen, depicting a necklace of wrens and bearing two lines from Michael's 1978 poem for his son Niall:

> *Beadsa ann d'ainneoin an bhais,*
> *Mar labhraionn duch is labhraionn par:*
>
> *'I will be there in spite of death*
> *For ink speaks and paper speaks:'*

On Sibelius's eighty-fifth birthday in 1950 the President of Finland motored out twenty miles from Helsinki to the composer's home in the countryside to pay the nation's respects. But when Michael Hartnett died the President of Ireland not only did not attend his funeral, but chose not to represent herself at it.

Such was the official view of a poet-scholar of our state and nation, in death as in life, except for one redeeming caveat. Just as the Finnish Government in 1897 – mark you, 1897! – awarded Sibelius a state pension for life, likewise in 1981 the Taoiseach Mr Charles J. Haughey supported the setting up of Aosdána whereby the State offered a measure of financial support to artists who had made 'an outstanding contribution to the arts', foremost among them Michael Hartnett. Apart from the companionship of Angela Liston, had it not been for that financial support from the State in the shape of Aosdána, Michael Hartnett would have died long years before he did and we would never have had the great, rich and strange poems of his last period such as his *Sibelius in Silence*.

226

The Hartnett of *Sibelius in Silence* is of the stature of Cézanne or Cavafy and I repudiate the myth of him as a *petit maître local*. I repudiate the myth of him as the performing chimpanzee of the bar stools, a myth which is the creation of those suburban commissars who forty years ago in the 1960s and 1970s had it in their power to give a dazzling young scholar-poet support but who scorned him with snobbery, ignorance and neglect. I am glad to report that I feel exuberantly and unrepentantly bitter at what they did to Michael Hartnett and I hope I always will feel so. To the memory of my dead friend and comrade, in the solitude of my own fate, I raise my trembling glass.

The Mystery of Harry Clifton

This is your saving grace – to restore mystery
To a common weal, and resurrect from disgrace
The non-political, kneeling in the unity
Of a moment's prayer ...

'Death of Thomas Merton' Harry Clifton (1982)

In 1994 I was invited by its editor Niall MacMonagle to write a foreword to *Lifelines 2*, the astutely-entitled anthology of favourite poems selected, so the subtitle stated, by 'famous people' in replies to letters of invitation from students of Wesley College, Dublin. In the course of reading a proof copy I came upon a poem which I had never read before and which startled me in a way which does not happen often to me when reading contemporary verse. The poem was entitled 'Vaucluse' and the name at the bottom of the poem was Harry Clifton. Not for the first time in my life I was puzzled by that name.

Like anyone else, I dare say, who has lived their life in and around Irish poetry, the name Harry Clifton was a name I was familiar with since boyhood; since about the age of fifteen when I read W.B. Yeats's late poem 'Lapis Lazuli' which begins with a dedication in parenthesis '(For Harry Clifton)'. Yeats's poem had been published in *New Poems* in 1938 and therefore the author of 'Vaucluse' could hardly be the same Harry Clifton as the dedicatee of 'Lapis Lazuli'. But it was just about possible. Or maybe he was a son. Or grandson. It seemed unlikely that, within the arena of Irish poetry, there were two Harry Cliftons belonging to separate and unconnected families. A biographical note at the back of *Lifelines 2* gave 1952 as the date of Harry Clifton's birth so a son or grandson seemed a credible explanation. I marvelled at the conjunction that the author of this startling poem 'Vaucluse' was the descendant of the dedicatee of 'Lapis Lazuli'.

I did not know Harry Clifton in 1994 nor had I ever met anyone who knew him. I formed an impression that he lived and worked in far-off distant lands in Africa and Asia. The sparse biographical information seemed fitting for one who was a descendant of the dedicatee of 'Lapis Lazuli' with its universal, sweeping evocations of other lands, other eras, other civilizations:

> On their own feet they came, or on shipboard,
> Camel-back, horse-back, ass-back, mule-back,
> Old civilisations put to the sword.
> Then they and their wisdom went to rack...

About the Harry Clifton to whom 'Lapis Lazuli' was dedicated I had never read nor heard anything since first reading the poem thirty-five years earlier and while I realized that it was impossible that he and the author of 'Vaucluse' were one and the same person, the nagging feeling persisted that they *were* one and the same person.

What I wish to attempt now is to think aloud about that first reading in 1994 of the poem entitled 'Vaucluse' and my subsequent readings of it down thirteen years and about how that poem led me into reading all the rest of Harry Clifton's poetry and prose culminating in a second reading experience in 2006, which, in the manner in which it startled me, was a comparable experience to reading 'Vaucluse' in 1994. In January 2006 while I was posted in Trinity College Dublin, Dr Philip Coleman one day left for me in the office of the School of English a large envelope (the sort used for mailing poster-size photographs); it contained a lettered (H) and signed copy of a broadsheet published by Dr Coleman under the imprint KORE BROADSHEETS # 10 which reproduced a poem by Harry Clifton entitled 'Benjamin Fondane Departs For The East'.

'Vaucluse' was submitted to the *Lifelines 2* anthology by the novelist Deirdre Madden, with the accompanying letter addressed to three Wesley College students:

> Dear Ewan, Aine and Christopher:
> My favourite poem is 'Vaucluse', by my husband Harry Clifton. It relates to a time before we were married, when I was spending some months in the south of France, and Harry came out to visit me. We went to Aix-en-Provence together, and to Marseilles. It's a marvellous poem, and it means a great deal to me.
> Good luck with 'Lifelines'.
> All best wishes
> Deirdre Madden

> Vaucluse

> *Cognac, like a gold sun*
> *Blazed in me, turning*
> *The landscape inside out –*
> *I had left the South*
> *An hour ago, and the train*
> *Through Arles, through Avignon*
> *Fed on electricity*

Overhead, and quickened my mind
With infinite platforms, cypress trees,
Stone villages, the granaries
Of Provence, and I saw again
France, like a blue afternoon
Genius makes hay in, and drink improves –
The worked fields, the yellow sheaves
In shockwaves, perceived
And lit from within, by love.
By then, I suppose,
You had made your own connections,
My chance, eventual girl,
And half Marseilles had closed
For the hot hours – the awnings of cafes
With nothingness in their shadows,
And the drink put away
For another day
Not ours …
                    I see, I remember
Coldly now, as I see ourselves
And the merchants from Africa, glozening
Liquor on the shelves
Of celebration, everyone dozing
In transmigratory dreams
Of heroin, garlic, and cloves –
And how we got there, you and I,
By trade route or intuition, seems,
Like charts for sale on the Occident streets
As fabulous, as obsolete
As a map of the known world.

But then again, how kind he was,
The dark patron *… and it lasted,*

That shot of cognac,
An hour, till the train
Occluded in grey rain
Above Lyons, and the Rhone Valley
Darkened. I would carry
Your books, your winter clothes
Through stations, streets of Paris
To a cold repose
In the North. We would meet again
In months to come, and years,
Exchanging consciousness, reason, and tears
Like beggars. Transfigured,
Not yet fallen from grace
I saw us, not as we are
But new in love, in the hallowed place
Of sources, the sacred fountains
Of Petrarch and René Char.

'Vaucluse' is first a love poem, secondly a train poem, thirdly a North and South of France poem. It consists of three passages of mostly short, three-stress lines. The phrase 'love poem' trips lightly off the tongue, but in the reality of literature an authentic love poem is a rare occurrence. Look at the last hundred years of Irish literature and how many authentic love poems will you come up with? Rarer still are poems of married love, which this poem also is. The moment, which is the occasion of the poem happens only once or twice in a lifetime and to catch it is almost impossible. Usually the writer winds up with a wodge of rhetoric dangling from a fork; memorable rhetoric sometimes but merely rhetoric. In the rat race of *ersatz* romance, an authentic love poem is a strange item.

The poem takes its title from the department in the south of France, one of the departments of Provence. Vaucluse is so-

named after the village of Fontaine-de-Vaucluse, the ancient
Vallis Clausa or 'Fountain of the Enclosed Valley' of Roman
times. The 'fountain' of Vaucluse is claimed to be the deep-
est spring well in the world. Lying under a 230-metre-high
cliff at the top of what in the days before tourism was a
secluded valley, the green spring can be docile or turbulent.
In the first century AD Seneca wrote of it: 'Where the impetu-
ous torrent escapes from the abyss, the spring is sacred
because of the unfathomable depth of its waters'. The spring
of Vaucluse is a kind of Provençal Delphi. Its waters form the
source of the river Sorgue, which flows through the old town
of L'Isle-sur-la-Sorgue, birthplace and home of the poet René
Char. The glorious climax of Harry Clifton's poem sings of:

> ... *the hallowed place*
> *Of sources, the sacred fountains*
> *Of Petrarch and René Char.*

A presiding genius of the first passage is Vincent Van Gogh
and one feels that the poet has specific paintings of Van Gogh
in mind: 'A Cornfield, with Cypresses' and 'Midday, after
Millet'. The reader is brought face to face with those unmis-
takeable corrugations of paint on the surface of canvas:

> *The worked fields, the yellow sheaves*
> *In shockwaves, perceived*
> *And lit from within, by love.*

I get the impression also of the poet co-opting Van Gogh in
the making of the image of the train being 'Fed on electricity/
Overhead'. That is a painting that Vincent did not himself get
to make but it is one which in Clifton's poem he is brought
back to make. I can see in that first passage the bent figure of
Van Gogh in a field near Arles painting the train from Mar-
seilles as it flashes past. Having trudged through the Francis

Bacon painting, ('Study for a Portrait of Van Gogh IV', 1957), he is presently ensconced on the edge of the Clifton poem.

A second presiding genius of the first passage is the eighteenth-century Irish philosopher George Berkeley whose central tenet of *esse est percipi* lies behind its lines.

The image of the train is vital to the poem as it is vital to all Clifton's work. The train in Clifton is a pre-lapsarian form of transport; so pre-lapsarian as if to seem an essential fixture of the furniture of the Garden of Eden. Trains in Clifton play a life-changing role; at once life-enhancing and life-destroying. The train seems to create the very world it is flashing through. The train splashes 'infinite platforms' on the canvas; the train throws up the very cypress trees it is shooting past; the train conjures up vistas of infinity – 'infinite platforms'. The poet announces that he has 'left the south' and we are left in no doubt by the end of the poem that the south is the equivalent of the Garden of Eden. Ironically the electricity of the train and its overhead wires are taking him northward darkly and away from the blue south and all its electric connections of love.

In the second passage the poet sketches the woman of the poem, the beloved, the bride-to-be whom he depicts in those four chosen words 'My chance, eventual girl'. In the cold light of sitting alone on the train speeding north, he recalls their meeting of only an hour or two previously; their having a drink together in a café in Marseilles. He tells us of 'the shelves of celebration', reminding us in our illness-beset culture in the north of the original purpose of alcohol which is to celebrate life, not destroy it. He imagines her now back in Marseilles in the hot hours and 'the awnings of cafes / With nothingness in their shadows'. A sculpted, pictorial image, a fusion of de Staël and Cézanne. He speaks of 'everyone dozing in transmigratory dreams' as if to suggest that the true element of humanity is the journey and the cosmos, not the static and the provincial. And he asks that question that all lovers finally cannot help but ask: by the power of what obscure agency did they have the good fortune to meet? Was it indeed good fortune or was it some kind of pre-ordained destiny, some form of providence?

The third and final passage of the triptych portrays the deity as being a 'dark *patron*' who is benign. By now the train has been travelling northward for an hour and it is past Lyons. In a sculpted, linguistic image the train is depicted as darkening after having been 'occluded in grey rain'. This is the darkness of the north, a radically other darkness to that of the shadows in Marseilles in the mid-afternoon. We learn that the narrator is carrying the books and winter clothes of the beloved to Paris in the cold north. A Rembrandt-like image of the beloved; she *is* her books, she *is* her winter clothes. Marriage is prefigured and defined as a state of 'exchanging consciousness, reason and tears / Like beggars.' What an astounding image. Could it also be out of Rembrandt? 'The Jewish Bride'?

We come to the climax of the poem. The transfiguration of the pair of lovers in Fontaine-de-Vaucluse and the invocation of the names of Petrarch and René Char. In depicting the transfiguration by love, Clifton adumbrates a theology of original sin; as we are, we are fallen; as transfigured by love, we are new. In these lines he achieves both a Camus-like lucidity as in *The First Man* and the innocence of Dylan Thomas's 'Fern Hill'. When I first read the last lines thirteen years ago, those two names, Petrarch and René Char, carried a powerful charge as they were meant to do and the strange fact of poetry and life is that after all these years they continue to carry that charge.

Petrarch. The fourteenth-century poet of love who lived

part of his early life in Avignon and later in Fontaine-de-Vau-cluse 'on the left bank of the Sorgue' as he tells us and in whose poetry are to be found images of the Fountain of the Enclosed Valley. He was, as well as being a poet, a humanist and scholar which is pertinent when we consider the intellectual basis of the lyricism of Harry Clifton; and he saw himself as a permanent dissident and exile everywhere (*'peregrinus ubique'*). Like Clifton, Petrarch believed a poet can be at home only in exile.

The copper-fastening name is that of René Char who spent a lifetime tracing the abyss of the mystery at the fountain of Vaucluse: 'poetry,' he wrote 'is, of all clear waters, the least likely to linger at the reflection of its bridges.' The name of René Char tastes of the Resistance, the *maquis*, rugby football and lyric poetry and it evokes the landscape of Provence in the area of the Vaucluse; that bare, mountainous, red landscape under blue skies. It's a name that also brings back to mind instantaneously the names of Martin Heidegger and Albert Camus; those lost worlds that are none the less real for being lost; maybe the more real for being lost.

In the story of my own life, it was in the early 1960s in connection with Heidegger that I first came upon the tracks of the poet René Char; Heidegger who, invoking the Pre-Socratic philosophers asked the same question that haunts the poetry of Harry Clifton: how should we dwell on earth? In the 1950s the disgraced German philosopher found a friend and disciple in the person of René Char. Heidegger, castigated for his dealings with the Nazi regime, found a sympathetic, congenial sanctuary in the Vaucluse in René Char, culminating in the legendary seminars at Le Thor. Char was as renowned for his exploits as a Resistance leader as for his poetry; the 'Capitaine Alexandre' of Resistance mythology. Later in reading of Albert Camus I came upon René Char

again. Camus had come to know René Char in 1945 and he
revered Char both as a poet and as a friend.

Twelve years later in 2006 I read for the first time Harry
Clifton's poem 'Benjamin Fondane Departs For The East'.

Benjamin Fondane Departs For The East

Look at us now, from the vanished years –
  Paris between the wars.
Penelopes and Juliets, pimps and racketeers
Of sugar and tobacco. Boys and girls
With stars on their lapels, who sleep on straw
Like everyone else, and carry out the slops.
And who could deny we're equals, under a Law
Annihilating us all! Conformists, resisters,
You I would never abandon, my own soul-sister,
Drinking brassy water from the taps

Of Drancy, where time and space are the antechamber
  To our latest idea of eternity –
Trains going east in convoys, sealed and numbered,
To an unknown destination, Pitchipoi
As the wits describe it, after the Yiddish tale –
A village in a clearing, zlotys changed for francs,
Children at their books, the old and frail
Looked after, and the rest suspiciously blank
On the postcards drifting like dead leaves
Back from that other world we are asked to believe in.

Death is not absolute! Two and two make five!
  My poems will survive!
Why not fly in the face of reason and scream
As Shestov says! Unscramble the anagram

Of my real name, which now is mud,
And tell Jean Wahl and Bachelard, bien pensants,
I forgive them, as they stalk the corridors
Of the Sorbonne, and the pages of the Cahiers du Sud.
I forgive them, for they know not who they are.
Irrational, fleeting, caught between wars,

Faking their own death, in thirteen nation-states,
     As the monies collapse
And the borders, and everyone transmigrates
Like souls, through the neutral space on the maps.
Athens and Jerusalem, Ulysses and the Wandering Jew –
There they all go, the living, the dead,
The one in the other ... Call them the Paris Crowd,
Unreal, uprooted, spectres drifting through,
The ashes of their ancestors in suitcases,
Bound for Buenos Aires, bound for the New.

In the steamroom dissipatings, the bathhouse stink,
     As the people of the Book
Undressed themselves, I learned at last how to think.
I saw the shame and beauty, and I shook
At patriarchs' aged knees, the love-handles of hips
And women's breasts, emerging, disappearing,
Standing, kneeling, waiting, finally stripped
Of civilisation – in their natural state.
At the heart of the orgy, I saw into the years
Beyond steam and faucets to the real Apocalypse.

And now they tell me 'Hide your poems, wait –
     Somewhere in Nineteen Eighty
Readers will find you ...' I see a Paris street,
Old letterbox, a drop-zone for the infinite

In a leaf-littered hallway, where a publisher long ago
Went out of business, and a young man searches
In the sibylline mess and the overflow
For a few lost words – my own soul-sister, my wife
Till death do us part, in the Eastern Marches –
And that, my friends, will be the afterlife.

The text is followed by a brief, italicised biographical note:

Romanian Jewish poet Benjamin Fondane (1898–1944), moved
to Paris in 1923. Deported from Drancy, he died in Birkenau.

The title 'Benjamin Fondane Departs For The East' reads as a
kind of public announcement at which the reader is invited to
behold and participate in the spectacle – *spectacle* in the
French sense of the phrase – of a Romanian-Jewish poet being
deported by train from a suburban railway station, Drancy,
near Paris to his incarceration and death in the concentration
camp at Auschwitz-Birkenau in Poland in 1944. The title has
a news-desk, circus ring to it. It carries within itself the incan-
tatory note of ringmaster and newsreel commentator. 'Hurry
up folks, gather round, stop press. Benjamin Fondane departs
for the East. Right now. Get your tickets. Roll up and watch
him. Watch his departure. Come along now. Hurry up.'

The poet in the first line assumes the voice of Fondane
himself and in that voice, sustaining it throughout the poem,
he paints for us scenes of the Holocaust particular to him and
his family, yet applicable to the entire Jewish race.

The voice is daring, insouciant, oracular, almost but not
quite arrogant. He invites us to look, and by implication stare
at him and his family and his people in their hour of maxi-
mum humiliation, anguish and degradation. His tone is
mocking, gossipy, resigned, bitter, ironic. A gay spirit in the
face of evil. 'Gaiety transfiguring all that dread.' He is
sparklingly bitter and passionately ironic. The poem is an

elegy, a declaration, a harangue, a wisdom-poem, a confession, a credo, a performance, above all, first and last, a cry, an articulate cry from the heart. It is a painting by, all at once, Chagall, Soutine and Jankel Adler.

The poem is comprised of six ten-line stanzas and in the opening stanza the voice of Fondane summons us to the world of 'Paris between the wars', 1918–1939, the world of *l'entre deux guerres'* as recalled by Eliot in 'East Coker', the ghettos where boys and girls 'sleep on straw ... and carry out the slops'. In the tone of Pushkin throwing down a challenge, Fondane launches a rhetorical question in a rant of scorn: 'And who could deny we're equals, under a Law / Annihilating us all?' Then he turns away from us, his audience, and addresses his sister, Lina, who was arrested with him on 7 March 1944 and whom Fondane was invited by his captors to abandon in exchange for his own freedom. He refused to abandon his sister whom Clifton portrays for us in an image of great tenderness as she drinks water from the taps, the 'brassy water' as he puts it, of Drancy.

The second stanza opens with another outburst of sarcasm in which Fondane describes Drancy as being the place 'where time and space are the antechamber / To our latest idea of eternity'. This modish idea is embodied in the form of 'trains going east in convoys'. His black humour deepens as he recounts how postcards used to arrive in Drancy from the east with pictures of children at kindergarten and the aged in retirement and with lots of blank space around the illustrations. In Drancy people used to joke about these postcards and they used to say how they came from a place called 'Pitchipoi', a fabled village paradise in Yiddish folklore that might have come straight out of a Chagall painting or an Isaac Babel story.

The third stanza opens with assertions of controlled,

rhyming hysteria. 'Death is not absolute! Two and two make five! My poems will survive!' We the readers are made to feel that the speaker regards these assertions as being at once true and ludicrous. Fondane invokes the name of Leon Shestov (1866–1938), the Russian-Jewish philosopher who was a dominant, controversial figure in the intelligentsia in Paris between the wars and whose credo proclaimed the futility of reason and the primacy of feeling. The speaker in the poem cries: 'Why not fly in the face of reason and scream / As Shestov says?' In his fury, almost mumbling to himself and flying in the face of reason, Fondane tells us he will drop his pseudonym or as he puts it, 'unscramble the anagram / Of my real name'.

Fondane was born Benjamin Wechsler in 1898 in Jassy in Moldavia in what is now the northeast of Romania. His uncles and his maternal grandfather were eminent Jewish intellectuals. Six languages were spoken in his home: Romanian, German, French, English, Yiddish and Hebrew. At the age of fourteen, he published poems under the name of Benjamin Fundoianu, taking his pen-name from the name of the countryside of his paternal ancestors. In Paris to which he emigrated in 1923 the Romanian Fundoianu became the French Fondane. Addressing the philosophers Jean Wahl and Gaston Bachelard, Fondane haughtily tells us that he forgives them. What is it he is forgiving them? Their rationalism; their being establishment stalwarts, sensible *'bien pensants'*. Fondane, in the manner of the Clifton of 'Vaucluse', dips his pen in the aura and romance of proper names, of 'the Sorbonne and the pages of the *Cahiers du Sud'*.

The poem is constructed like an Irish High Cross with each stanza a discrete panel depicting a different episode of the Holocaust while the narrative thread of Fondane's voice weaves its fierce, delicate interleave. The fourth stanza is a

picture of what Clifton calls 'the Paris Crowd', the heart of
the Jewish Diaspora exiled and drifting in Europe and beyond.
Again that signature Clifton word, 'transmigrates', and the
conflation of economics, politics, geography, anthropology
and history: 'and everyone transmigrates / Like souls,
through the neutral space on maps.' Again the invocation and
romance of proper names: 'Athens and Jerusalem, Ulysses
and the Wandering Jew'. These refer also to the major book-
titles of Fondane's life; the title of Shestov's magnum opus,
Athens and Jerusalem (1938) and the title of Fondane's own
magnum opus 'Ulysses' (1933), which in his private short-
hand he referred to as 'the Wandering Jew'. Echoes of Eliot
and Baudelaire from *The Waste Land* and from 'Les Sept
Vieillards': '*Fourmillante cité, cité pleine de rêves / Où le
spectre en plein jour raccroche le passant*': 'Unreal city /
Under the brown fog of a winter dawn'; 'There they all go, the
living and the dead / The one in the other ... Call them the
Paris Crowd / Unreal, uprooted'. Here we are locked into the
nightmare world of the stateless immigrant, the torment of
being an alien at everyone's mercy, the bureaucratic inferno
of work permits, ration coupons and identity cards. Alluding
to Fondane's own voyages to Argentina in 1929 and 1936, the
speaker in the poem sees these apparitions as 'spectres drift-
ing through, / The ashes of their ancestors in suitcases, /
Bound for Buenos Aires'. As well the felicitous rhyming of
'suitcases' with 'Buenos Aires', we may note the partial tran-
scription of one of the opening lines of Fondane's poem
'Ulysses' dedicated to his brother-in-law Armand Pascal;
'Armand your ashes weigh so heavily in my suitcase'. 'Bound
for Buenos Aires' is also, I surmise, an evocation of Witold
Gombrowicz who escaped to Buenos Aires (by mistake!) in
1939 and who, I believe, is a tutelary antecedent of Clifton's.

In the fifth stanza we arrive at the nadir of the Holocaust,

but at the zenith of Fondane's own perception of it as under-
stood and communicated by Clifton. Fondane asserts that
only by travelling into this ultimate debacle did he become
capable of thinking for himself. This is a catastrophic claim.
For it was in philosophy that Fondane had been primarily
engaged in the journals and halls of Paris in the 1920s and
1930s. He was the epitome of the poet-philosopher. Along
with his teacher and mentor Shestov he had come to form
the leading prong of attack on one side of the intense debate
between religious existentialism and secular rationalism. In
Clifton's poem, Fondane is echoing Simone Weil: 'You could
not be born at a better period than the present, when we have
lost everything' (Simone Weil, *Gravity and Grace*, p. 156).

In the fifth stanza we see again in Clifton's technique the
emergence of the sensibility of Rembrandt. For who else but
Rembrandt could be behind these lines in which Fondane
reports how, having arrived at the concentration camp, he
'shook / At patriarchs' aged knees, the love-handles of hips /
And women's breasts, emerging, disappearing, / Standing,
kneeling, waiting'. It is not seemly to dwell on images of pri-
vate horror and desolation but in this instance it behoves us
to repeat these words and consider them as we would stand
before a picture by Rembrandt: 'and I shook / At patriarchs'
aged knees, the love-handles of hips / And women's breasts,
emerging, disappearing, / Standing, kneeling, waiting'. It
behoves us to focus on that one phrase 'the love-handles of
hips / And women's breasts' and ask ourselves where we
might have seen this image before and by whose hand: 'the
love-handles of hips / And women's breasts'.

But all that sacred delft and holy hardware of God's cre-
ation is, in the concentration camp, about to be 'finally
stripped / Of civilisation'. This is 'the heart of the orgy'. This
is what happens in concentration camps; and, Fondane had

argued for twenty years, in social structures of the modern era, in their systematic, mechanical, totally impersonal materialism. The 'people of the Book' are treated not as the people of the Book but as fuel of the Political Machine and the Abstract Idea; not with respect but with hateful contempt.

In the sixth and final stanza Fondane considers what being a poet may have meant to him and what may be meant by the concept of 'the afterlife', if anything; by such notions as 'fame' and 'immortality'. He is vouchsafed a glimpse into the future, into the 1980s – forty years after his death – and he sees a nondescript street in Paris and the office of a defunct publisher in whose letter box a young man seeking after poetry comes upon wind-blown copies of Fondane's own poems. The last line reads: 'And that, my friends, will be the afterlife.' The letterbox, 'a drop-zone for the infinite', is located in a 'leaf-littered hallway'. Are poems also, it is being asked, like the dead leaves of postcards from Pitchipoi / Auschwitz drifting 'back from that other world we are asked to believe in'?

So that is what it may mean to have been a poet. To have lived your life in obscurity, a kind of hiding one's life away on the basis of a weird faith that sometime after your death, say forty or fifty years after your death, there is the possibility that some young man lost in his own journey may unearth your poems – 'a few lost words' – and bring them to light.

The tone of voice in the poem is the key to the author's sense of Fondane. It is an outraged voice, an audacious voice, an angry voice, a non-conformist voice. And when you look at Fondane's life story, at the totality of it, at all forty-six years of it, you see that that is what above all else he was: a non-conformist. In 1916 at the age of eighteen the precocious young Jew wrote: 'And I wept in the Garden of Gethsemane and I died on the Cross and I rose from the dead not on the

third day but in the souls of those who understood me.'
Already a modernist as an adolescent in the Romanian
provinces before World War One; a high modernist, Fran-
cophile, dissident in Bucharest in the years after World War
One; an exile in Paris from 1923 until his murder in 1944.

In Paris Fondane not only stood at the cutting edge of phi-
losophy and poetry, he was ahead of the cutting edge. He was
the avant-garde of the avant-garde. From early on in Paris, he
was out there with Picabia, Brancusi, Man Ray, Artaud,
Tzara. For him the central, fundamental fact of human exis-
tence was the absurdity of death. He was the archetypal
Romanian Jewish émigré and, in the photographs that sur-
vive of him, he looks the part; gay, handsome, laughing, intel-
lectual; enormous, arched, black eyebrows; wide, glittering
eyes; cigarette dangling from the corner of the mouth; jacket
draped over the shoulders; multicoloured scarf. There is a
marvellous photograph from 1938 of Fondane with his wife
Geneviève Tissier in which both of them are sparkling with
the joy of life.

For Fondane the cinema was where it was at in art; and
the cinema at its purest for him was by definition surrealist.
In poetry his hero was Rimbaud. His first book of poems in
French, published in 1928 with a photograph by Man Ray,
was entitled *Cinépoèmes*.

In 1931 the Argentinian woman of letters Victoria
Ocampo founded the journal *Sur*, a cosmopolitan journal of
art and literature, based in Buenos Aires. She published Fon-
dane from 1931 to 1940. She arranged for him to visit Buenos
Aires in 1929 and 1936 to present avant-garde films and to
participate in conferences. These three-week voyages across
the Atlantic Ocean by way of Dakar and Rio de Janeiro were
of massive importance in Fondane's life as a poet, providing
him with material for his epic poem 'Ulysses'. Another

source of inspiration was Tennyson's poem 'Ulysses' written in 1833:

> *To follow knowledge like a sinking star*
> *Beyond the utmost bound of human thought*

Such are the consanguinities that lift poetry to its proper level in the human story; from a twenty-first-century suburban-raised Irishman to a vagabond twentieth-century Romanian Jew to a nineteenth-century, lordly, English poet laureate.

With the Occupation of Paris in 1940 Fondane became nonchalant. When the Germans ordered that Jews wear yellow stars on their lapels, he ignored the order. His friends marvelled at his big, warm voice greeting them in the streets with his trademark *'Alors,* what's the news?' To a nosey baroness at a literary party he announced *'Je suis Victor Hugo'*. On 7 March 1944, betrayed by his concierge, he was arrested along with his sister Lina and taken to the prefecture at Ile de la Cité. Having refused the offer of freedom to stay by the side of his sister he was deported from Drancy to Auschwitz-Birkenau on 30 May 1944. He had four months to live. The choice he was forced into making in Drancy, a choice not only between life and death, but between his sister and his wife, Clifton transmutes into an almost unbearably tender image of Fondane making his sister his bride. In Clifton's poem Fondane suddenly turns to his sister and addresses her as ' my own soul-sister, my wife / Till death do us part, in the Eastern Marches'.

Witnesses have testified how Fondane ran a kind of literary salon in Auschwitz. In a corner of a bunkhouse, although ill and weak and singled out by the *capos* for derision and mockery, Fondane regaled his comrades with memories of Paris in the twenties and with readings from his epic poem

'Ulysses'. The doctor who attended him, Lazar Moscovici, wrote of how Fondane's 'warm voice was that of the fireside storytellers of old in Romania dazzling children with the wonders of tales of fairies and dragons.' Moscovici tells us how 'in the evenings of the last weeks of his life Fondane recited his poem 'Ulysses' which had become an elegy for the Jewish race and which symbolised his fate. And with what tenderness he spoke to us of his wife Geneviève, of his own den in Paris, of his books and his paintings ... of brotherhood and humanity.'

On the morning of 2 October 1944, in freezing rain, Fondane was loaded onto a lorry to take him to his death. The philosopher and fellow-countryman of Fondane, E. Cioran wrote: '... Fondane was resigned to his lot ... there was in him a peculiar complicity with the inevitable ... only this can explain his refusal to take any precaution, of which the rudimentary would have been to change his country of residence ...' This testimony is in accord with all we know of Fondane's heroic, casual attitude to life. But Cioran also added:

> Fondane was a superior man. Someone noble, above ordinary things. He refused to abandon Lina and accept his liberation. He had risen above normal miseries: as a man he was superior to Man. He had gone beyond the world in his own career, without pride or demonstrativeness – he was incapable of that. He was a man set apart, by that extraordinary nobility ...

In other words, it might be proper to ascribe to Fondane something of the sanctity of known martyrs such as Bonhoeffer. Probably Fondane would have eschewed the term 'sanctity' but as we see and hear and witness him in Clifton's poem we are encouraged and permitted to ascribe to him the mysterious condition of sanctity.

When Fondane died at the hands of the Nazis his poetry died with him and it was to be fifty years before his *Collected*

Poems were published in Paris in 1996 and in 2004 a critical biography, *Benjamin Fondane* by Olivier Salazar-Ferrer. In 1993, in Kfar-Saba in Israel, the inauguration took place of 'the Society for Benjamin Fondane Studies'. Such is 'the after-life' of the poet.

The reader will bring to Clifton's poem his or her own knowledge of Fondane. In my own case I became aware of Benjamin Fondane in 1965 in London when in David Gascoyne's *Collected Poems* (1965) I read his 1942 poem 'To Benjamin Fondane'. This is a matter of significance to me because I can see in Fondane an antecedent of Gascoyne, the visionary English poet, visionary in the mystic pieties of Samuel Palmer as well as in the revelations of Blake and Hölderlin. In 1986 the magazine *Aquarius* published Gascoyne's essay 'Meetings with Benjamin Fondane'.

In 1978 I met Francis Stuart for the first time and not long after in one of numerous conversations with him from 1978 until 2000, the year of his death, Francis Stuart cited to me the name of Benjamin Fondane as being one of the – for him – significant figures of European literature. Fondane was possibly an unofficial member of Stuart's own pantheon, which he called 'the High Consistory', although Fondane does not feature in Stuart's novel of that name. Fondane does, however, feature in an earlier Stuart novel, *The Pillar of Cloud* (1948). In an essay on Fondane in 2005 in the *Dublin Review* Harry Clifton remarks on the poignant significance of Stuart being a primary transmitter, so to speak, in the English language of Fondane.

That Fondane, a Jewish martyr of the Holocaust, was close to Stuart's heart and that Stuart featured him in his novel and translated his poetry are heartbreaking facts when one recalls the abuse heaped on Stuart for his alleged Nazi sympathies. The fact of the matter is that Stuart, like Fondane and Gascoyne and Clifton is a diasporist in all things; that outsider-ness might be described as the Jewish aspect of Stuart.

Taking together the two poems, 'Vaucluse' and 'Benjamin Fondane Departs For The East' we see that both poems are based on a train journey; the one representing the journey from and into all that is good in this life, the journey made under the sign of love; the other, a journey into the heart of evil, made under the sign of extraordinary courage; the one sings of the beatific fountains of the Enclosed Valley, the other depicts the vile fountains of the gas chambers of Auschwitz; both poems evoke and invoke the lives of poets; both poems put a value on poetry in the affairs of mankind. Each poem is driven by a specific energy: 'Vaucluse' by the energy of love; and 'Benjamin Fondane Departs For The East' by the energy of anger. In another poem of married love, 'The Liberal Cage', originally published in 1988 alongside 'Vau-cluse', Clifton had written:

> *But listen ... not in doubt,*
> *Contentment, or in pure mind,*
> *But in anger alone, will we find*
> *The key that lets us out.*

Part of the mystery of Harry Clifton is how and why a child of post-war Ireland, a child of the middle-class, garden sub-urbs of post-war Dublin took it upon himself to speak in the person of a Romanian-Jewish intellectual who was born more than an hundred years ago in Moldavia and, in doing so in the form of a poem in the English language, succeeded in catch-ing the authentic voice of the Romanian Jew. The obstacles to such an achievement may be gauged by considering the 1982 sculpture of James Joyce, a contemporary of Fondane's, outside the Newman Building in University College Dublin. Apparently Joyce, it is more a representation of a Trotskyite militiaman than of Joyce whereas Clifton's Fondane is carved from inside the soul of the man as he stands among the charnel houses of the European nightmare. Clifton has depicted both the spiritual reality of Fondane's personality as well as the circumstance of his tragedy. Whereas Joe McCaul the Irish sculptor of the Irishman Joyce has not experienced Joyce, the Irishman Clifton has experienced the Romanian Jewish Fondane and, by his success in entering into his subjectivity, communicated him to us in the music of his poetry. The seeds of Clifton's achievement were sown thirty years earlier when in his master's thesis ('Imaginative Absolute in Wallace Stevens', UCD, Dept. of Metaphysics, 1975) he investigated Hume's theory of imagination 'as *sympathy* where the imagination translates an idea into an impression in order to participate sympathetically in the experience of another' (Clifton, c.f. Hume *A Treatise of Human Nature*, pp. 385–386). Clifton followed up his 1975 research with an apprenticeship of thirty years in writing poetry during which he sought to recreate the life-experiences of thinkers and poets, among them Thomas Merton, Dag Hammarskjold, Hart Crane, Dostoyevsky, Silone, Kirkegaard, and Hopkins.

In 1987 in his Raven Arts Press pamphlet 'Martyrs and Metaphors' Cólm Tóibín momentarily illuminated Harry Clifton's suburban upbringing when he wrote (p. 16) that Clifton was 'brought up in the suburbs of Dublin: an Ireland which had no official recognition'. To be a child of the Dublin suburbs in the 1950s and 1960s was to be displaced, alien, disorientated, almost stateless.

Considering the œuvre of Harry Clifton in the light of 'Vaucluse' and 'Benjamin Fondane Departs For The East', seven volumes of poetry and two volumes of prose, not to mention multifarious fugitive publication in journals and newspapers, one is struck by the persistence of particular preoccupations.

First, there is Clifton's fascination with trains. It is there in his first volume of poems, published at the age of twenty-five, *The Walls of Carthage* (1977), in a poem entitled 'Two Stations in Paris' which constitute two still lifes of the Gare du Nord and the Gare St Lazare. Again an image of the overhead lines feeding electricity to the trains:

> *Blueprint of metal tangents – curving away*
> *Into what human distance, separation pure*
> *At the end of an alien day?*

The ticket machine is seen as

> *the photo*
> *Electric imprimatur*
> *Of a passenger gate*

A long-range snapshot sings of

> *Cantilevered sublime*
> *Where everyone but the pigeons*
> *Is an alien, and time*
> *Is its own religion.*

His sixth collection, *Night Train through the Brenner*, taking its title from an account of a train journey from Munich to Florence in 1989, contains the poem 'Watershed' which begins

> *On the spine of Italy*
> *Our train had come to a standstill*

It contains also 'The Marriage Feast', a magical poem linking the marriage process to that sacramental moment in a railway station when the uncoupling of carriages and the switching of tracks takes place.

Secondly, there is Clifton's obsession with Europe's primary sources and forgotten beginnings; its water tables and

watersheds being keened over, one is made to feel, by Hera-
clitus and Parmenides as well as by René Char and Petrarch.
Physical health, spiritual health, Clifton seems to be remind-
ing us, are one and the same and they will be rediscovered
only in the sources of primeval Europe and not in the artifi-
cial spas of megasonic wealth and so, in 'Taking the Waters'
(1994), he writes:

> *There are taps that flow, all day and all night,*
> *From the depths of Europe,*
> *Inexhaustible, taken for granted,*
>
> *Slaking our casual thirsts*
> *At a railway station*
> *Heading south, or here in the Abruzzo*
>
> *Bursting cold from an iron standpipe*
> *While our blind mouths*
> *Suck at essentials, straight from the water table ...*
>
> *History passes, only the waters remain,*
>
> *Bubbling up, through their carbon sheets,*
> *To the other side of catastrophe*
> *Where we drink at a forgotten source,*
>
> *Through the old crust of Europe*
> *Centuries deep*

The opening line of his 1994 poem 'Watershed', 'On the spine
of Italy ...' gave Clifton the title of his prose journal of four
seasons in a mountain-top village in the Abruzzi, which is
also a chronicle of water and about water and to water, a nar-
rative of snow and ice and melt-water and mountain torrents.

In *On the Spine of Italy* water is physically omnipresent and the whole book bears out the truth of its epigraph, 'The greatest poverty is not to live / In a physical world', lines from Wallace Stevens's late poem 'Esthétique du Mal'.

Thirdly, there is the vision of woman as the beloved in 'Vaucluse' and 'Benjamin Fondane Departs For The East', which in the shadowy, shuttered world of call-girls and street-walkers in his earlier books is tantamount to a tearing apart of the curtains at dawn to reveal the transfigured person. In the earlier books woman is either inaccessible self-containment or a 'monsoon girl' in a brothel delineated in what in *The Field Day Anthology of Irish Writing* (1991), Declan Kiberd described as Clifton's 'distinctive, personal fever and chill'.

Into this cityscape of sexual estrangement, 'Vaucluse' and 'Benjamin Fondane Departs For The East' burst like aislings. In 'Vaucluse', transfigured by love, the woman becomes a real person, 'my chance, eventual girl', and in 'Benjamin Fondane Departs For The East' there is the exquisite idea of the bride as 'soul-sister'. Back in 1988, 'Vaucluse' released in Clifton's poetry fountains of spousal love. In 2003 in his book *God in France*, there is a short poem entitled 'Bare Arm' in which we observe two strangers, a married woman and a married man, glimpse one another in dormer windows in the roof-tops of Paris. It is a sort of Edward Hopper/Edouard Vuillard epiphany:

> *Naked, in the small hours*
> *Coming from showers*
> *And lovemaking, two spouses*
> *In opposite houses*
>
> *Pausing, in the lit frame*
> *Of revelation,*

> *Not knowing each other's name,*
> *Uncaring, unconditional*
>
> *For once, two creatures*
> *Awake, while everyone slept,*
> *Alive in the forest*
> *Of second nature*

Fourthly, throughout Clifton's work one is conscious of the presence of Rembrandt. This is not surprising if we consider his short story 'The Rembrandt Series', a portrait of a Dublin civil servant in love for a lifetime with Rembrandt.

Lastly there is Clifton's golden obsession with Paris. His new book of poems forthcoming from Wake Forest University Press is entitled *Secular Eden: Paris Notebooks 1994–2004.*

In 2005 in his volume entitled *Harbour Lights* Derek Mahon published a poem with the same title as Yeats's poem of 1938 'Lapis Lazuli' and employing the same rubric of dedication as Yeats had employed sixty-seven years earlier: a name in parenthesis and that name being Harry Clifton.

(For Harry Clifton)

Once again we are jolted by the mystery of Harry Clifton. We are confronted also in the first lines of Mahon's poem with a chunk of lapis lazuli sitting on the poet's desk, 'a complex chunk … night-formed in sun-struck Afghanistan … A royal blue loved since the earth began / because, like the swirling sea, it never dates.' At the end of the second stanza Mahon hints at the identity of the Harry Clifton of his dedication. He writes:

> *Dim in the half-light of conventional rain*
> *We start at the squeal of Berkeley's telephone.*

The Hercule Poirot antennae of the alert, cultured reader will recall the publication in 2000 by the Lilliput Press of the volume *Berkeley's Telephone and Other Fictions*. The alert, cultured reader will also by this stage have read the second volume of Roy Foster's biography of W.B. Yeats in which we learn that the Harry Clifton to whom Yeats dedicated his poem was a poet also but that he was born in 1907, the son of Talbot and Violet Clifton, and died in 1978. His three volumes of verse were entitled *Dielma and Other Poems* (1932), *Flight* (1934) and *Gleams Britain's Day* (1942). The alert, cultured reader finally will have learned from the Christmas 2006 edition of the journal *Irish Pages* that the Harry Clifton of 'Vaucluse' and 'Benjamin Fondane Departs For The East' had for his mother a South American woman of Chilean extraction while his father was a migrant Irishman of Fenian, republican background.

In the concluding stanza of Mahon's poem we are vouchsafed a glimpse of a young woman on the Eurostar, the London-Paris train, a vignette we might expect to find in a Harry Clifton poem, and she is in the act of reading a book. The poet, offering to us an image of her book as a slate of lapis lazuli, portrays her as she searches its pages

> ... *for the rich and rare.*
> *Hope lies with her as it always does really*
> *And the twinkling sages in the Deux Magots*
> *First glimpsed by a student forty years ago*
> *On a continent like a plain of lapis lazuli*
> *And the Eurostar glides into the Gare du Nord.*

Gare du Nord was the name also of the white rabbit beloved of Francis Stuart whose first wife was a young woman in whom W.B. Yeats had a certain interest; pieces of a patchwork mystery familiar to Mahon. And is Mahon also sketching the possibility that Harry Clifton may be one of the three sages whom Yeats discerned in the texture of his lapis lazuli stone? Perhaps, especially if the book the young woman on the train is reading is a book by Harry Clifton.

Here is what Yeats saw in that ten-and-a-half inches high tablet of lapis lazuli which Harry Clifton, son of Talbot and Violet Clifton, gave him for his seventieth birthday on 4 July 1935:

> *Two Chinamen, behind them a third,*
> *Are carved in lapis lazuli,*
> *Over them flies a long-legged bird,*
> *A symbol of longevity;*
> *The third, doubtless a serving-man,*
> *Carries a musical instrument.*

Perhaps we may also discern in the discolouration, cracks and dents of the three wise men of the Deux Magots as seen by Derek Mahon, the crouched, handsome figures of Benjamin Fondane and René Char. How well they knew one another one cannot be certain but in 1930s Paris they moved in the same circles. On 14 February 1930, Benjamin Fondane was sitting in the Bar Maldoror in Montparnasse when the bar was gate-crashed by André Breton accompanied by René Char, Louis Aragon, Paul Eluard and other surrealists who were protesting the commercial exploitation of the revered surrealist figure of the Count de Lautréamont. Fisticuffs may have ensued; certainly, according to Fondane's account, the women in the bar threw napkins at the aggressors.

Let us stroll down Boulevard Raspail from Montparnasse to the more sedate atmosphere of St Germain and, taking coffee in the Deux Magots, let us, by grace of the two blocks of lapis lazuli as depicted by W.B. Yeats and Derek Mahon, discern in their configurations the profiles of Benjamin Fondane and René Char, two modern heroes who inspired two startling poems in the imaginative conscience of Harry Clifton, son of Charlie and Dorothy Clifton. If we do so, we may want to conclude that the face of the third carrying a musical instrument and 'doubtless a serving-man' is that of the same Harry Clifton who gave us these two redemption songs of the Vaucluse and of Auschwitz, two poems branded by an authenticity of primal fire as absolute as geological time, an authenticity which Clifton himself depicted in one of the first poems he ever published, 'Null Beauty' (*The Walls of Carthage*, 1977):

> *I have a stone about me,*
> *Round as I know round,*
> *So without peculiarities*
> *That I feel free*
>
> *To imagine as I can.*
> *Beyond the fact of stone,*
> *A before and to come*
> *It could never disclose …*
>
> *I can only rediscover it.*
> *I can only make queries,*
> *Draw what fire I can*
> *From a cold, null beauty.*

BIBLIOGRAPHY
Harry Clifton: *The Walls of Carthage*, Gallery Books, 1977; *Office of the Salt Merchant*, Gallery Books, 1979; *Comparative Lives*, Gallery Books, 1982; *The Liberal Cage*, Gallery Books, 1988; *The Desert Route*, Gallery Books, 1992; *Night Train Through The Brenner*, Gallery Books, 1994; *On the Spine of Italy*, MacMillan, 1999;

Paul Durcan

Berkeley's Telephone, Lilliput, 2000; *God In France,* Metre Editions, 2003; *Secular Eden: Paris Notebooks 1994–2004,* Wake Forest University Press, 2007; *Imaginative Absolute In Wallace Stevens,* M.A. Thesis, Dept of Metaphysics, UCD, 1975; Benjamin Fondane: *Le Mal des Fantômes,* Paris-Mediterranées / L'Ether Vague-Patrice Thierry, 1996; Olivier Salazar-Ferrer: *Benjamin Fondane,* Oxus, Paris, 2004; Derek Mahon: *Harbour Lights,* Gallery Books, 2005; W.B. Yeats: *The Poems,* edited Daniel Albright, Everyman's Library, 1992; Michael Hartnett: *Collected Poems,* Gallery Books, 2001; David Burnett-James: *Sibelius,* Ominbus Press, 1989; Erik Tawaststjerna: *Sibelius,* trans. Robert Layton, 3 vols, Faber, 1976, 1986, 1997.

Notes on Contributors

JOHN MONTAGUE

John Montague was born in Brooklyn, New York in 1929 and
brought up in County Tyrone. He was educated at St Patrick's
College, Armagh and University College, Dublin. His collec-
tions are *Poisoned Lands* (1961), *A Chosen Light* (1967),
Tides (1970), *The Rough Field* (1972), *A Slow Dance* (1975),
The Great Cloak (1978), *The Dead Kingdom* (1984), *Mount
Eagle* (1988), *The Love Poems* (1992), *Time in Armagh* (1993),
Smashing The Piano (1999) and *Drunken Sailor* (2004). He
has also published a book of short stories, *Death of a Chief-
tain* (1964), a novella, *The Lost Notebook* (1987), selected
American writings published in 1991, *Born in Brooklyn*, and
edited *The Faber Book of Irish Verse* (1974). *Selected Poems*
appeared in 1982, *New Selected Poems* in 1990 and the *Col-
lected Poems* in 1995. A collection of prose pieces, *The Fig-
ure in the Cave*, was published in 1990 and short stories, *An
Occasion of Sin*, in 1992.

NUALA NI DHOMHNAILL

Nuala Ní Dhomhnaill was born in Lancashire in 1952 and
grew up in the Kerry Gaeltacht. She graduated from University

College, Cork. Her collections are *An Dealg Droighin* (1981), *Féar Suaithinseach* (1984), *Feis* (1991) and *Cead Aighnis* (1998). Her books include *Selected Poems*, translated by Michael Hartnett (1996), *Pharaoh's Daughter*, translated by several hands (1990), *The Astrakhan Cloak*, translated by Paul Muldoon (1992) and *The Water Horse* (1999). Nuala Ní Dhomhnaill's work has also been translated by Ciaran Carson, Seamus Heaney, Derek Mahon and Medbh McGuckian.

PAUL DURCAN

Paul Durcan was born in Dublin in 1944. He was educated at Gonzaga College and University College, Cork. His collections are *Endsville* (1967), *O Westport in the Light of Asia Minor* (1975), *Teresa's Bar* (1976), *Sam's Cross* (1978), *Jesus, Break His Fall* (1980), *Ark of the North* (1982), *Jumping the Traintracks with Angela* (1984), *The Berlin Wall Café* (1985), *Going Home to Russia* (1987), *Daddy, Daddy* (1990), *Crazy About Women* (1991), *Give Me Your Hand* (1994), *Christmas Day* (1996), *Greetings to our Friends in Brazil* (1999), *Cries of an Irish Caveman* (2001) and *The Art of Life* (2004). *The Selected Paul Durcan* was published in 1983 and *A Snail in My Prime: New and Selected Poems* appeared in 1993. *The Laughter of Mothers* was published by Harvill Secker in 2007.

SEAMUS HEANEY

Seamus Heaney was born in 1939 in County Derry. His collections are *Death of a Naturalist* (1966), *Door into the Dark* (1969), *Wintering Out* (1972), *North* (1975), *Field Work* (1979), *Station Island* (1984), *The Haw Lantern* (1987), *Seeing Things* (1991), *The Spirit Level* (1996), *Electric Light* (2001) and *District and Circle* (2006). *Seamus Heaney's Selected Poems 1965–1975* appeared in 1980 and his *New Selected Poems 1966–1987* in 1990. *Opened Ground: Poems 1966–96* appeared in 1998. He has also published *Preoccupations: Selected Prose 1968–1978* (1980), a version of the Middle Irish tale, *Sweeney Astray* (1984), lectures and other critical writings published as *The Government of the Tongue* (1988), essays, *The Place of Writing* (1989), a play, *The Cure at Troy* (1990), verse translations, *The Midnight Verdict* (1993), *The Redress of Poetry: Oxford Lectures* (1995), *Crediting Poetry: The Nobel Lecture* (1995), a translation of *Beowulf* (1999), and *The Burial at Thebes*, a version of Sophocles' *Antigone* in 2004. *Finders Keepers: Selected Prose 1971–2001* was published by Faber & Faber in 2002.

DONNELL DEENY

Sir Donnell Deeny is the founding and present Chairman of the Ireland Chair of Poetry Trust and a former Chairman of the Arts Council of Northern Ireland. He is a judge of the High Court of Justice in Northern Ireland.

GABRIEL ROSENSTOCK

Gabriel Rosenstock is a poet, haikuist and author/translator of over a hundred books. His latest titles are the bilingual volume *Bliain an Bhandé/Year of the Goddess* (Dedalus) and the spiritual diary *Dialann Anama* (Coiscéim).

Trustees 1998–2007